IRA Terror on Britain's Streets 1939–1940

DICK KIRBY

has also written:

Rough Justice – Memoirs of a Flying Squad officer

The Real Sweeney

You're Nicked!

Villains

The Guv'nors – Ten of Scotland Yard's Greatest Detectives

The Sweeney – The First Sixty Years of Scotland Yard's Crimebusting

Flying Squad 1919–1978

Scotland Yard's Ghost Squad
The Secret Weapon against Post-War Crime

The Brave Blue Line
100 Years of Metropolitan Police Gallantry

Death on the Beat
Police Officers killed in the Line of Duty

The Scourge of Soho
The Controversial Career of SAS Hero
Detective Sergeant Harry Challenor MM

Whitechapel's Sherlock Holmes
The Casebook of Fred Wensley OBE, KPM
Victorian Crimebuster

The Wrong Man
The Shooting of Steven Waldorf and
The Hunt for David Martin

Laid Bare
The Nude Murders and
The Hunt for 'Jack the Stripper'

London's Gangs at War

Operation Countryman
The Flawed Enquiry into London Police Corruption

Scotland Yard's Gangbuster
Bert Wickstead's Most Celebrated Cases

The Mayfair Mafia
The Lives and Crimes of the Messina Brothers

Scotland Yard's Flying Squad
100 Years of Crime Fighting

Scotland Yard's Murder Squad

The Racetrack Gangs
Four Decades of Doping, Intimidation & Violent Crime

IRA Terror on Britain's Streets 1939–1940

The Wartime Bombing Campaign and Hitler Connection

DICK KIRBY

Foreword by

SIMON CRAWSHAW QPM
Former Deputy Assistant Commissioner
New Scotland Yard

PEN & SWORD
TRUE CRIME

First published in Great Britain in 2021 by
Pen & Sword True Crime
An imprint of
Pen & Sword Books Ltd
Yorkshire – Philadelphia

Copyright © Dick Kirby 2021

ISBN 978 1 52678 642 5

The right of Dick Kirby to be identified as Author of this work has been asserted by him in accordance with the Copyright, Designs and Patents Act 1988.

A CIP catalogue record for this book is available from the British Library.

All rights reserved. No part of this book may be reproduced or transmitted in any form or by any means, electronic or mechanical including photocopying, recording or by any information storage and retrieval system, without permission from the Publisher in writing.

Printed and bound in the UK by TJ Books Ltd, Padstow, Cornwall

FSC www.fsc.org MIX Paper from responsible sources FSC® C013056

Pen & Sword Books Limited incorporates the imprints of Atlas, Archaeology, Aviation, Discovery, Family History, Fiction, History, Maritime, Military, Military Classics, Politics, Select, Transport, True Crime, Air World, Frontline Publishing, Leo Cooper, Remember When, Seaforth Publishing, The Praetorian Press, Wharncliffe Local History, Wharncliffe Transport, Wharncliffe True Crime and White Owl.

For a complete list of Pen & Sword titles please contact

PEN & SWORD BOOKS LIMITED
47 Church Street, Barnsley, South Yorkshire, S70 2AS, England
E-mail: enquiries@pen-and-sword.co.uk
Website: www.pen-and-sword.co.uk

Or
PEN AND SWORD BOOKS
1950 Lawrence Rd, Havertown, PA 19083, USA
E-mail: Uspen-and-sword@casematepublishers.com
Website: www.penandswordbooks.com

To Ann

Hers was a proud and noble face,
A secret heart, and eyes
Like water in a lonely place
Beneath unclouded skies.

A bed, a chest, a faded mat,
And broken chairs a few,
Were all we had to grace our flat
In Hazel Avenue.

James Elroy Flecker
The Ballad of Camden Town

Praise for Dick Kirby's Books

'His style of writing pulls no punches and he tells it the way it is. Highly recommended.' **POLICE HISTORY SOCIETY MAGAZINE**

'These are the real-life accounts of a tough London cop.' **DAILY EXPRESS**

'All of the stories are told with Dick Kirby's acerbic black humour in a compelling style, by a detective who was there.' **AMERICAN POLICE BEAT**

'New Scotland Yard legends are vividly brought to life by a man who had walked the walk, the Flying Squad's own Dick Kirby.' **JOSEPH WAMBAUGH, AUTHOR OF THE CHOIRBOYS**

'It's a rollercoaster ride; detectives who took crime by the scruff of its neck and wouldn't let go.' **EAST ANGLIAN DAILY TIMES**

'I am delighted that Dick Kirby has written this book. I am sure those who read it will realize how very hazardous the life of a policeman is.' **MICHAEL WINNER**

'Kirby looks to untangle facts from speculation and questions everything.' **GET WEST LONDON**

'Ex-cop Dick Kirby has now laid bare the Krays' empire.' **DAILY STAR**

'A vivid and fascinating account of policing some of the era's most serious crimes, written by an experienced and retired police officer.' **THE LAW SOCIETY GAZETTE**

'Real *Boys Own* stuff, this. Tinged with a wry sense of humour makes this an excellent read.' **METROPOLITAN POLICE HISTORY SOCIETY**

'This is a fast-paced, riveting read, made even more enjoyable by Kirby's trademark humour.' **TANGLED WEB**

'This is simply the best book about police gallantry ever written and arguably the best book about any sort of gallantry awards. It comes with our highest possible recommendation.' **HISTORY BY THE YARD**

'A sensational and gripping account.' **PEGASUS YEARBOOK**

'Dick Kirby pulls no punches as he looks in depth at some of the most infamous names from the criminal underworld.' **MEDIA DRUM WORLD**

'Murder, torture and extortion all feature prominently as Mr Kirby investigates some of the most famous incidents of the post-war era.' **DAILY MAIL**

'Old-school, but effective – how the Met took the fight to the underworld.' **THE SCOTSMAN**

Contents

About the Author

Dick Kirby was born in 1943 in the East End of London and joined the Metropolitan Police in 1967. Half of his twenty-six years' service as a detective was spent with the Yard's Serious Crime Squad and the Flying Squad.

Married, with four children and five grandchildren, Kirby lives in a Suffolk village with his wife. He appears on television and radio and can be relied upon to provide forthright views on spineless senior police officers and other politicians, with their insipid, absurd and mendacious claims on how they intend to defeat serious crime and reclaim the streets.

He contributes regularly to newspapers and magazines, reviews books, films and music and writes memoirs, biographies and true crime books, which are widely quoted – this is his twenty-first.

Kirby can be visited on his website: www.dickkirby.com

Acknowledgements

My thanks go to Simon Crawshaw, one of the Yard's finest operational Deputy Assistant Commissioners, for taking the trouble to read through the book and add a thoughtful and perceptive foreword. As always, thanks also go to Brigadier Henry Wilson for his help and encouragement, together with the rest of the staff at Pen & Sword Books: Matt Jones, Tara Moran, Jon Wilkinson for his brilliant, imaginative jacket designs, and George Chamier, to whom I'm most grateful for his eagle-eyed editing.

In addition, I received much-needed help from: Clive Bishop; Corrine Brazier, Subject Matter Expert, West Midlands Police; Sioban Clarke, Women's Police Historian; Chief Constable Andy Cooke QPM, Merseyside Police; Karen Crutchlow, West Midlands Police; Jackie Eggleton, Metropolitan Women Police Association; Eryll Fabian; Mike Fabian; Bob Fenton QGM, the Ex-CID Officers' Association; Paul Finegan, Curator, Dartmoor Prison Museum; Hazel Fothergill, PA to the Chief Constable, Merseyside Police; Mark Henry; Chief Constable Ian Hopkins QPM, Greater Manchester Police; Martin D. Lyddall; Kate McNichol, PA to the Chief Constable, West Midlands Police; Jayne Milne, PA to ACC Vanessa Jardine, West Midlands Police; Alan Moss; Michael Nesbitt; Chris Nolan; Susi Rogol, editor, the *London Police Pensioner*; John Royle; Graham Sutherland; and Chief Constable Dave Thompson QPM, West Midlands Police.

My thanks for the use of their photographs go to Karen Crutchlow and Chris Shortland; others come from the author's collection. While every effort has been made to trace copyright holders, Pen & Sword Books and the author apologize for any inadvertent omissions.

As always, my thanks go to my daughter, Suzanne Cowper, and her husband, Steve for their unfailing assistance in reaching out into the incomprehensible mysteries of cyberspace for me, as well as the love and support of their children, Emma Cowper B Mus, Jessica Cowper B Mus and Harry Cowper.

The same applies to the rest of my family: my daughter Barbara Jerreat, her husband Rich and their children, Sam and Annie Grace Jerreat, my sons Mark and Robert Kirby, and most of all to my dear one, Ann, who for almost sixty years has kept me for much of our life on an almost even keel.

Dick Kirby
Suffolk, 2020

Foreword

Simon Crawshaw QPM

Former Deputy Assistant Commissioner
'C' Department (Operations),
New Scotland Yard

The Dick Kirby whom I knew as an energetic Flying Squad detective sergeant, forty years ago, has replaced his handcuffs with a pen; now, as a successful author, he's still as energetic – and just as forthright.

In this hard-hitting book, his outspokenness is evident; he wastes no time in attempting to discuss – as some authors have – whether or not there was any possible justification for the Irish terrorists' actions.

In describing – often, in frightening detail – the carnage which resulted from the IRA's mainland offensive during 1939–1940, Kirby's book focuses on the stoicism and gallantry of many of the average British citizens who suddenly found themselves in terrifying situations; plus the tremendous work carried out by police forces throughout the United Kingdom. Much of this work was done by the Metropolitan Police's Special Branch, and because, at one stage of my career, I was the commander of that unit, I know only too well the huge amount of dedication and expertise that the men and women of 'The Branch' were able to inject into the fight against terrorism.

During the IRA's 15-month-long campaign on the mainland they set off, or attempted to, 265 explosions, during which seven innocent members of the public were killed and 117 others injured.

However, Dick Kirby's book describes in detail how 99 of the terrorists were convicted, which led to a total of 1,021 years' imprisonment for them.

This book is a testament to the inspirational commitment and bravery of those police officers.

Prologue

Just before 10 o'clock on the evening of Saturday, 24 June 1939, there were shattering explosions in quick succession in the vicinity of Piccadilly Circus, central London. The first was at the Westminster Bank; diners at the nearby Monico Restaurant saw a ginger-haired man jump out of a taxi, throw a parcel on to the pavement and climb back into the taxi, which quickly drove off. A night watchman saw a light on the ground which was followed by an immediate explosion. Considerable damage was done to the bank, windows were blown out, pedestrians were cut by the flying glass, and amongst those knocked over by the force of the blast was a man blown down the steps to Piccadilly Circus Underground Station. James Barlow, a 17-year-old delivery boy, was blown into the road with a fragment of glass embedded in his left eye and nearly run over by a taxi; surgeons were unable to operate and reported that he had been left with no sight in that eye. Another young man, 18-year-old Henry White, was also hit in the eye by a metal splinter and he, like Barlow, was taken to the Royal Westminster Ophthalmic Hospital.

Manhole covers were blown completely out of the ground, and as some fifty diners at a nearby Chinese restaurant rushed into the street, so a second explosion occurred at Lloyds Bank, at the corner of Piccadilly and Sackville Street, which was so violent it was heard two miles away in Vauxhall.

Just before the second explosion, a Mr H. W. Service had been drinking at a bar in a nearby hotel when five or six men rushed in, one of them telling the barman, 'Give us a drink, quickly!' Then came the explosion which, Mr Service stated, 'startled us all, but it did not seem to startle these men', some of whom, he said, 'spoke with Irish accents' – and they left, without finishing their drinks.

The Italian Tourism Organization was damaged, and the blast shattered shop windows 70 yards away; diners in a nearby restaurant were unable to leave until heaps of masonry dislodged by the blast had been cleared away.

But out in the street there were cries of 'Lynch him, kill him, string him up from a lamppost!' and a man who had been seen running towards St James' Church, Piccadilly, possibly to seek sanctuary in consecrated ground, was seized and roughly manhandled by a crowd, punched by the men and whacked by women holding rolled-up newspapers, before being rescued by whistle-blowing constables and taken away in an ambulance. He was one of two dozen men rounded up and taken in by the police for questioning. All of them were later released without charge; they had to be. Despite the fact that devastation such as this had been perpetuated on a regular basis for the past five months, with 130 explosions, a gormless Parliament had thought it more pressing to place the Street Playgrounds Act on the statute book. Legislation to counter this particular brand of destruction, with powers to detain suspects for up to five days, would not be enacted until two months after these events.

Meanwhile, panic-stricken people poured out of restaurants, hotels and theatres into streets filled with broken glass; and this was just the beginning.

An hour after the first explosion, a bomb was thrown through the window of Lloyds Bank at the corner of the Aldwych and Wellington Street. Panelled woodwork was ripped from the walls, outside ironwork was twisted and blown for a considerable distance and people waiting for a bus outside the bank were showered with shattered fragments from the bank's nine plate-glass windows. Among those struck by the splintered woodwork and glass were a man and a woman who were boarding a bus, the driver of the bus and a police officer; they were taken to Charing Cross Hospital, as was a child, and Mr W. J. Stevens a disabled newspaper seller.

A further bomb, posted through the letter box of the Midland Bank in Park Lane at the junction with Aldford Street, exploded with such force that the complete frontage of the premises was blown out, hitting a taxi and hospitalizing the driver; the bank's front door was flung 20 yards across Park Lane, embedding itself in the railings of Hyde Park. A huge window frame on the Aldford Street side of the premises was blown out on to the pavement. Gelignite with short fuses had been used in all of these explosions.

Incendiary bombs planted in pillar boxes in Nottingham Place and in the Marylebone Road, outside Madame Tussaud's wax-works museum, exploded and destroyed the letters therein; and inside Madame Tussaud's more incendiaries exploded in the 'Chamber of Horrors', just as a few late visitors were leaving. A search of the premises was immediately carried out; another explosion occurred in 'The Hall of Kings', and the exhibition manager, Mr F. W. Smith, discovered a further device in 'The Red Riding Hood Tableau' hidden under the wolf's pillow.

'I picked it up and was putting it in a bucket of water when it exploded, knocking me on my back', said Mr Smith, adding, almost as an afterthought to minimize his heroic efforts, 'The flash was fierce but my glasses protected my eyes and I was not hurt.'

Mr Smith was very fortunate; although he described himself as 'not hurt', nineteen other people were.

Another bomb was discovered by Thomas Hawkett, a cloakroom attendant at Oxford Circus Underground station, who dropped it into a bucket of water; and fortunately, that was not the only one that was made safe . . .

* * *

As the first bombs exploded by Piccadilly Circus, 38-year-old Detective Inspector Robert Fabian – he would later be immortalized as 'Fabian of the Yard' – was typing a report at nearby Vine Street police station. Dashing to the scene of the explosions, accompanied by Detective Sergeant Percy Burgess and Detective Constable Saul, Fabian was faced with a scene of complete devastation. As well as the rest of the damage, the blast had caught the frontage of the Etam shop, and lingerie fluttered in the breeze; the cigars and cigar boxes that had been blown through the shattered window of Van Raalte & Sons tobacconist's shop now littered the pavements. Suddenly, Fabian spotted something else, a brown paper parcel, fastened with string; and that was not all – there were two strips of black adhesive tape, and when he picked it up, the parcel was hot in his hands and he was left in no doubt that he was handling a viable explosive device. Shouting at Burgess and Saul to keep the crowd of onlookers back – they were assisted by Police Constables 68 'D' Butler and 79 'D' Attwood – Fabian desperately looked around for some sort of receptacle to hold water, but none was to be found.

At that moment, the fire brigade arrived and Fabian asked for a bucket of water. 'What do you think we represent – Southend?' replied a fire brigade officer, displaying a sort of chirpy, cheerful Cockney humour which, given the circumstances, was ludicrously inappropriate. But Fabian realized, with the parcel getting hotter and hotter, that something had to be done – right now! Kneeling down by the kerb and taking out his pocket knife, he cut through the adhesive tape and opened one end of the parcel. Putting his hand inside, he drew out a greasy 4oz stick of Polar Ammon gelignite. One by one, Fabian then withdrew ten sticks of gelignite from the parcel; from one of them protruded a pencil fuse, which he pulled from the gelignite and placed in his pocket. The ten sticks he set out apart on the pavement, so that if one detonated, hopefully the others would not. But although he had retrieved one detonator, what if there were more hidden in the other sticks? So to make sure, Fabian cut through the sticks, quite unaware that the slightest spark from the blade of his pocket knife could cause the gelignite to detonate. Finally, he saw in the parcel a small pile of grey powder, in the middle of which was a green rubber balloon with a brown wax cylinder inside. He tore the balloon apart and the acid inside it burned his hands – had the parcel remained undisturbed, once the acid had eaten its way through the wax, the bomb would have detonated.

Picking up the pieces of gelignite, Fabian and his colleagues put them into some of Messrs Van Raalte's discarded cigar boxes and gingerly carried them the 100 yards to Vine Street police station where, in the hallway, they were tipped into a line of water-filled fire buckets. Fabian, a married man with a 13-year-old son, expelled a deep sigh of relief. During his eighteen years' police service he had established a reputation for bravery, but he had never been called upon to carry out a task as daunting as this.

Fabian's senior officer, Divisional Detective Inspector Peter Beveridge, who attended the station that night, was in no doubt that his subordinate's actions had saved the lives of many onlookers. Upon his recommendation, Fabian received his thirty-third commendation from the commissioner, was awarded £15 from the Bow Street Reward Fund and, on 6 February 1940, was presented with the King's Police Medal for gallantry at Buckingham Palace. King George VI told him, 'I am pleased to make your acquaintance and congratulate you on your gallantry.'

There was also another, unofficial reward, this one from the underworld. A few days prior to his attendance at the palace, Fabian received a bronze medal, about the size of an old penny on a blue silk ribbon, with laurel leaves on one side; inscribed on the other were the words:

> To Detective Inspector Bob Fabian,
> For Bravery, 24-6-39,
> from The Boys.

* * *

The following day, Cardinal Arthur Hinsley, the Catholic Archbishop of Westminster, speaking from the Holy Trinity Church,

Brook Green, roundly denounced the bombings as 'cowardly and atrocious outrages', adding that the penalty for Catholics plotting against the church or the state was excommunication. Unfortunately, those strictures were not reciprocated by the cardinal's opposite number in Dublin, or by the IRA, who with breathtaking hypocrisy wrote back to the cardinal on 29 June from their General Headquarters at Dublin:

> May it please Your Eminence,
>
> We have read with pained surprise your condemnations of certain incidents in England. As a Prince of the Catholic Church we expected that, if in the assumed interests of your own country you found it necessary or desirable to use the prestige of the Church to defend your country's aggression in Ireland, you would have refrained from using religion to the level of political diatribe.

The incident that involved Fabian was just one in a whole series of mainland explosions which had commenced five months previously, courtesy of the Irish Republican Army; and it would certainly not be the last. In the fifteen months' duration of this murderous campaign there would be senseless carnage and destruction; and in the nine months that followed the bombing in and around Piccadilly, there would be an escalation of explosions and death.

This is how it all came about.

Introduction

'Look at the Irish!' exclaimed Macgillivray, a high-up official (albeit a fictional one) at Scotland Yard, in John Buchan's 1924 novel *The Three Hostages*. In a choleric frame of mind, he went on to say, 'They are the cleverest propagandists extant, and managed to persuade most people that they were a brave, generous, humorous, talented, warm-hearted race, cruelly yoked to a dull, mercantile England, when God knows they were exactly the opposite.'

'Macgillivray, I may remark, is an Ulsterman', explains the narrator, Sir Richard Hannay, to his readers, adding, 'and has his prejudices' (although Hannay, given his opinions about black and Jewish people, was certainly no better and probably a lot worse).

But jingoistic – not to mention prejudiced – though those views of the fictional detective were, there would then have been plenty who agreed with them.

Ireland – Éire in the south, Ulster in the north – is known, due to its lush landscape, as 'The Emerald Isle'. To say that politically it has also been a troubled Isle, is rather like saying that the Allied troops who inhabited the trenches in Flanders during the First World War had a slightly uncomfortable time. The intractably opposed views of Catholics and Protestants, Republicans and Unionists, have led to centuries of discord.

It is not the intention of this book to delve too deeply into the political history of Ireland; rather, it is to concentrate on what became known as the Irish Republican Army (IRA), who during the nineteenth and twentieth century wished to rid themselves by force of the resident British establishment, civil and military, in order to establish an independent Irish Republic.

At the beginning of the twentieth century, although Irish Catholics had long hated what they saw as repressive British rule, the whole island of Ireland was still part of the United Kingdom. Many Irish people emigrated to America, others – perhaps illogically – to England. Although most of the religious disabilities suffered by Catholics in Ireland had been removed by the middle of the nineteenth century, an independence movement continued to exist, and a very strong Irish-American group came to England in January 1867, set up headquarters in London and devised plans to storm Chester Castle, in order to steal guns and ammunition, which they intended to use in an uprising in Ireland to overthrow the government.

In March, a number of Fenians, as they were known – calling themselves the Irish Republican Brotherhood, the forerunners of the IRA – were arrested in Manchester; and later, when thirty other Fenians attacked the Black Maria which was taking two of them to prison, they shot and killed a Police Sergeant Brett, and the two men escaped. They were later arrested in London and remanded in Pentonville prison. However, on 11 December 1867, the Dublin Police received information that an escape was planned and informed the Metropolitan Police Commissioner, Sir Richard Mayne KCB – who took no action whatsoever. The Dublin authorities also informed the prison governor, who did. The governor kept the two prisoners out of the exercise yard and when, on 13 December, Fenians pushed a barrel of gunpowder against the wall of the prison which detonated, killing six people immediately, mortally wounding nine more and injuring a further 120, the two detainees were not amongst the casualties. The explosion had destroyed sixty yards of the perimeter wall, as well as several houses opposite, and Mayne's outrageous excuse for his sedulous inactivity was that he had been informed that the Fenians intended to blow the wall *up*, instead of *down*, and he therefore thought that the authorities should have been looking for subterranean burrowers. In fact, the sabotage team had been spotted the previous day, by a police constable, shoving a large barrel against the prison wall and lighting a fuse which spluttered and went out, before loading the barrel on to a cart and pushing it away. The fact that this was a clue as to the plotters' intentions, plus the fact that the observing officer gormlessly did nothing, was neither here nor there. Told by the Home Office that he had made 'a damned fool of himself', Mayne nevertheless remained in office, and died the following year.

This was followed by what was known as the Fenian dynamite campaign, which was carried out on mainland Britain between 1881 and 1885, principally in London, Liverpool and Glasgow. The targets were infrastructure, government, police and military establishments, and the resultant explosions caused widespread damage, in which over eighty people sustained injuries (detonations at Paddington and Westminster Bridge Underground stations accounted for seventy of these); in Lancashire, a young boy was killed, as were three of the bombers during an attack on London Bridge in 1884.

In 1883, to combat this offensive, Sir Howard Vincent KCMG, the Metropolitan Police's Assistant Commissioner (Crime), was instructed to set up an 'Irish Bureau' at Great Scotland Yard which initially comprised a dozen (mainly Irish) officers. There followed a brisk exchange of information between what initially became known as the Special Irish Branch at Scotland Yard and Dublin, and thanks to the efforts of informants, a number of arrests were carried out. Unfortunately, no pertinent information was received in time to take action on 30 May 1884; on this date three bombs were set off in London, one of which was placed in a urinal directly underneath the first floor Special Irish Branch office at Scotland Yard. There were no fatalities, but the office was destroyed and with it, many of the records pertaining to Fenian suspects, although one of the bombers responsible was later killed in the London Bridge incident.

On 24 January 1885, three bombs exploded in the House of Commons Chamber, Westminster Hall and the banqueting room of the Tower of London. Two police officers (one of whom, Police Constable William Cole, is the only police officer ever to be awarded the Albert Medal for gallantry), two women and two children were seriously injured, and two Fenians were arrested. PC Cole was later reported as being 'still deaf but the deafness is less marked than it was'. Two weeks later, after the final incident when dynamite was found at Harrow Road, the Fenians appeared at the Old Bailey in May 1885 and were sentenced to penal servitude for life – after which the bombing offensive fizzled out. The 'Irish' was dropped from the designation of Special Branch, the personnel was increased to twenty-two and mainland Britain was spared the explosive depredations of the Fenians – or, as they would later become known, the Irish Republican Army (IRA) – for the next half-century.

* * *

In the last years of the nineteenth and the early years of the twentieth century, the efforts of Irish nationalists were mostly aimed at achieving 'home rule' (devolution, it would be called nowadays) by peaceful, parliamentary means. However, when an Act was finally passed in 1912 granting home rule to the whole of Ireland, this provoked further trouble. Protestant Unionists in Ulster, fiercely loyal to the UK, were outraged at the idea of being ruled by Catholics, who were in the majority in Ireland as a whole, and declared themselves prepared to fight to resist home rule. In response, the Irish Republican Brotherhood in the south proclaimed its desire for complete independence. Both sides began buying arms.

The coming of the First World War in 1914 put on hold the implementation of home rule, but it did not quench the passion of extreme Irish nationalists. In Easter week 1916, the Irish Republican Brotherhood seized a number of key buildings in Dublin and proclaimed an Irish republic. The Easter Rising, as it is known, lasted barely a week; the British Army was sent in, and after some street fighting the Rising was rapidly put down.

Not many Irish people had supported the Easter Rising, but the British government's foolish and vindictive treatment of the captured rebels (sixteen were executed by firing squad, including James Connolly, who had been so badly injured that he could not stand up) converted many people to the republican cause. And in December 1918, when a general election was held, 73 out of the 106 Irish seats were won by the Republican party, Sinn Féin ('Ourselves Alone'), who refused to take their seats at Westminster; instead, the following year, they formed a Parliament in Dublin, the Dáil Éireann. This was, of course, completely unacceptable to Unionists. Sinn Féin then formed their own government, declaring Ireland to be an independent republic; therefore there were now two competing administrations in Dublin, the British and the Republican.

Although Sinn Féin stated that it was opposed to the use of force, the IRA was not; the Royal Irish Constabulary (RIC) was regarded as a tool of the British government, and egged on by the Republican newspaper, *An tÓglách*, a campaign of violence was launched against their members, two of whom were murdered. There was also an assassination attempt on the Lord Lieutenant of Ireland, and with this escalation of ferocity, some 800 'special constables' were sent from England – many of them former soldiers – who had no police training and were known as the 'Black and Tans'. Their numbers rose to 7,000 and, reinforcing the ranks of the RIC, they too became targets for the IRA, who fought back strongly. As the casualties mounted on both sides during the ensuing conflict, the Black and Tans regarded any republican (whether affiliated to the IRA or not) as fair game, attacking them and burning their homes and businesses.

As well as being untrained, the Black and Tans were completely out of control; at Trim, Co. Meath they looted then set fire to forty houses, as well as shops, a factory and the Town Hall. On another occasion, at Croke Park, Dublin, they opened fire at a football match, killing twelve spectators and wounding sixty.

Understandably, feelings were bitter towards the Black and Tans, and songs and poems were devoted to the retaliation carried out against them:

On the eighteenth day of November,
Just outside the town of Macroom,
The Tans in their big Crossley tenders
Came roaring along to their doom.
But the boys of the column were waiting
With hand grenades primed on the spot,
And the Irish Republican Army
Made shit of the whole fucking lot!

With lyrics like that, and depredations carried out by both sides, there was no hope of a peaceful settlement; buildings were torched and attacks carried out on the mainland against relatives of members of the RIC. Firearms were used, and members of the IRA were sent to penal servitude. The Anglo-Irish treaty, partitioning the island into Northern Ireland, to remain part of the UK, and the Irish Free State in the south, a self-governing dominion but still within the British Commonwealth, was signed on 6 December 1921. The treaty was rejected by both the IRA and the President of Sinn Féin, Éamon de Valera, but the Dáil approved it by 64 to 57 votes; this led to a civil war in the south which was known as *Cogadh na gCarad* – 'the friends' war'.

In the violence that followed, there were some 2,000 fatalities, including 77 IRA men executed by the Irish Government; a further 12,000 were imprisoned. Upon being told that a plan was afoot to overthrow the Free State Government, as well as to commit a series of outrages in mainland Britain, in 1923 the Home Secretary issued deportation orders on 110 suspects, who were duly expelled and detained in Mountjoy Prison, Dublin. In fact, these expulsions were ruled by the House of Lords to be completely illegal; the prisoners were released, paid compensation and returned to England. Special Branch officers were obliged to issue travel warrants to enable the prisoners to return home – all except the seven who were stopped in possession of firearms.

And that, for the time being, was that. The IRA declared a ceasefire on 24 May 1923, Éamon de Valera (who had been imprisoned for a year in 1923) formed the Fianna Fáil party in 1926, Special Branch kept a wary eye on Republican meetings and peace reigned once more – or so it appeared.

* * *

Seán Russell was a thoroughly hardline member of the IRA who had never abandoned the concept of uniting Ireland by confronting the British on the mainland. He had been interned and imprisoned – and following a 41-day hunger strike, during which he boasted that by one day he had 'outdone Christ', in 1926 he had gone to Russia to ask for firearms for the IRA. In 1936, Russell had become Quartermaster-General of the IRA and two years later, now aged thirty-eight, he took control of operations. He received substantial financial backing from J. J. McGarrity, a Tyrone-born businessman and leading member of *Clan na Gael*, the American branch of the IRA, and recruited Jim O'Donovan, also a veteran Republican, to produce a plan to force the British to leave Ireland completely, and to commence a series of explosions at strategic targets in mainland Britain if they failed to do so.

The document was known as 'The 'S' Plan'. It was erroneously thought that the 'S' stood for 'Seán's Plan', but in fact, it stood for 'sabotage'.

However, before that happened, armaments had to be accumulated in Britain so that in the event of an anticipated refusal by the British Government, the sabotage plan could immediately be implemented. It was thought that there were somewhere between 5,000 and 30,000 members of the IRA, both men and women, and IRA sympathizers on the mainland were contacted to provide storage for arms, details of possible targets and information regarding the movements of firearms and explosives. Nevertheless, IRA officials who visited the mainland in spring 1938 reported that 'In general, it can be said that the state of the organization in units which exist, is poor and loose, and militarily should be described as almost elementary.'

Senior members of the IRA also arrived and when, in the summer of 1938, three such members – Jimmy Joe Reynolds, Peader O'Flaherty and Denis O'Connell – were stopped by police in a car in Green Lane, Ilford, Essex, they were found to be in possession of a large quantity of potassium chlorate. This, in itself, was not an offence. Potassium chlorate, a compound containing potassium, chlorine and oxygen, had industrial uses, such as the manufacture of pesticide. The three men politely answered the questions put to them and produced a receipt for the chemical, which had been legitimately purchased. They provided their names and addresses and were permitted to go on their way.

But although no offences appeared to have been committed, one of the officers was distinctly unhappy and, returning to Ilford police station at 40 High Road, reported his misgivings to the station officer. After recording details of the incident in the station's large, dun-coloured Occurrence Book, the officer also informed Special Branch.

They, too, were aware that possession of potassium chlorate was not an offence; but they also knew that when it was mixed with sulphur or phosphorus it became an extremely powerful explosive. Additionally, when it was mixed with aluminium, kerosene, very fine coal dust or even sawdust, it became an explosive of varying power.

Consequently, a clandestine visit was paid to the address in Dagenham where the men had been lodging; no explosives or arms were found, but in a jacket a notebook was discovered which revealed the details of a number of known IRA activists. By now, Jimmy Joe Reynolds, the recently appointed officer commanding IRA operations in England, had returned to Dublin, where it appears he was wearing two hats. His other task was to blow up British customs posts, and it was while he was planning to do this, with two other IRA members – John James Kelly and Charles McCafferty – who were priming a landmine, it exploded prematurely, killing them all. Reynolds last words were, 'Stand back, John James, there's been a wee mistake' – as indeed there had. The loss of three important members of the IRA was distressing, but it was also turned to that organization's advantage. It became part of IRA folklore to claim that they had realized that the bomb was timed to explode just when civilians would be leaving a nearby cinema, and given the IRA's respect for the sanctity for civilian lives, the fuse was compassionately being adjusted on the timing device – when up it went. The same considerations did not apply when two days later, on 30 November 1938, six customs posts were destroyed by the same landmines, one of them at Tullydonnel, where a police patrol narrowly escaped death.

But at 1.15am on 19 October 1938, coincidentally once more in Ilford – this time in the High Road – a police sergeant saw a man carrying a car tyre. He followed him to a garage, where the man – coincidentally the same Denis O'Connell who had been stopped by police a few hundred yards away, several months previously – met up with another Irishman, James Joseph O'Toole; and when the officer searched a van that was in their possession he discovered four barrels which were found to contain potassium chlorate and also magnetic oxide of iron. The latter substance was also not in itself an explosive, but when mixed with aluminium and other elements it made thermite, which was used in incendiary bombs. When questioned, O'Connell stated,

'The stuff was on the van when it was handed us at Wembley by a friend whose name, I think, is Ferguson.'

This time, O'Connell was not permitted to go on his way; he and O'Toole were taken to Ilford Police station, and after Mick Ferguson was interviewed by police, he vanished. Ferguson, who as the IRA's CO of Longford Battalion had been arrested for murder in 1934, would resurface a few months later when he was scooped up in a series of arrests, by this time using the name of James Michael Lyons.

Charged with possessing an explosive substance under such circumstances as to suggest they did not have it for a lawful purpose, O'Connell and O'Toole refused to enter a plea at the Old Bailey; and after they declined the offer of legal aid, Sir Gerald Dodson QC, the Recorder of London, directed that a plea of not guilty should be entered. Having been found guilty, each was sentenced to nine months' imprisonment.

So this represented a couple of setbacks for the 'S' plan – but not for long.

CHAPTER 1

The 'S' Plan

O'Donovan's plan was hugely ambitious, but unrealistic given the resources available. He believed that both propaganda and direct action should be utilized. The initial concept was to concentrate on military subjects, aerodromes, dockyards and stores, but this was rejected since these establishments were well guarded by military personnel. What was not mentioned (but was an inescapable fact) was that in the event of attack, the military were likely to open fire, and that would never do. Armaments factories were also considered; however, their security was thought to be too strict. Attacks on the country's fire brigades and water supplies were seen as being counter-productive. Not for long, though; both these aspects of Britain's key services and industries would later be targeted.

Instead, it was decided to concentrate on telephone and telegraph systems, underground cables coupled with gas and electricity supplies, government offices and banks, in an effort to disrupt and do the maximum damage to the British economy. These targets, they felt, were far more likely to succeed.

During 1938, O'Donovan took time off from his job as a manager for the state-owned Electricity Supply Board and spent five months training volunteers in the art of bomb-making. Potassium chlorate was mixed with paraffin wax and heated in a saucepan using a wooden – not metal – spoon. The resultant mix was then placed in a container, but to set it off, a fuse connected to a detonator was required. The ingredients needed were sulphuric acid, magnesium, sugar and balloons. Sulphuric acid was sealed in a wax container and then inserted, initially into one balloon or two inside each other, although later, condoms were considered more reliable. When the balloon was squeezed, the wax container would break, permitting the acid to escape and burn through the rubber, then come into contact with the magnesium, which would burn, melting the sugar surrounding the fuse. That would then ignite, travelling along to the detonator to set off the volatile mix – which, due to its similarity in looks to the popular poultry stuffing, became known as 'Paxo'.

Next, on 27 December, teams of saboteurs were infiltrated into the mainland. Charles Casey, Seamus McGuiness and Eoin MacNamee went to London; Rory Campbell and Patrick Fleming travelled to Manchester, and Joe Deighan, Gerald Quigley and Michael Cleary to Liverpool; Jackie Kearns and Sean Fuller arrived in Birmingham, and Peter Walsh in Glasgow. Some of these names will resurface in the pages that follow.

They were the professionals; some of the pupils trained in Dublin and elsewhere proved to be adept at bomb-making; others, given the paucity of their education, proved less than reliable. These volunteers were infiltrated into England's main towns and cities and told not to mix with other Irish people or go to clubs or dance halls frequented by the local Irish population (since they were likely to be under surveillance by the police and/or the security services). Many of them, who had never previously strayed from their villages, were like fish out of water. They were likely to be betrayed by their accents, as well as by suspicious English landladies, and if they were caught, this might drag in their more sophisticated counterparts, who were able to adopt English or Scots accents. All types of explosives, including 'Paxo', dynamite and gelignite, as well as funding, were brought into England by members of *Cumann na mBann*, the IRA's women's organization; they would be less conspicuous and less likely to be known to members of the security services.

O'Donovan was keen to emphasize that the IRA's intention was to avoid casualties, and without further delay, it's time to review this ambiguous statement. O'Donovan wanted people to believe that he wished to keep civilian casualties to a minimum, but it makes sense to kick this ridiculous and hypocritical piece of cant straight into touch.

When bombs are detonated in a public place, it is inescapable that before very long, someone is going to be seriously injured or killed. Clear? It is to you and me but was not, apparently, to the fanatical or the gormless depositors of those bombs.

But the ambiguity can be cleared up: when O'Donovan was referring to 'casualties', he meant harm coming to any member of the IRA – nobody else.

Now for the letter sent not only to the Foreign Secretary, Lord Halifax, in London, but also to heads of government and political parties worldwide, in justification of the atrocities that would follow. Dated 12 January 1939, it read:

> Your Excellency,
>
> I have the honour to inform you that the Government of the Irish Republic, as having its first duty towards the people,

the establishment and maintenance of peace and order, herewith demand the withdrawal of all British armed forces stationed in Ireland. These forces are an active incitement to turmoil and civil strife, not only being a symbol of hostile occupation but in their effect and potentialities as an invading army. It is secondly the duty of the Government to establish relations of friendship between the Irish and all other peoples and to achieve this we must insist upon the withdrawal of British troops from our country and a declaration from your Government renouncing all claims to interfere in its domestic policy or external affairs. The Irish people have no cause of hostility to any European nation, even those nations whose natural development may bring them into conflict with British interests, and we are desirous of making it clear that we shall in no event take part in a war of aggression against any people or permit the nation to be regarded as having any community or identity of interest with Britain that would make us liable to attack by British enemies. The occupation of our territory by troops of another nation and the persistent subvention here of activities directly against the expressed national will and in the interests of a foreign power, prevent the expansion and development of our institution in consonance with our social needs and purposes, and must cease. Neither the Government of the Irish Republic nor the Irish people are actuated by any feelings of hostility to the people of Britain. Rather would we welcome a better understanding but this can be brought about only on the basis that each of the two peoples should be absolutely free to pursue its own course unhampered by the other. We shall regret if this fundamental condition is ignored and we are compelled to intervene actively in the military or commercial life of your country as your Government are now intervening in ours. The Government of the Irish Republic believes that a period of four days is sufficient notice for your Government to signify its intention in the matter of military evacuation and for the issue of your Declaration of Abdication in respect of our country. Our Government reserves the right of appropriate action without further notice if upon the expiration of this period of grace, these conditions remain unfulfilled.

Signed on behalf of the Republican Government and the Army

Council of Oglaigh na h-eireann

(Irish Republican Army)

Stephen Hayes, Patrick Fleming, Peadar O'Flaherty, George Plunkett, Lawrence Grogan, Sean Russell.

The idea that all British troops could be withdrawn in four days was nonsensical, as the signatories knew it must be, even if the

British Government had decided to acquiesce to these demands, which they most certainly would not have.

A phone call was made by the Home Office to Dublin: did de Valera's Government intend to wage war on England? They did not. Therefore the letter was stored away in that section of the files that all Government departments (including the police) reserve for what are colloquially known as 'nutters'.

It would have made sense for the letter to be forwarded to the Special Branch, who were better aware of the activities of the more nihilistic inhabitants of the Emerald Isle than their Foreign Office counterparts; but it wasn't.

* * *

The campaign commenced, as promised, on Monday 16 January 1939, with the first detonation occurring at 5 o'clock in the morning. A bomb exploded, tilting one of the pylons of the electricity grid which crossed the Alnwick and Rothbury Road, Northumberland, although the electricity supply was not disrupted; nor was it when a bomb exploded on a bridge carrying cables over the Grand Union Canal to Willesden power station, or following an explosion at the control room for the Central Electricity Board at Southwark.

Several men, one of them carrying a suitcase, had been seen at Southwark shortly before the explosion. Glass from their shattered windows rained down on many sleeping residents nearby, who were cut and shocked and many of whom rushed out into the streets. The blast blew out the windows of the Noah's Ark public house, as it did at the Queen's Head, where the door was practically torn from its hinges; and one of two curates asleep in St Peter's Curate House, next to the electricity control room, was covered in broken glass from his shattered bedroom window. Every window of the Thames Embankment Rescue Mission at nearby Summer Street was blown out.

Almost simultaneous explosions in Manchester covered a half-mile radius. Witnesses to the damage caused by an explosion at the William Deacon's Bank in Whitworth Street stated that it looked as though it had been bombed. Flames burst through a large hole in the pavement, the exterior and windows of the building were badly damaged by flying pieces of flagstone, as were the roofs, 50 feet above street level, of Lancaster House and the Union Bank, 25 yards away on the opposite side of the street. One piece of flagstone punctured a hole in the roof of India House, which was 80 feet above street level. Almost opposite the art gallery in

Princess Street, another bomb exploded, shattering underground electric cables and causing an escape of gas.

But by far the worst damage in Manchester that day was caused by a bomb which exploded at the corner of Newton Street and Hilton Street. It had been planted under three manhole covers leading to electricity cables and it blew 24-year-old Albert Ross high into the air, sending him crashing into Thomas Wash, who was walking a few yards behind him. Mr Wash survived, suffering from severe shock; Albert Ross, with both legs fractured and his spine broken in two places, did not. He died in the Royal Infirmary three hours later. So much for the IRA's sanctimonious crooning four days earlier that they 'had no feelings of hostility towards the people of Britain'.

Traffic was badly disrupted, and although it was initially suggested that the explosions were the result of an electrical fault, Captain C. W. Ede, an Inspector of Explosives for the Home Office (who would figure prominently as an expert in the Broadgate bombing, six months later), arrived to make an inspection. For hours afterwards, a gas main blazed in a 12-square-foot crater at the site of the murder, and workmen had to dig at eleven points in the street to relieve the gas pressure.

By now, Walter Tricker, the Home Office official responsible, had come to the conclusion that his decision to file away that IRA letter of ultimatum might have been a trifle hasty; it was retrieved and sent to New Scotland Yard's Special Branch – furthermore, it was leaked to the press.

Two bombs attached to a pylon carrying high tension cables across a field at Great Barr, just outside Birmingham, had exploded shattering three of the four steel legs, one of them being blown 45 yards away, although the cables were not brought down; a third bomb failed to explode. At 6.20 that morning there was a severe explosion on a steel bridge carrying some of the main extra high-tension trunk feeders from Hams Hall power station and two of the principal water mains supplying the station. The bridge was distorted and two of the cables were severed. But a large unexploded bomb comprised of stolen dynamite which had twin cables of flexible wire attached to it was discovered wedged in position beneath cables on another bridge, a short distance away from the scene of the explosion.

This brought Detective Chief Inspector Leonard Burt of C1 Department at the Yard, a highly experienced detective with twenty-seven years' service, racing to the scene, together with Mr H. E. Watts, the Chief Inspector of Explosives at the Home Office. They both waded knee-deep in mud to inspect the device.

'Thank goodness this is your job', Burt remarked to Watts. He then added, rather nervously, 'Do these things often go wrong when you dismantle them?'

'Sometimes', the expert replied laconically as he got to work, and after a few tense minutes he qualified his remark by telling Burt, 'But these won't!'

So that was one device which had been recovered intact, but there were more: a bag containing dynamite and gelignite was found by a passer-by attached to an electricity pylon carrying supplies over the Manchester Ship Canal at Barton, between Manchester and Warrington. The alarm clock had been set to detonate the explosives at 6 o'clock. Unfortunately, the bomber had failed to wind the clock up sufficiently and it had stopped at 12.35, so that, too, was sent to the Home Office for further examination, as was another unexploded bomb found at Clarence Dock, Liverpool.

However, despite Walter Tricker's rather gormless response to the IRA threat, Special Branch had a template for arrests: the list of names found in the jacket of the IRA team at the Dagenham address some six months previously. But of course, the IRA were unaware of this – and when Special Branch got to work so quickly after the initial explosions, the terrorists came to the conclusion that the IRA teams in England were riddled with informants. This put the bombers on the back foot from the start.

Chapter 2

Arrests

Given the number of terrorists involved, Special Branch quite clearly had insufficient personnel to cater for the numbers of searches and arrests to be carried out; therefore the Commissioner, Sir Philip Game, who as a lieutenant colonel during the First World War had won the DSO and been mentioned five times in dispatches, and was known as the 'listening' commissioner, listened to Albert Canning, the head of the Special Branch. Sir Philip authorized the secondment of a number of experienced CID officers, mainly from Scotland Yard and especially from the Flying Squad. Formed in 1919, this very tough band of adventurers were hugely disinclined to take 'no' for an answer, from anybody.

At 6 o'clock on the morning following the explosions, Detective Sergeant Coveney and Special Branch officers went to the Roundwood Road, Willesden address of Lawrence Lyons which, his landlady stated, he had taken in the name of 'Turner'. Coveney searched Lyons' room, finding a 6mm rifle and twenty-four rounds of ammunition. Later, at Littlebrook Power Station Construction at Dartford, he saw Lyons and arrested him. When he was later charged with possession of the rifle, Lyons replied, 'I object to the words "with intent to endanger life".'

Ten minutes after the first search, Detective Inspector Frank Bridges searched a flat at Viaduct Street, Bethnal Green which was occupied by Charles James Casey and where, under the bed, was found a brown suitcase containing two Colt revolvers, a Mauser pistol and seventy rounds of ammunition; Casey acknowledged the items were his property and he also admitted that he did not possess a firearms certificate. Additionally, he had no reasonable explanation for his possession of a mortar and pestle, a quantity of white powder, an exercise book containing chemical formulae and methods of making explosives, a book on machine gun tactics and a membership card of the IRA.

At 8.40am that morning, Detective Inspector Arthur Newton raided George Brendan Kane's address at Harold Road, Sutton where, in his bedroom, he found a locked suitcase; upon opening it, he found a Mauser automatic pistol and three rounds of ammunition, plus a spare magazine, wrapped up in a shirt. Kane admitted it was his case; inside it was an envelope addressed to Harold Kane. However, when Newton asked if he had a firearms certificate, Kane replied, 'No' and pointing to the pistol said, 'It's not mine.' He was also in possession of a four-page report giving locations of gasworks, electric power houses, post offices and sorting offices.

One of the most interesting finds was at Mornington Crescent at 6.05am on 18 January, when Detective Inspector Harold Keeble impolitely kicked in the door of a room occupied by Daniel Fitzpatrick and two seventeen-year-olds: Jack Logue and Francis James Burns. Keeble found an attaché case containing eighty-eight 2oz cartridges of gelignite tied up in brown paper bearing a Liverpool address and a galvanometer,[1] as well as a brown suitcase containing white powder, seventeen electric detonators and coils of fuse. Another suitcase held white powder, and the room contained an abundance of brown adhesive paper, a home-made copper wire sifter and brown paper bags. Two further suitcases were empty but contained traces of white powder. There was also a revolver holster, which Fitzpatrick admitted was his; and when Keeble's associate, Detective Sergeant McDougall, asked, 'Where's the article that fits this holster?' Fitzpatrick replied, 'If I'd had it in bed with me, you would all be unlucky!' It was an impetuous remark which Fitzpatrick regretted and thought it prudent to later deny making.

Keeble also found a letter in a chest of drawers. It was signed by Logue – Keeble was later able to say he knew this because he had seen him write his signature – and although Logue later said, 'I have no recollection of writing it', it read as follows:

> Dear Joe,
>
> This is to tell you that I cannot see you as arranged about the pipe on Saturday but when it suits your convenience you can let me know either by post or phone. I think I gave you my number last time I saw you. I hope you are still in the same mind. You can tell the others the reason. I think we have waited long enough. There are two good lads with me who know their 'Ps' and 'Qs' and are practically in the same boat as I am except they are still all right with the Army. You know one of them. I will not disclose his name here but I'll tell you when I see you again . . .

---

[1] An instrument for detecting and measuring small electric currents

When they were charged, the two teenagers made no reply but Fitzpatrick replied, 'I have something to say about it. The stuff was under my bed. Nobody had any knowledge of it, except myself.' A few seconds later, he added, 'I was the only one of the three of us that knew anything about it.'

Gerald Francis Wharton was found in possession of the second most interesting find, a quantity of potassium chlorate and magnetic oxide under circumstances that he did not have it in his possession for a lawful purpose, at his address in Camden Road by Detective Inspector Thompson, who was told, 'They were not knowingly in my possession.' He was also in possession of a questionnaire for the IRA on which could be written the applicant's name, address, unit in Ireland and length of time in the Army, as well as 103 balloons which, he stated, were for 'Christmas decorations'.

But by the time those defendants appeared, once more on remand at Bow Street Police Court on 2 February 1939 before Sir Rollo Graham-Campbell sitting in No 3 Court, there were additional faces; it appeared that somebody had been talking.

When Detective Inspector Sydney Barnes called at Michael O'Shea's address at Clewar Crescent, Harold Weald, he discovered four revolvers, a rifle and thirty-eight rounds of ammunition, plus three 1cwt drums containing aluminium powder and addressed to 21 Great Marlborough Street – the site of Marlborough Street Police Court. Among sixty documents found there was one headed 'The 'S' Plan', in which it was stated that the beginning of winter was a good time to commence operations, describing possible targets and referring to the letter which would be sent to Lord Halifax. Also included in this treasure trove of evidence was a telegram in code which, when deciphered, read:

> You will carry out first series of operations at 6am Monday 16th. See that where clock mines are used, they will explode at the above given time. No excuse will be received for not carrying out this order.

No excuse was necessary; the three bombs had exploded as ordered. Another coded telegram, dated 20 January – following the first wave of arrests but just prior to O'Shea's – read, 'Cease operations until further notice. Will communicate with you shortly. Congratulations.'

A letter dated 11 January addressed to 'The Commandant, London Unit' finished with the words, 'Make sure no stuff of any kind has been left over at Healy's, Fordington Road.'

It was true, no explosive material was found at John Healy's home address at Fordington Road when it was searched by Detective Inspector Charles Buckle; however, Healy was also the proprietor of a social club, and it was there that two tons of potassium chlorate and one ton of black iron oxide, for which Healy had paid £64, had been delivered. It was also discovered that Healy had distributed these items during December 1938 and January 1939. Four of the kegs were removed to Camden Town goods yard, painted white on top and had 'Soda' stencilled on them; these were forwarded to Liverpool. Eight more barrels were loaded on to a lorry and taken to Manchester. When he was charged, Healy replied, 'I didn't have it for an unlawful object; I had it there for commercial purposes.'

Detective Inspector Tansley searched the room at Cambridge Street, Pimlico occupied by Michael Preston and found a receipt for an excess fare from Liverpool to Manchester, a locked suitcase, a receipt for fifty Post Office envelopes, seventy-seven sheets of Government notepaper, a folder with names of aerodromes, 'shadow' factories,[2] military intelligence, a misspelt document marked 'Manuel [*sic*] of Instruction' which related to incendiary materials, Kelly's London Post Office map, a diary, a receipt for 2½ gross of balloons and receipts from a scientific glass-blowing company. There were also papers giving the strength of explosives and a list of explosives with the words 'London', 'Liverpool' and 'Birmingham'. Asked to provide an explanation for these items, Preston replied, 'I will not make a statement'. Like Lawrence Lyons, Preston had also used the name 'Turner' when he ordered eight gallons of sulphuric acid. The following day, Inspector Cooper asked Preston to account for data in his possession relating to explosives, to which he replied, 'I don't wish to say anything at the moment.'

He was probably wise not to. He had refused to give his occupation, and his name was not Michael Preston; it was Patrick Fleming, he was the IRA's OC London and he was one of the signatories to the letter addressed to Lord Halifax.

Peter Stuart was in possession of a large amount of property at his address in New Oxford Street which included an RAF uniform and an airman's cap, a postman's uniform, workman's dungarees, eleven parcels wrapped in paper containing black and white powder, a pestle and mortar, insulating tape, 1,000 balloons,

---

2 Shadow factories were devised in 1935 to try to meet the urgent need for additional aircraft in the event of a second war with Germany.

a packet of registered envelopes and two packets of envelopes marked 'O.H.M.S. Post Office'. A diary contained the names of twenty well-known stores and shops, with the words, 'Concentrate on Oxford Street, Regent Street, Piccadilly and Prince's Arcade'. There was also the matter of the thirty-nine sticks of gelignite, four electric detonators and a 40lb drum of aluminium powder. Asked by Detective Inspector Whitehead why he needed the explosives, he replied, 'No', but a few moments later qualified the remark by saying, 'We want an Irish republic.'

He neglected to inform the inspector that his name was really Peter Walsh and that he was the IRA's operations officer. Coincidentally, a letter was found at O'Shea's address which read in part: 'Success or failure of all operations to be carried out by your battalion rests to a great extent on you. You are responsible . . . If you think an operation cannot be carried out without men being arrested or civilians killed, you are at liberty to call the operations off.' The writer described himself as 'Operation Officer, Britain' and signed the letter with the same initials as used by Peter Stuart.

But by now the evidence was all coming together, and the Attorney General authorized the charge of conspiracy to cause explosions in the United Kingdom likely to endanger life or cause serious damage to property.

Chapter 3

Court Appearances

By 14 February, No. 3 Court at Bow Street was getting distinctly crowded, with the arrival of five more male prisoners and one woman, Molly Gallagher. Her room, which she shared with another woman at Thornhill Square, had been searched by Detective Inspector Whitehead, who found two rucksacks each containing packets of white powder and a suitcase containing traces of white and aluminium powder; there were also receipts for the purchase of copper gauze, paraffin wax and a pestle and mortar, as well as receipts from '8th Battalion, F.O.' and '9th Battalion, O.C.' A Christmas card signed 'P. Stuart' was found, as was an address book containing Kane's address. Miss Gallagher disclaimed all knowledge of the items.

The evidence concerning Michael John Lyons, charged with possessing an explosive substance, was said to be 'weak', and the magistrate discharged him.

But evidence from Detective Sergeant Cain of the Special Branch revealed that when he searched the premises of Charles McCarthy and his sons, Thomas and Daniel, at Sixth Avenue, Manor Park, he found a suitcase containing three balloons, white powder, three lengths of powder fuse, one of which was fitted to a detonator, and two alarm clocks, with a halfpenny in the timing apparatus of one and a farthing in the other. Two boxes of detonators were found and eighty-seven balloons, as well as maps of London, Essex and Birmingham and a newspaper with accounts of explosions in central London. Daniel McCarthy stated, 'My father and brother Tom have not the slightest knowledge of the stuff found.'

The daughter of Charles McCarthy told the magistrate that her father and brother Thomas were innocent and that she had assisted the police in the arrest of her other brother, Daniel. Sergeant Cain admitted that that was indeed the case.

When Detective Inspector Frank Bridges searched the coal cellar at Ashmore Road, Paddington, the home of John Ryan, and found a damaged corrugated iron drum, Ryan told him, 'That stuff that was in it, I've put on the garden, as I wanted to make room for my coal'; he later made a statement saying that he had agreed to store three drums of aluminium powder for a man who had previously lodged with him.

At John Mitchell's address Detective Inspector Baker found four gallon bottles marked 'Poison', three of which were full and one half-full.

More prisoners were joining the throng; on 17 February 1939, Detective Golding went to a house at Belle Vue Terrace, Hendon and in the presence of the occupants, James and Daniel McCafferty, discovered an attaché case under a bed. In it was an alarm clock fitted with timing apparatus, wires and a halfpenny attached to the alarm section. 'That's mine', said Daniel, while James said, 'I think this is victimization.'

The day following the arrest of the brothers McCafferty, James Patrick Connolly received a visit from Detective Sergeant Arthur Fretwell at his lodgings at Hargrave Park. When Fretwell lifted a suitcase from a wardrobe, Connolly entreated him, 'Go steady with that case.' He told Fretwell that the case belonged to his co-lodger, Francis McGowan, and an inspection of it revealed nine brown paper parcels, some containing white and grey powder, four with lengths of magnesium tape, and a hot water bottle containing turpentine. It was sufficient to ensure the arrest of both men.

In order to show that this was a nationwide conspiracy, evidence was now called from Liverpool.

On 19 January there had been an attempt to cause an explosion at the base of an electricity pylon in a field at Moss Lane, Windle, Lancashire. Four paper parcels containing potassium chlorate, paraffin wax, two gelignite sticks and a detonator were discovered, two tied to the pylon and two on the ground. Dual cables protruded from each of the parcels and were attached to an alarm clock and a battery. A local officer, Police Sergeant Duxberry, who discovered them cut the wires, and a fingerprint examination of the device's alarm clock revealed a left thumbprint. Detective Chief Inspector Fred Cherrill of the Yard's Fingerprint Branch was able to identify it as belonging to 29-year-old Michael Cleary, a member of the IRA who had been infiltrated into the Liverpool area, using the name Michael Joseph Mason, as one of a gang of bombers.

A week previously, on 12 January, two suitcases labelled 'N. Mason, King Street, Garston, Liverpool' were deposited at Acton GWR Station. A week later, when the cases were at Paddington Station parcels office, liquid was seen running from one of them and they were found to contain three half-gallon bottles of sulphuric acid.

On 3 February, both Mason and Joseph Walker were seen at a house in Great Nelson Street, Liverpool by Detective Inspector Pritchard of that force; Mason gave his name as Hynes. Six electrical leads were found in a dressing table drawer, to which Walker stated, 'I know nothing about them'.

But in Mason's pocket was a letter, headed 'Ireland' which read:

> Dear M,
>
> I hope the boys and self have got over the first onslaught of the enemy. Has the increased activity militated against further action for the present? Has the D/T P.F. been to see you yet? We sent him over a week ago and have not heard from him since. I hope he is not run to earth. We got a report of J.D's accident. Perhaps it is all for the best. The first blower has had a wonderful effect here. One or two more would get us the desired effect. If you have any urgent message or require anything you may be able to get a female courier . . . P.S. We have Eileen K.[1] on the job, part-time now.

Both men had London bus tickets and a map of the London Underground, and Mason was asked about a £10 note he had in his possession. He initially told Detective Sergeant Grundy that it had been sent by his sister but then, realizing that the officer would certainly investigate such a claim, he denied it. But when Sergeant Grundy suggested that the money had been sent to him by Peter Stuart in London, Mason made the astonishing and incriminating reply: 'I refuse to discuss Stuart, and if you mention his name in the statement, I will refuse to sign it.'

Now further evidence, other than that from the police, was forthcoming. Isabel Haillez lodged in the same house as Molly Gallagher and said that 'on numerous occasions' a man who she believed was Gallagher's brother had called at the house; one Sunday he had taken a yellow suitcase which appeared to be full upstairs, followed by Gallagher carrying a green suitcase. When she was shown a suitcase in court, she identified it as the one Molly Gallagher was carrying, at which stage Gallagher screamed from the dock, 'I'm not going to have lies told!'

Miss Haillez told the court that the man had had cylindrical packages under his arm and that when Gallagher left for work in the morning she was carrying a parcel of a similar shape. But the most important statement was when the witness described

[1] Eileen K. may have been an alias; at any rate, she does not appear in this narrative.

assisting her landlady to clean the house and recalled finding what she believed to be salt, which she threw on the fire. There was a hissing sound, before the substance burned with a large blue flame.

When Detective Sergeant Cain had searched the address of the McCafferty brothers, one of the items he found was an exercise book bearing the impression of writing underneath a page that had been torn out. Detective Sergeant (later Detective Superintendent) George Salter from the Forensic Science Laboratory had made a photographic enlargement of the impressions which revealed several names and addresses, one of which was 'Gerry Wharton, Camden Road, N. Waterford City Unit'. Daniel McCafferty carefully inspected the photograph before declaring with profound stupidity, 'It's a forgery.'

Now it was the turn of the scientific experts.

Mr H. E. Watts, who had dismantled the charge at Hams Hall power station in the presence of a distinctly nervous DCI Burt, informed the court that he had carried out six other anti-demolition jobs in Warwickshire, Staffordshire and Worcestershire on the same day and provided evidence about the alarm clocks with the halfpenny attached found in the McCafferty brothers possession.

'When the alarm goes off', explained Mr Watts, 'the halfpenny rotates. When it reaches the bottom, it presses a spring on to a piece of naked copper wire and that completes an electrical circuit. I have made experiments with the clocks and an electric detonator and I could do so in court, if necessary?'

'I don't think that is necessary,' replied Sir Rollo quickly, and swiftly went on to the next witness, Mr Frederick Harold Dupré, a chemical adviser to the explosives department at the Home Office.

Dupré gave the results of the testing of a number of items which had been submitted to him, including potassium chlorate, paraffin wax, black oxide of iron, hydrochloric acid, gelignite, aluminium, a rubber hot water bottle containing an inflammable liquid, sulphuric acid and rubber balloons. Put very simply, Mr Dupré said, when mixed, aluminium powder and black oxide of iron became thermite; placing the sulphuric acid in the balloons would rot the rubber, and then contact with a layer of chlorate of sugar placed on top of some thermite could be used to ignite it.

After the luckless civil servant, Walter Charles Tricker, produced the letter sent to Lord Halifax, Sir Rollo Graham-Campbell had no hesitation in committing the prisoners to stand their trial at the Old Bailey.

Chapter 4

The First of the London Trials

It was probably considered that to try all of the defendants together might prove unwieldy; therefore they were split into groups, and the trial of Mason, Stuart, Preston, Casey, Healy, Lyons, Walker, O'Shea and Kane commenced at the Old Bailey on 22 March 1939.

From a defence point of view, they were perhaps unfortunate that their cases were to be heard before Mr Justice Humphreys. Called to the Bar in 1889, Humphreys' career was devoted almost exclusively to prosecuting, as he did with great success in the trials of Oscar Wilde, Crippen, the poisoner Frederick Henry Seddon, George Joseph Smith (of 'the brides in the bath' case), the treason trial of Sir Roger Casement and the highly controversial Thompson and Bywaters murder case.

Now aged seventy-one, he was regarded as popular and witty by his colleagues, although in court he was said to be fierce and intimidating. An early intimation of this was when Charles James Casey, having initially refused to come up into court from the cells, after a struggle with the warders fell panting on the floor of the dock.

'Give him a chair and let him sit', said Mr Justice Humphreys, but Casey continued to struggle. 'Let him stand or sit or lie, whichever he prefers', then remarked the unsympathetic judge, so Casey remained on the floor until he realized that he would be trodden on by the other defendants on their way into the dock, whereupon he got up and sat down.

Asked to plead to the indictment, Casey and the other first four defendants refused to do so, each replying, 'I am a soldier of the Irish Republican Army.' The judge directed that pleas of not guilty be entered, and these pleas were tendered by the remaining defendants.

The case was outlined by the Attorney General, Sir Donald Somervell, and the witnesses were duly called. When DCI Cherrill gave evidence of finding Mason's thumbprint on an alarm clock found at Windle, the Judge told Mason, 'This evidence affects you, seriously. Do you desire to put any question?' Mason declined to do so.

Dr G. Roche Lynch, a Home Office analyst, stated that he had examined a cap belonging to Joseph Walker and that it had sparkled with minute fragments of aluminium.

Peter Stuart wanted a proclamation regarding the Irish Republic read aloud in court, but when he began disputing which part of it should be read, Mr Justice Humphreys told him sternly, 'Don't argue with me.'

He was more considerate – or so it seemed – in the case of James Lyons, who was not represented, when he invited Lyons to cross-examine expert witnesses. 'If there is anything you do not understand, tell me', he said. 'I want to help you all I can.'

Some of those present in court may have come to the conclusion that in making that statement, Mr Justice Humphreys' tongue was firmly in his cheek.

None of those who refused to plead wished to give evidence or call witnesses.

Walker and Healy, on oath, both stated that they had not conspired with anyone, were men of good character and not members of the IRA. Healy stated that he had acquired the two tons of chlorate of potash in order to manufacture throat pastilles, although when the Attorney General said that two tons of that mixture would produce 14 million pastilles, even the defendants had to join in the laughter.

O'Shea stated that two men had come to his address on the day before he was arrested and handed him the three drums of aluminium powder, not informing him what they contained but advising him not to tell anybody about them, or 'We'll see you later'. As for the rifle that was found, he had never seen it before, nor, indeed, any of the other men in the dock.

The judge invited Mason to make a statement in his defence. First, he stated that although he and Walker had lived in the same house, Walker knew nothing of his affairs. He then said:

> I am not a criminal. I am fighting for the freedom of my country. For hundreds of years, Irishmen have fought for freedom and will continue to fight as long as any part of their country is occupied by the British.

Now it was Stuart's turn. He declared:

> I am not a criminal. What I did was my duty as a soldier of the Irish Republic to protest against the coercion of the Irish people by the British and the suppression of the Irish people. I don't care what sentence I get in this court. I know the fight

> will go on. If, when I come out, the fight is still going on, I shall take part in it again.

Mr Justice Humphreys looked thoughtfully at Stuart for a moment before quietly saying, 'Just repeat that, will you?' and Stuart obliged, replying, 'If Ireland is not free when I come out, I shall carry on the fight again. Ireland will be free and I shall see it free, I know.'

Preston turned towards the jury and declared:

> At the onset of this trial, I refused to plead or ask for legal aid to defend myself. Had I done so that would have been a pitiful apology to the British Government for my action and I would not do that. England's policy towards the Irish people has always been one of shooting, hanging or gaoling. We have stood up to that and we can stand up to it still . . .

The judge's voice cut across the rest of his words. 'That will do, Preston', he said. 'I've listened to enough of this nonsense.'

Abandoning his rhetoric, Preston said that he took full responsibility for the purchases of acid and aluminium powder, adding that Healy had no way of knowing that he was connected with the Irish Republican Army.

Lyons read a statement claiming, with jaw-dropping hypocrisy, that because the British Government had refused to comply with the IRA's demands it could not wash its hands of responsibility for the bombings. When he made a reference to partition, the judge told him, 'I won't have politics introduced', and when Lyons ignored him, the judge closed the argument with the words, 'I have told you, I will not allow any reference to Northern Ireland. It has nothing whatever to do with this case.'

Summing up to the jury on 28 March, Mr Justice Humphreys told them:

> There is complete freedom of thought in this country and any person who takes the view that Ireland or Scotland or the Isle of Man or the Isle of Wight ought to be severed from the British Crown and become a republic is perfectly entitled to hold that view. Moreover, there is here complete freedom of utterance of thought and such a person is entitled to express his views and by writing, or by speech to induce others, if he can, to be converted to his views. All that is permissible and that is what is called political propaganda. But when a person ceases to employ these constitutional methods of altering the position of part of a British Dominion and employs methods

> of terrorism, incendiarism, causing of explosions and rendering the life of respectable law-abiding citizens impossible, then it is that the Crown – represented in this case by the Attorney General – steps in and invites those who are responsible for the administration of the criminal law – that is magistrates, juries and judges – to act, and act firmly, in doing what they can to suppress such illegal and dangerous acts. These men are not in the dock because they advocate an Irish Republic but because it is alleged against them that they used methods which cannot be tolerated in any civilised country. You and I need not stop to consider whether it is really possible in these days of education – or so-called education – that people can really and honestly hold the view that they are assisting their country to become a Republic by destroying the telephones, electric lights, the public buildings and the private buildings of people who live in another country. It may appear to be a perfectly ridiculous question, and we need not stop to discuss it.

The jury retired for one hour and fifty minutes. Walker was found not guilty of possessing nine electrical leads for an unlawful object, and Kane was acquitted of possessing a pistol with intent to endanger life or property. However, midway through the trial, Kane had pleaded guilty to conspiracies to cause explosions and commit arson, and everybody else in the dock was found guilty of those offences.

'My name is not Mason', said that defendant. 'I would like to be sentenced in my real name; it is Cleary.'

Having been told that Mason had come to the country in 1938 and had taken over the post of OC, IRA Great Britain, the Judge said, 'It is quite clear that you are an incendiary. You were personally engaged in an attempt to blow up one of the pylons . . . I regard you as the worst of the men in the dock.' He was then sentenced to seventeen years' penal servitude.

Telling Stuart that he had been acting as operations officer and was obviously one of the leaders of the conspiracy, the Judge sentenced him to fifteen years' penal servitude.

After Preston informed the judge, 'My correct name is not Preston; it is Fleming', Mr Justice Humphreys told him, 'Undoubtedly, you were an active person in the inner councils of this criminal association, but I think your part in the matter has not been proved to be as serious as that of the other two I have just sentenced.' Twelve years' penal servitude.

Sentencing Casey – who told the court that he had done his duty in assisting the IRA – to fourteen years' penal servitude, Mr Justice Humphreys told him, 'Yours is a very bad case, indeed.

That book which the jury have seen shows that you were the most active person in discovering ways and means of making explosives and how to use them and the list of the things found in your premises is very serious indeed.'

Healy still protested his innocence, but the Judge described him as 'the introducer of other persons . . . to obtain what they would describe as munitions of war' and sentenced him to ten years' penal servitude, as he did Lyons, on entering the dock, sprang to attention and cried, 'I have done my duty and God save Ireland!'

The Judge told him, 'You are very much in the same position as Healy but . . . you have chosen to glorify your misdeeds and you have kept that up to the end.'

Kane, who described himself as OC of the local IRA in the neighbourhood of Sutton and Epsom, was sentenced to seven years' penal servitude, with the Judge remarking that had he pleaded guilty right from the outset, he would have saved public time and money. O'Shea received five years' penal servitude, and after the jury foreman confirmed to the Judge that they believed Walker had been a subordinate to Mason, he was sentenced to eighteen months' hard labour.

Hardly had the judge told the Attorney General that he thought the police had 'acted with acumen and celerity in making the arrests', than the next batch of prisoners was wheeled into court.

CHAPTER 5

The Remainder of the London Trials

Daniel Fitzpatrick and Daniel McCarthy refused to plead; the rest, who pleaded not guilty to similar charges to their predecessors, were John Mitchell, Jack Logue, Francis Burns, the father and son Charles and Thomas McCarthy, John Ryan and Gerald Wharton.

After a two-day trial, the Judge summed up in his customary robust fashion:

> This case alleges a gigantic conspiracy – and it *is* a gigantic conspiracy. Conspiracy in itself is a criminal offence. It is a very serious thing and it ought to be. It is not an attack on an individual but on a nation. There is ample evidence to justify you in coming to a conclusion that there was an abominable conspiracy which evidenced itself in January this year and which is going on now and has not come to an end, the headquarters of which are in Dublin and which conspiracy perhaps cannot be ended by any English police, however active and courageous they are, unless and until the head of the conspiracy is killed by a police force which is not English, because an English police force cannot go into Dublin.

Daniel McCarthy, who had initially refused to plead, pleaded guilty to possession of explosives, which let his father and brother off the hook; they were both acquitted and outside the court were congratulated by members of their family, as well as by Special Branch officers, Detective Inspector Thompson shaking hands with Charles McCarthy.

Everybody else was found guilty of all the offences, and Inspector Thompson stepped into the witness box to inform the court of the defendants' characters. The ringleader – quite rightly – was said to be Gerald Wharton, and the court heard that he was a member of the IRA and in 1920 had been sentenced to two years' imprisonment for offences under the Defence of the Realm Act. Having fought against the British Government, he was released in February 1922; when an Irish Government was appointed, he fought them as well. After being involved in a number of skirmishes, Wharton was sentenced to two years' hard labour; once in prison, he helped to make an escape tunnel but was removed to another camp before it was completed. Released in December 1924, he claimed to be suffering from rheumatism as a result of his captivity and asked the Irish Government for a pension.

Wharton told the Judge that he wished to make a statement, and the Judge replied, 'I will hear anything you have to say relevant to your sentence and why your sentence should be reduced; I will not listen to any political speech.'

To this, Wharton replied:

> This is certainly not a political speech. I have a wife and a young baby and a baby not yet born; I also have a father and mother whom I may never see again – they believe and know I am innocent of the charges. I want to say I abhor these bombings as much as anybody. I had never known the IRA contemplated such action until I heard the 'S' Plan read out in Bow Street. I had never heard of potassium chlorate or balloons in connexion with explosives. As for my past record, many Cabinet Ministers in the Government of Eire have the same record. These things happened twenty years ago. These past records do not prevent our people from being friendly with each other. In reference to a letter of mine which was mentioned during the case, that was not meant in any way to be offensive to the British people whom I have worked with and learned to appreciate for the past twelve years.

Sentencing him to ten years' penal servitude, Mr Justice Humphreys said:

> You are a rebel against all constituted authority. You were a member of that gang which committed murders of British officers and others, up to 1922. There was then constituted a different Government in Ireland. You rebelled against that and fought against that and gloried in a letter which I have been reading. You have stated in a letter, what I have no doubt is perfectly true, that the only reason you came to England was because you could get better wages here; and I have no reason to doubt what you have said in the letter was true – that you hate the English and that it was a pain and grief to you that living in England, you had to listen to your children singing 'God Save the King'. You are a hypocrite and in my view, you are the worst and most dangerous of the gang that is now before me.

Logue was a member of the IRA who had neglected to attend his drills in Belfast and had been tarred for it; he was sentenced to three years' borstal detention. After the Judge asked Burns for some statement which would permit him to place him on probation, Burns hesitated, then chose to reply, 'I have nothing to say, except that I am in sympathy with the rest of the men sentenced.' The offer of leniency was then kicked smartly into touch, and he, too, was sentenced to three years' borstal detention.

Fitzpatrick, who occupied the same lodgings as Logue and Burns, had convictions in Belfast, where he was regarded by the local police as being a vicious and active member of the IRA. Sentencing him to eight years' penal servitude, the Judge told him:

> You are the man who is responsible for the appearance in the dock and the conviction of the two young men, Logue and Burns. Without you, I am satisfied they would never have been here; you are responsible for their downfall. You are also the person who, when arrested by the police, regretted that you had not a pistol with you.

The Judge did not believe that Mitchell was 'quite as active as the others', but in telling him that the evidence that had convicted him was 'overwhelming', he sentenced him to five years' penal servitude.

McCarthy, Inspector Thompson told the court, had been influenced by Casey and others of his type, and a letter handed up to the Judge stated that McCarthy was suffering from religious mania which cleverer people had capitalized upon, suggesting to him that their purposes were consistent with his religious beliefs. In fact, said his barrister, his own defence had been prejudiced by his insistence that his father and brother were not in any way to blame.

But the 'terribly serious' list of articles in his possession plus the fact that he had shown no repentance necessitated, said the Judge, even at the tender age of nineteen, a sentence of four years' penal servitude.

'Dull-witted' and 'simple-minded' was the way Inspector Thompson described Ryan, saying that he had done all he could to help the police trace the man who left the stuff with him. The Judge agreed with this assessment but, he stated, it was impossible to allow people to act as Ryan had done, and the British people were entitled to be protected. He sentenced Ryan to eighteen months' imprisonment.

Closing the proceedings with a fulsome tribute to the police (and a sideways swipe at the Dublin authorities), the Judge said, 'They have shown very great diligence and very great intelligence without very much assistance from any other body in bringing to justice these dangerous people; they are to be congratulated.' The last of the prisoners was brought into court on 4 April.

* * *

After the Judge had heard all of the evidence, during which the court was told that the alarm clock in the McCafferty brothers' possession could not be used to wake anybody up in the morning – 'Unless', the Judge stated caustically, 'you like to be woken up by gelignite' – he summed up, saying:

> Some persons, I believe, are astonished by the ideas prevailing in this country with regard to the administration of criminal law. They think we aim too far in the direction of assuring to accused persons a fair and impartial trial. I do not myself take that view. I believe the best way of administering justice is to try to give to every person, however recalcitrant he may be, exactly the same form of trial as to any other person. These men say they are members of the IRA. There is no such thing, because there is no Irish Republic.

The jurors did not bother to leave the court in order to find the McCafferty brothers, Francis McGowan, James Connelly and Molly Gallagher guilty, and Mr Justice Humphreys assured the jury, 'I don't see how you could have found any other verdict.'

Mentioning that Molly Gallagher's family had been known to Special Branch as ardent supporters of the IRA for many years, and that despite Inspector Thompson's best efforts, Margaret Edgeworth, with whom Gallagher had shared a room, was in Dublin – 'At large in Dublin and likely to remain at large', was the Judge's caustic comment – Gallagher was told that 'If you were free, your friends would soon get hold of you and you would come under the same influence as before.' She was sentenced to three years' borstal detention.

James McCafferty told the court, 'The verdict was wrong. We were found guilty in a good cause. Up the Republic!'

To this, the Judge replied:

> You tell me almost in words – you do tell me by your behaviour – that when you come out of prison your present

> intention is to continue in the course you have followed in the past. That being so, my duty to the public is to see that you don't at least take part in any such criminal activities for a substantial period of time.

James McCafferty was then sentenced to five years' penal servitude, and brother Daniel (shouting 'Up the Republic!' as he left the dock) to four and a half years' penal servitude.

Francis McGowan and James Connolly had pleas of not guilty recorded after each stated, 'As a soldier of the Irish Republic, I refuse to plead.' Although Inspector Thompson said that there was nothing against their characters, Mr Justice Humphreys told them, 'These infernal machines – because that is what they are – are exactly similar to those found in possession of one of the undoubted leaders in England of this terrorist gang, Peter Stuart', and sentenced McGowan and Connolly to seven and six and a half years' penal servitude, respectively. 'Up the Republic!' shouted both men as they were led off to the cells.

Gerald Wharton's stay in the cells was a short one; utilizing the legal system of the country he despised, he appealed his conviction on 13 June 1939. The Lord Chief Justice stated that 'It could not be disputed that a substantial case had been made against Wharton' and that 'He was shown to be in possession of explosive substances . . . but there has been a misdirection and a non-direction on essential matters' – and one extremely guilty terrorist walked free, although he was later arrested and deported.

* * *

Too late to join Healy and the other conspirators in the dock was John Percival Martin, who was arrested on 11 March. Healy had arranged for a shipment of aluminium powder to be delivered to an address at Horn Lane, Acton, and Martin had been identified as the person who had accepted the delivery and signed a receipt.

The police discovered that Martin was lodging at an address in Gower Street with another man, James Pearce McGuiness. Potassium chlorate was found at the address, and McGuiness was arrested a week later.

At Bow Street Police Court, Sir Rollo Graham-Campbell complimented McGuiness on the way he had conducted his defence: 'You have cross-examined extremely well', he said, but nevertheless he committed both men for trial at the Old Bailey.

Although both refused to plead – a sure indication to many jurors that they were guilty – Detective Inspector Rogers agreed, in cross-examination by McGuiness, that although McGuiness had taken part in several identification parades, he had not been picked out. The evidence against him was fairly circumstantial, and he was found not guilty and discharged.

Martin, found guilty, delivered the following statement from the dock:

> We of the Irish Republican Army have no fear of prison. A twenty, thirty or even fifty years' sentence or even death has no fear for us. We are fighting for an ideal. If, after my release, Ireland has any connection with the British, I will, without hesitation take my position of attack with the same zeal as heretofore. The place of every true Irishman is behind the stock of his rifle.

The Recorder of London, Sir Gerald Dodson, put Martin back for sentence until other trials involving explosives had finished; and when he appeared again on 4 May he said that he was not eighteen as previously stated and that his real name was Pearse McLaughlin, and he repeated that what he had done was his duty as a soldier of the IRA.

Detective Inspector Thompson stated that Martin had come to the country early in January, and that before the explosions had occurred he was in touch with sections of the IRA in London and apparently had known all that was going to happen.

'Who gives him his money?' asked the Recorder, and when he was told that it was the IRA, Martin shouted, 'That's a lie – we accept no payment for carrying out our duty!' The Recorder sentenced him to ten years' penal servitude, without comment.

Chapter 6

Charges in Wales and Manchester

Contained in Michael Preston's diary were details of a certain cycle dealer named Timothy Dacey with an address at Metal Street, Roath, Cardiff; and Scotland Yard urged the local police to pay him a visit without delay. On the evening of the same day as Preston's arrest, police discovered two parcels at Dacey's premises; one contained twenty sticks of gelignite, the other, sixteen detonators.

On his second appearance at Cardiff Police Court a further remand was sought, and Mr Horace Davies, Dacey's defending solicitor, made a strong plea to have this refused. However, Mr Leslie Owen, on behalf of the Director of Public Prosecutions, told the bench:

> There is no need for me to tell you of the seriousness of the charge. Permission to proceed with the case is being obtained after examinations have been made of certain articles.

Committed to Glamorgan Assizes, Dacey stated that he had never been to Ireland, was not a member of the IRA and knew nothing of explosives. He said that two Irishmen who appeared rather apprehensive had brought the parcels to his shop; why, he had no idea. He was told that they would call back later and pay him for keeping their goods there. Who they were, or where to find them, he could not say, since he had had no further communication with them. The first time he was aware of the contents of the parcels was when the police opened them. It might almost have sounded convincing, except for the fact that a copy of *Wolfe Tone Weekly*, the official newspaper of the IRA, was found in his shop.[1]

Having been found guilty on 1 March 1939 and sentenced to seven years' penal servitude, Dacey was told by Mr Justice Cassels:

> This is not a country in which explosive substances can be harboured for unlawful objects. The danger to life and

[1] Wolfe Tone, who died in 1798 after leading a rebellion against British rule in Ireland, was regarded as the father of Irish Republicanism.

> property through the unlawful use of explosives is so great that Parliament has provided that such an offence shall be severely dealt with.

* * *

The same charges that had been brought at the Old Bailey would soon be preferred against persons detained in Manchester on the same day as the London arrests. As a result of careful enquiries concerning the three explosions in Manchester, the arrests were carried out the following day, commencing at 11.50pm on Tuesday, 17 January and finishing at 6.30am the following morning. Patrick Walsh, Michael Rory Campbell, Patrick Deviney, Jack Glenn, Joseph Broderick, Denis Duggan and Patrick O'Connell were arrested by Detective Superintendent William Page for collectively being in possession of six barrels, each containing 1 cwt of potassium chlorate, a large quantity of powdered charcoal, forty sticks of gelignite, a box of candles, a solidified composition of paraffin wax and potassium chlorate and three matchboxes containing sugar and potassium chlorate.

Walsh was questioned about the three explosions in Manchester the previous day and told the officers that he had some stuff upstairs that two men had told him was beeswax and asked him to look after for them. There they found four barrels, a sack containing fine black powder and three shopping bags containing similar powder. Pressed as to what had happened to the other barrels, Walsh hesitated before claiming they had been removed two weeks previously – but declined to say who by.

Campbell and O'Connell were arrested at a house in Alexandra Road South, Manchester, where documents relating to IRA activities were found, plus maps of Manchester and Salford marking police stations, fire stations, military barracks and railway stations.

Campbell told Superintendent Page, 'What I did, I did for Ireland', and O'Connell agreed, saying, 'That goes for me, too.'

An alarm clock, which had been found with explosives at Barton, bore O'Connell's fingerprints.

A copy of 'Battalion Orders' was found at Parkfield Street, Rusholme, where Patrick Deviney and Jack Glenn were arrested, which set out directions demanding strict compliance and ending with the words, 'Failure to comply with the above orders calls for immediate military action against any officer or volunteer who commits himself and if necessary, the death penalty will be carried out.'

Questioned about a car found in a garage, Deviney stated, 'If I hadn't used it, I would have been shot.'

Glenn admitted removing two barrels of explosives to an address in Salford but said, 'I'm not having the explosions.'

When Joseph Broderick (whose address was, coincidentally, in Salford) was charged, he replied, 'I'm not standing for this. Paddy and Jack Glenn brought the stuff to me and Duggan – that's the boss at the club – gave me the gelignite and told me to look after it.'

Ralph Howard, the Deputy Chief Constable, who raided Broderick's address, would later say, 'He was far more alarmed about his mother-in-law than about us. The old lady was the owner of the house and was very indignant.'

Charged under the Explosive Substances Act, 1883, the men appeared at Manchester City Police Court, and when they were remanded in custody, Michael Campbell shouted, 'Before we leave the court, I wish to state that against the occupation of the English in Ireland I wish to utter a protest!'

This gave the stipendiary magistrate, Mr J. Wellesley Orr a fair idea of the way matters were going to proceed.

At the next remand, two women – Mary Glenn and Nora Glenn, sisters of Jack Glenn – joined their brother and six other men in the dock.

During the search of a house in Dryden Street, police found barrels of explosives inside a nailed-up wardrobe, and forty-eight sticks of gelignite and two Mills bombs under the floorboards. In the same hiding place a sketch was found marked 'S.W.E. control' which was an exact plan of the control room at Bristol of the electricity grid for South-West England, together with four sheets headed 'Methods of War', which provided the reader with a rousing list of ways to disrupt life in England.

At this point, Mary Glenn walked in. She was searched, and a letter addressed to a person named Bridie was found, which read in part:

> We have to keep things quiet for a bit and trust in God for the best. Don't say too much when you write to me, as our letters may be opened and don't be surprised if you hear we are in gaol, as we all expect to be picked up if anything happens.

More documents were found which referred to the use of incendiaries and which stated, 'We will not only attack England's might but the morale of her people. That is one of our objectives.' Three alarm clocks were also found, two of them bearing the fingerprints of Mary Glenn and Michael Rory Campbell. Documentation found in Nora Glenn's bedroom suggested her job was to keep documents and accounts.

When they were charged with the same offence as the male defendants, both women replied that they knew nothing about it. The defendants were later committed to stand their trial at Manchester Assizes.

* * *

Some sixty officers were deployed, inside and outside the Manchester Assizes, on 6 March 1939; everyone entering the building was scrutinized, and no one was allowed into the public gallery.

Patrick Walsh, Michael Rory Campbell, Patrick Deviney, Jack Glenn, Joseph Broderick, Denis Duggan, Patrick O'Connell and Mary and Nora Glenn were all charged with several offences, including the most serious, possession of explosive substances with intent to endanger life.

Their numbers had now been increased following the detention of John Gavahan who, when he was arrested, warned the superintendent, 'Although you've got us, the cause will go on. Something will probably happen in Liverpool, tonight' – although nothing did. However, something did happen the following night, when a bomb exploded, damaging the wall of Liverpool's Walton Gaol, where a number of IRA prisoners were being held. Damage was minimal and the wall was not breached, although a passer-by was badly shocked by the blast.

The trial judge was Mr Justice Stable – Sir Wintringham Norton Stable MC as was. Approaching his fifty-first birthday, he had only been appointed to the High Court just over three months previously.

Campbell, Jack Glenn, Duggan, O'Connell and Gavahan refused to plead, and after the jury had considered that they were 'mute of malice' as opposed to 'mute by visitation of God', pleas of not guilty were entered for them which coincided with the pleas tendered by the other defendants.

David Maxwell Fyfe KC, MP set out the facts for the prosecution – and although none of the prisoners were charged with the three explosions in Manchester, one of which resulted in the death of Albert Ross, those details nevertheless formed a great deal of the address to the jury.

Evidence was given by Miss L. K. Crossland, who owned the house at Parkfield Street, Rusholme, that Nora and Mary Glenn had originally lived there and that their cousin Deviney and brother Jack had then moved in. The sisters had later moved out but, stated Miss Crossland, on the night before the bombings, neither of the men had returned to the premises before she had retired, at 11.30pm.

Detective Inspector Forster gave evidence that when he had arrested Jack Glenn he had found a piece of cable and a copy of IRA battalion orders in his overcoat pocket. Glenn, who until then had remained 'mute of malice', suddenly found his voice and, jumping to his feet, shouted, 'You're a liar!'

The Judge suggested various forms of cross-examination that Glenn could subject the officer to, but the best he could do was declare, 'It's only a police frame-up.'

Walsh stated that he had never been a member of the IRA and had no idea that any of the substances found in his house were explosive or dangerous; his wife, Sybil, agreed.

Mary Glenn denied that she had ever seen the incriminating letter found in her handbag which, she said, was not in her handwriting, but the Judge asked her to spell the words 'Lonely' and 'Until', which featured in the letter. She wrote the words down, and then the Judge informed the jury that in the letter, 'until' was spelt 'untill' and 'lonely' was spelt 'lonley'. In the Judge's notebook Glenn had written 'untill' and 'lonly'.

Deviney, in a statement from the dock, denied telling the police that had he not used his car, he would be shot and he was unaware that the material he had conveyed in his car was explosives; he had done so merely 'to be obliging'.

The Judge's summing-up lasted four hours and was a model of fairness to the defendants. On the Judge's directions, Nora Glenn and Joseph Broderick – the latter perhaps surprisingly, given his comments when he was arrested – were discharged, and after the jury had deliberated for one hour, Patrick Walsh was acquitted. Not so the others.

Inspector E. J. Pierpoint stated that Campbell had for several years been known as an extremist in Ireland, and in passing sentence, the Judge – in what was described as 'cold and deliberate tones' – said:

> The jury have found you guilty on the clearest possible evidence of being engaged in a conspiracy of a diabolical character, a conspiracy to pass far beyond the realm of plotting and planning – it had taken shape in the form of action. It is as apparent to me as it must have been apparent to you that if you had succeeded and the explosions which you planned had taken place, the lives of perfectly innocent people who knew nothing of you and of whom you knew nothing would have

> been imperilled. One harmless life was destroyed by one of the explosions which I have no doubt you had actively planned, if yours was not actually the hand which put the explosive apparatus in position.

Campbell was then sentenced to a total of twenty years' penal servitude, whereupon he shouted, 'Well, it was all for a good cause and I would do it again – God save Ireland!' and a woman in the well of the court screamed, 'Rory! Rory!' A warder clapped his hand over Campbell's mouth and, following a furious struggle in the dock, he was overpowered by three or four warders and dragged off to the cells.

Telling O'Connell, 'You have been found guilty on the clearest possible evidence of a diabolical conspiracy', the Judge sentenced him to a total of twenty years' penal servitude. Shouting loudly, O'Connell was hustled down the dock steps.

The Judge had already demonstrated his shrewdness when he asked Mary Glenn to spell two incriminating words; and now he did so again when Deviney was brought up for sentence. He said, 'One of the officers said when you were arrested that you said, "I had to take the car out that night or I should have been shot". You denied that in court. Was it true?'

'No, it was not', replied Deviney.

'You were not acting under compulsion?' asked the Judge. 'You were not acting in fear of your life?'

'No', replied Deviney. 'Just merely to oblige.'

'In spite of what you have said to me now', said the Judge, 'I shall take in your case a comparatively merciful view', and he sentenced him to concurrent terms of fourteen years' penal servitude.

Duggan and John Glenn were each sentenced to twenty years' penal servitude, the former twice shouting 'Up the Republic!' and the latter, 'God save Ireland!' as both were hurried to the cells.

Dealing next with 22-year-old Mary Glenn, Mr Justice Stable told her:

> You have been convicted of taking part in this evil conspiracy. It is a lamentable thing and a painful duty to sentence a woman of your age. The days of youth mean so much to you and so much more than for a man.

After being sentenced to a total of seven years' penal servitude, she managed, like her brother, to shout 'God save Ireland!' before a warder clapped his hand over her mouth and she was taken from the dock.

The same defiant shout came from John Gavahan after the Judge told him that 'It passes human belief that a married man of thirty-two, with two children, should take part in such a conspiracy, which must sooner or later have involved wanton and indiscriminate destruction of some perfectly innocent persons' and sentenced him to twenty years' penal servitude.

Thanking the jury and the prosecution counsel for their endeavours, Mr Justice Stable added:

> I should like to compliment all the police officers engaged, not only for the rapidity with which they got on the tracks of these outrageous happenings, but on the quite admirable way in which the case has been prepared. If they had had a year to do it in, it could not have been done better; I hope my words will reach the proper quarter.

The last word in the case went to the acquitted Patrick Walsh, whose house had contained the huge cache of explosives. He told a reporter, 'I'm glad to be able to go home, now it's all over. I'm finished with Ireland.'

CHAPTER 7

Arrests in Birmingham, Scotland and Liverpool

It was not only the police of London and Manchester who had been busy; Birmingham, Scotland and Liverpool had been hard at work as well.

On 8 February Detective Inspector Sanders led a team of Birmingham CID officers into a house at Wheelys Road, Edgbaston, where a search was carried out. Hugh McClusky was one of the occupants present; between 1929 and 1934 he had lived in America, but on 28 July 1937, the occasion of a royal visit to Belfast, seven men attacked police who were guarding some decorations, inflicting some serious injuries. McClusky was one of two men arrested, and he received twelve months' hard labour.

Another of those in the house was Robert McCann, who had been sent to hard labour for twelve months in Belfast for possessing documents concerned with the IRA; and lastly, there was 19-year-old Thomas Magill, who was responsible for an attaché case containing two sticks of magnesium, three tins containing metallic sodium and a quantity of magnesium scrapings. In a food cupboard was found a bundle of fine wire mesh, together with other articles for use in making explosives or incendiaries.

When McClusky was searched, he told the officers:

> It's all right. We haven't got a gun. If we had, we should have put a bullet through all of you. You caught us napping. I'm better off inside. I'm shutting up as one of our fellows went to Australia and they got him there.

McCann's speech was less lengthy. 'I'm saying nothing' he said. 'I should like to know how you knew I was here. They chased me from home.'

Magill helpfully told the officers, 'I'll take responsibility.'

But that was all he did say; both he and McCann refused to plead at Birmingham Assizes; the jury found them 'mute of malice', and McClusky pleaded not guilty.

Detective Inspector Sanders gave evidence in full, and the prosecuting counsel told Mr Justice Oliver that other officers could corroborate the inspector's evidence. The Judge was having none of it.

> There is no reason why they should. If Magill and McCann do not choose to take any part in this trial, they will have to take the consequences. I do not see why the time of the court should be wasted by proving things over and over again.

Hugh Edmond Watts of the Home Office (he now had a doctorate) gave a demonstration in the witness box of what happened when he applied a match to the wire mesh found in the food cupboard at the men's lodgings. It burned brilliantly, and Dr Watts said it could be used for firing a bomb.

At the conclusion of the prosecution evidence, McCann still had nothing to say, although from the dock he declared:

> I would like to make it clear to the jury that so far as Hugh McClusky was concerned in this transaction, he was only in the house because he had nowhere else to go . . . I could not tell him there was anything in the house or he probably would not have come.

McClusky did give evidence from the witness box, saying that he had come to the mainland in January, he knew nothing about the items found at the house, he was not a member of the IRA and he *definitely* did not make a statement regarding putting a bullet through the police. However, after a very brief retirement, the jury found the three men guilty, and Detective Inspector Sanders told the court:

> Magill is an active and aggressive member of the IRA. Information has come to hand that following the arrest of leaders of that army last December, he was appointed to an important position in that concern and it is possible that he may have been sent to this country to take part in subversive activity.

It may be gleaned from his previous comments that Mr Justice Oliver would deal with them in a particularly robust matter, and before sentencing on 20 March he did so, saying:

> I know your kind too well to think there is the slightest hope you will ever be sorry. There is at this moment in this society in which we live nothing worse as you and your like. You are

> about as dangerous as mad dogs and perhaps, not much more responsible.

Telling Magill that he could not deal with him as a boy of nineteen but would have to deal with him as what he was, a source of potential danger, the Judge sentenced him to seven years' penal servitude.

McClusky was sentenced to ten years' penal servitude, as was McCann (described by Inspector Sanders as 'a dangerous man'), who grasped the dock rail and shouted, 'Long live the Republic!' before being dragged away.

* * *

But before the court proceedings at Birmingham had concluded, there were odd happenings some 302 miles to the north.

Two men – with no known connection to the IRA – using skeleton keys broke into a store at Barleyside colliery, near Falkirk and stole 200lbs of gelignite and 300 detonators. Arthur Lynch Scobbie and William Anderson told Sheriff Substitute Hendy[1] at Falkirk on 27 March that they had been bribed by men from Glasgow to steal the explosives, which were removed by car and were required for poaching purposes; and Scobbie and Anderson were each sentenced to nine months' imprisonment.

But while the men who bribed them had Glaswegian accents, they were not the genuine article, nor were the stolen explosives for poaching.

Scottish police arrested Terence McSherry, Samuel Kennedy and Francis McNeece, three diehard IRA men, and they, together with Matthew Somerville, were accused of being concerned in the theft of gelignite and detonators from the Falkirk colliery and making preparation to store the items in a pit beneath the floor of a garage. McSherry had the details of a man – probably Peter Stuart (whom we have already met) – who had since been sentenced to penal servitude, and it was McSherry and McNeece who removed the explosives in a car.

They appeared at a heavily guarded Glasgow Sheriff's Court on 29 May and were committed for trial at Stirling High Court, where McSherry refused to enter a plea, stating that as a citizen of the Irish Republic and a soldier of the IRA, he refused to recognize the charges. The others simply entered pleas of not guilty.

---

[1] A Sheriff Substitute is an under-sheriff, who usually hears cases in the first instance.

The evidence was presented, the star witness being William Anderson, who told the court that he had received approaches from the accused to steal the explosives from the colliery where he had once worked, having been told that he and Scobbie would be 'well paid'.

Asked if he wished to say anything with regard to the evidence, McSherry had plenty to say, and despite a number of interruptions from the Judge, Lord Wark, this was it:

> I think that I am entitled to give you an explanation as to what has taken place in Scotland and England. In January of this year, the Army Council of the IRA sent a note to the British Foreign Secretary demanding the withdrawal of all British troops from Northern Ireland. All representations failed. The British Government did not take action and a series of explosions took place throughout England. I hold the British Government responsible for those explosions that have taken place and will continue to take place until the demands set out in the ultimatum be granted . . . So long as Ireland remains partitioned it is the duty of all Irishmen to treat English rule with contempt, wherever it exists . . . I do not make any apologies to any man in this world for my association with this organization which has endeavoured in the past and is still endeavouring to ensure the independence of my country. I stand by the proclamation of the IRA.

And that – with the assurance that the charges brought against him were 'a deliberation fabrication' – was the kind of pompous and exculpatory speech on behalf of himself and his brother terrorists guaranteed to do them no good whatsoever. All were found guilty on 9 June 1939.

Although Sommerville was sentenced to eighteen months' imprisonment, his conviction was quashed at the Scottish Court of Appeal in Edinburgh on 6 July. Not so the others. Terence McSweeney smiled as the trio were sentenced to penal servitude: ten years for him, seven for McNessa and five for Kennedy.

The most worrying aspect of the case was that no trace of the gelignite or detonators could be found.

* * *

A further case was heard at Manchester Assizes, again before Mr Justice Stable.

On 29 January, Chief Superintendent Moore of Liverpool CID and his men had raided a block of lock-up garages in

Litley Road, Liverpool. There they found an enormous quantity of explosives (including the potassium chlorate which Healy had shipped from Camden Town), plus 258 sticks of gelignite, 129 detonators, an alarm clock, a gas mask, cloth ammunition carriers and two revolvers and ammunition. As a result, they went to a house in Great Howard Street, Liverpool, where a rifle, a daylight signalling lamp, a Morse code key and books on machine guns and a military manual were found. Six men were arrested and charged with conspiring with John Healy and others to cause explosions likely to endanger life.

John Joseph Hannon, a 27-year-old docker, was asked to plead at the Assize Court; predictably, he shouted, 'I am a soldier of the Irish Republic! I cannot plead for pardon in this English court of law', and he and the other five defendants had pleas of not guilty recorded.

It was an odd trial, with one of the defendants stating that he ran 'The Irish Republican Army Dramatic Society' from his house; when a witness, one Harry Goldberg, came into court, he refused to go into the witness box, whereupon an usher and three detectives seized hold of him and propelled him feet-first into the box, where they held his arms. This caused Hannon to shout, 'Up the Republic!', and with two warders pushing him down on to his seat, Hannon shouted, 'To hell with that, boy!' – although it's not clear to whom those remarks were directed.

Goldberg adamantly refused to give any evidence whatsoever – it was suggested to the other defendants that he had been brought to one of their houses for court-martial proceedings over an offence under IRA standing orders, which was denied – and he was dealt with for contempt of court. Hannon was warned by the judge against any further outbursts, or 'You may find yourself in the same position as Goldberg; now, be careful.'

The Judge had upheld several objections from the defence regarding certain evidence and exhibits which the police intended to produce. At the conclusion of the case, the other five defendants were acquitted – despite one of them having a bottle of sulphuric acid and a revolver in his possession and another admitting having had four kegs of potassium chlorate delivered to his business premises – the Judge telling them that 'During the last four days you have stood in very grave peril, a peril from which you have escaped because of the integrity of the jury.' This was Judge-speak for 'Think yourselves bloody lucky!'

Inevitably, John Joseph Hannon was convicted, and Detective Inspector Sullivan told the Judge that although Hannon was a man of good character, he had been actively engaged with the IRA movement in Liverpool for some time, in his capacity as finance officer, and had received his instructions from Dublin. From the dock, Hannon said, 'I don't query the verdict in any respect.'

Passing sentence on 17 March 1939, Mr Justice Stable said:

> You have been found guilty by the verdict of the jury of having been an active participant in a most diabolical criminal conspiracy. With the correctness of the jury's verdict, I completely concur. You yourself have had the manhood to say that you don't query the verdict. I find it quite incomprehensible how anybody with a normal amount of intelligence who honestly entertains, as he quite honestly and quite properly may, the political conviction that the future of Ireland should not be directed in any shape or form by the Government of this country, should be engaged in a criminal conspiracy the object of which is to terrorise the people of this country so that they will put pressure on their Government to compel the Government of this country to interfere with what is happening in your own country. It seems the most crazy scheme that ever was created by the mind of man. It is clear that you have been a party to this widespread conspiracy to cause explosions which have already involved the destruction of perfectly innocent human life. A more wanton and indiscriminate murder – for that was what it was – it is impossible to consider. You probably know that not many days ago, a number of your associates were sentenced to 20 years' penal servitude. In this case, it may be your good fortune that, although the evidence that you were actively concerned in this conspiracy was as plain as a pikestaff, there has not been the evidence of the same degree of active participation in what was done as there was in the case of the people before me, last week. I am going to stretch leniency to the extreme limit to which, in my view, it can be stretched.

He then sentenced Hannon to a total of seven years' penal servitude, which concluded the proceedings at Manchester.

* * *

During the rest of that period, there were several other arrests. When Thomas McDermott was detained in Liverpool in possession of a revolver, he told the police somewhat ambiguously, 'I've been expecting this, ever since my pals were locked up.'

John McGeough was arrested in Birmingham after police searched his address on 13 March; inside a locked suitcase they discovered a gas mask and six rounds of ammunition for use in pistols and revolvers. He admitted being a member of the IRA, which he had joined, he stated, 'to learn Irish dancing'. When he appeared at a court in Birmingham and was asked if he would use the ammunition for furthering the aims of the IRA, McGeough replied, 'If ordered'. Asked whether, if he had a revolver and was ordered to, he would shoot anybody with it, McGeough unwisely replied, 'I refuse to answer that question.'

Appearing at Birmingham Quarter Sessions on 9 May 1939, he was found guilty of possessing ammunition in order that other persons might endanger life and was sentenced to five years' penal servitude. His roommate, who was found in possession of sixty-six assorted rounds of ammunition, was less voluble, and the charges against him were dismissed.

Leonard Eric Groves was arrested in possession of 150 detonators, two 2oz Polar Ammon cartridges and twelve pieces of safety fuse, although it transpired that this was for purposes other than terrorism – safe-blowing was particularly prevalent at that time – and the same applied when James Kelly and Edward Charles O'Donnell appeared at Lambeth Police Court, charged with having in their possession three cartridges of explosives. Mr H. A. K. Morgan for the prosecution informed the Bench that the defendants had no connection with the IRA and that they had the explosives for 'the comparatively innocent (though unlawful) purpose of blowing safes'.

Salesman William Henry Bowman appeared at Liverpool Police Court on 14 February 1939, charged with possession of a Webley revolver, and breathed an audible sigh of relief after the prosecutor was quick to inform the Stipendiary Magistrate that the prisoner 'had no connection whatsoever with the IRA'. Mr Bowman was fined a merciful £10.

Surely the most bizarre case to come before the courts was after Patrick O'Hanlon informed the clientele of a packed Lanarkshire public house that he was 'a de Valera man' and possessed sufficient explosives in his house to 'blow up the whole of Scotland'. One can't make comments like that and expect to blush unseen, and the local constabulary soon paid a visit to his address, where they discovered 4oz of an explosive substance, an explosive named Samsonite and a cartridge of gelignite. It was not quite the quantity required, as he had informed the astonished listeners in the pub, 'to begin at Edinburgh Castle and blow it up, then tackle Glasgow', but it was a start.

Proceedings descended into broad farce when it was pointed out at Airdrie Sheriff Court on 21 March 1939 that the maximum fine for possessing these commodities without a licence was sixpence. Sheriff Gillies fined O'Hanlon £1 (with the alternative of ten days' imprisonment) for causing a breach of the peace, and in respect of the explosives the defendant was admonished.

Couldn't make it up, could you?

* * *

So, to bring matters up to date, following almost immediately the explosions in the London and Manchester areas, a number of people had been arrested and premises raided, and firearms and enormous amounts of explosive material were seized. It had resulted in forty-one people being convicted of terrorism offences, with a total of 280 years' incarceration being imposed on them.

Thanks to the promptness of the police, and due to the number of arrests and the confiscation of so much explosive material, it looked as though the IRA's 'S' plan had been quashed just as soon as it commenced.

Don't you believe it.

The police had hardly scratched the surface of the plot; the terror in the streets had barely got underway.

CHAPTER 8

The Panic Spreads

Following the initial January arrests, there was a lull in the bombing for two weeks; then, on 3 February, it resumed with a vengeance.

At 5.55am a bomb exploded in the luggage office of Tottenham Court Road Underground Station, wrecking the interior, blowing the office's door across the ticket hall and breaking the leg of Harry Eyre, the foreman ticket collector; another member of staff was treated for multiple abrasions and shock.

Twenty-five minutes later, two stations away on the Piccadilly Line, it was the turn of Leicester Square. There was a tremendous explosion in the luggage office, and although Albert Brice was delivering milk on the other side of the brick wall which divided the luggage office from the main building, he was struck by debris, knocked down and seriously injured; he was one of five people hospitalized. Pathé News reported that this was the work of 'politicians of the underworld'.

Documents found in a house in Belfast suggested that bombs were going to be set off at Buckingham Palace and in government buildings, and guards were stationed night and day in the grounds of Royal Lodge, Windsor Great Park, where the King, the Queen and the two princesses were staying for the weekend. Visitors to the state apartments at Windsor Castle were asked to display the contents of their bags before entry, and the number of police officers at Chequers was increased prior to the Prime Minister's arrival.

On Sunday, 5 February, there was a rush of incendiary bombs in Coventry; balloons filled with nitric acid inside envelopes had been used at Woolworths in Smithford Street, at Marks & Spencer, in the furniture department of Owen & Owen Ltd and in the packing department of Burton's the tailors; fortunately, all the fires were extinguished before serious damage was caused.[1]

[1] These explosions, as well as the attack at Walton Gaol, were apparently the work of Tom Byrne, also known as Tomás Ó Broin; he was never convicted.

In Bristol, a note was found in a petrol storage depot which read: 'BEWARE. These tanks are the next to be blown up', but although firearms were issued to the police, the tanks remained unmolested; it was not part of the 'S' Plan to issue warnings. Then there were further threats and warnings: someone purporting to be 'The Chief of the IRA in Cardiff' threatened to blow up the offices of the *South Wales Echo* and Bow Street Police Court, unless IRA volunteers held there were released – but they weren't, and the buildings remained unscathed.

Although the IRA had been declared an illegal organization by the Irish Free State under the Declaration of Unlawful Organization Order, 1936, the regulation had been used sparingly. But now, on 8 February, in an effort to curtail the activities of the IRA within the Irish Free State and the United Kingdom, two bills giving the Government of Ireland extraordinary powers were introduced in the Dáil. The first became the Treason Act; it imposed the death penalty on persons guilty of treason and applied whether the act was committed within or without the boundaries of the state. The second, the Offences against the State Act, permitted the police to search, arrest and intern without trial persons contravening the Act; it also declared seditious any suggestion in any publication that the Government of Ireland was unlawful.

On 9 February, *The Times* reported:

> The signatories of the ridiculous ultimatum to Great Britain are men of no account. Nobody in this country would have taken them seriously, but for the recent outrages in Great Britain. As a political force in Éire, the IRA simply does not count.

Nevertheless, the public was becoming understandably jumpy; it was thought that there might be a bomb outrage at the England/Ireland rugby international at Twickenham on 10 February, because an incendiary bomb had exploded in the saloon of the *St David*, the night boat from Rosslare, when it docked at Fishguard and after the passengers, many of whom were going to attend the match, had disembarked. Therefore, watchmen patrolled the ground during the night before the match, and catering staff, plus others whose duties took them inside the ground, were required to produce their credentials. The public's jumpiness increased when sixteen rounds of revolver ammunition were found on a train in Ilford which might – or might not – have had some connection with the bombing campaign. Certainly, the public and the press were inclined to think so.

Home Office explosive experts went to the Catering Trades Employment Exchange in Denmark Street when a canister wrapped in brown paper bearing the letters 'IRA' was pushed through the letterbox – a member of the staff threw it into a bucket of water – and the item was taken away for examination. The same applied to what was thought to be a homemade bomb found on the seat of a trolleybus in Farringdon Road. The conductor quickly handed it to a police officer on point duty, who just as quickly chucked it into a horse trough.

Once more there was a lull in the bombers' activities, for just three weeks, but on 2 March an explosion occurred at 2.20am on the aqueduct which carried the Grand Union Canal over the North Circular Road, near Stonebridge Park. The word 'DIE' had been written in letters two feet high on the parapet. Part of the aqueduct's stonework was shattered, with some of the masonry falling on to the roadway, but the damage was not severe. Although eight feet of concrete was blown away, it was just as well that the aqueduct was not breached, since there was not a single lock between Paddington and Uxbridge, and thus 50 million gallons of water contained in the 5-mile stretch of the canal, weighing over a quarter of a million tons, would have deluged north London. As the commentator for Pathé News observed, 'Be thankful this latest piece of insanity has failed.'

Police enquiries revealed that a postman had seen four men with a wooden box stepping from a black car standing near the aqueduct; a railway employee had seen a man wearing a light overcoat at the same location; and an attendant in a nearby café stated that two men carrying suitcases had called the night before the explosion.

There was a similar explosion, the same day, at the Birmingham Navigation Canal near Ball's Hill Bridge, Staffordshire. A bomb had been placed in a culvert under the main Walsall to Stonecross section, but although brickwork was blown out at each end of the culvert, the cracks which appeared in the embankment were not large or deep enough to permit water to escape.

That weekend, incendiary devices exploded at 2.00am in Birmingham, at Messrs Henry's in the High Street and Messrs Edward Grey Ltd in Bull Street, followed four hours later by another explosion at Grey's. Extinguishing the flames, firemen discovered a quantity of balloons filled with acid, as well as inflammable material. The same materials were found, the same day, by a sorter at Francis Road Post Office in London's Victoria.

Two days after the explosion at Stonebridge Park, a few miles away at Park Avenue Bridge, Willesden Green, a Metropolitan

Railway worker, a Mr Henry George West, saw four men carrying boxes from a car to the railway embankment. He stopped one of the men, there was a struggle and the two fell down the embankment. The man shouted, 'Shoot, Paddy!' and a shot was fired but missed Mr West. The men disappeared, no explosion occurred and the police were called; later, three men were taken into Cannon Row police station but were released after questioning.

That may have been to the bombers' advantage. Four days later, on 8 March, a bomb wired to an alarm clock was discovered near the asbestos covering of a high tension cable about 70 yards away from the LMS railway bridge at Acton Lane, Willesden; police officers disconnected the leads.

A fire damaged two coaches of the Wolverhampton to London express train on 11 March, although the chief of Oldbury Fire Brigade was of the opinion that the fire had been caused by a spark from the engine. Perhaps it had. Whenever anything of the kind happened, people were inclined to jump to conclusions, so much so that when Daniel Joseph O'Connor, a 21-year-old petrol pump attendant, appeared at Marylebone Police Court charged with possession of a revolver, he pleaded with the Magistrate, Mr Lawrence Dunne, to put him on probation for life, as long as he could stay in England. Assured that Mr O'Connor had a good character and no involvement with the IRA, the Magistrate took the merciful course and fined him £5.

Less amusing was the attack on inspection chambers connected with the Post Office system in Coventry which was carried out on 23 March. The first explosion at Cheylesmore shattered the glass in 120 windows and caused heavy pieces of metal to smash into an engineering works opposite, damaging overhead and underground telephone lines. It was fortunate that the blast occurred at 7.15am; had it been an hour later, the area would have been filled with men on their way to work.

Three hours later, a similar explosion occurred at a telephone junction box in Quinton Road; iron fragments of the box and pieces of concrete were flung over a wide area, some of them crashing through the glass roofs of nearby factories, fortunately without causing any casualties.

The same could not be said at lunchtime that day, when a third explosion occurred in an inspection chamber outside a transformer station at Gosford Green. The blast tore the boughs off roadside trees, and flying debris struck a passer-by. Tragedy was averted that afternoon, when the driver of a corporation bus noted smoke coming from a manhole in Coundon Way; he accelerated past, and although two windows in the bus were shattered when a bomb went off, it escaped the full force of the blast and no one was injured. But the explosion caused the heavy iron manhole cover to crash through the roof of St Osburg's Roman Catholic Presbytery, landing in a room which the housekeeper had fortunately just left. As a result of the explosions, 1,000 telephone lines were put out of action.

A stolen, unoccupied car was destroyed after a bomb left inside it exploded, and houses at 91 and 93 Balsall Heath Road, Birmingham, which were set on fire, were extensively damaged. Some of the occupants had to be rescued from the upper windows, and five adjacent houses had their windows and a front door blown in and their roofs stripped of tiles. The whereabouts of several Irishmen who had lived nearby were sought by police.

So it might be thought that the terrorists were having matters all their own way. They weren't.

Chapter 9

The Attack on Hammersmith Bridge

Six days after the car explosion in Birmingham, on 28 March at about 11.00pm, a telephone call was made by a man giving the name of Chessman to the London office of the car hire company, Godfrey Davis Ltd, requesting a car and driver to meet him at Hammersmith and take him to Ewell.

A car driven by Clifford Moffatt was duly dispatched, arriving at Hammersmith half an hour later. Four men got into the car, one of whom identified himself as Chessman – in fact, he was Edward John Connell, who had become a member of the IRA in 1932; another was 'William Browne', whose real name was William Gaughran. When they got to Tolworth, Moffatt was told to stop the car, whereupon the four men got out and Browne produced what was believed to be a pistol; after he was overpowered, Moffatt was told, 'We've got to do a job and we want your car for it.' Browne took Moffatt's chauffeur's cap, got into the driver's seat and the car resumed its journey, stopping somewhere near Hammersmith, whereupon Connell and another man got out, telling the others, 'Keep your eye on the chauffeur.'

Ten minutes later, they returned carrying suitcases, the car drove off again and eventually arrived at Hammersmith Bridge.

Connell told Browne, 'Pull up on the slope, so that you can make a quick getaway.'

Connell and one of the other men got out, each carrying a suitcase, then returned almost immediately, and the car drove off, stopping in Hammersmith Broadway. There was the sound of an explosion and Connell said, 'Did you hear that bang? Did you see a flash?'

Browne replied, 'I didn't see a flash but I heard a bang.'

'The other one's a long time going off but I know what's happened', said Connell. 'The first one's set the other one off.'

However, he was wrong. The explosives had been primed and the suitcases placed in position when a pedestrian crossed the bridge from Barnes towards Hammersmith. That man was Frederick William Henry Maurice Child, a 42-year-old hairdresser, who had seen active service in France during the First World War and had been wounded whilst serving with the Honourable

Artillery Company. He noticed a suitcase lying on the lower of two suspension chains of the bridge and saw that it was smoking. He prised open the locks of the suitcase, which he estimated to weigh 28–30lbs, realized that a bomb was inside and, although he had no idea of the length of the fuse, closed the suitcase, and with great coolness climbed through the chains of the footpath and threw it into the Thames. The bomb exploded, sending a column of water 60 feet into the air; the second bomb then exploded about five seconds later on the west side of the bridge, causing considerable damage.

Stiffening girders and suspension chains on Hammersmith Bridge were twisted and damaged, and windows were shattered in houses several hundred yards away. All vehicular traffic was stopped from crossing the bridge, six Green Line bus routes were diverted and while four police officers (instead of just one) patrolled the bridge and river patrols were doubled, pedestrians were allowed to cross using the downstream footway. The cost of repairs to put the bridge back into what was referred to as 'a useable condition' was estimated at £1,000; it would take a month before traffic could cross it again.

'This happened almost on the eve of the boat race', expostulated the Pathé News commentator, adding caustically, 'What kind thoughts these maniacs entertain!'

Meanwhile, back on the day of the explosions, Moffatt was allowed to leave the car and was running towards a telephone kiosk, when he saw a police officer. They then got into Moffatt's abandoned car and, although the four men had split up, they spotted Browne and Connell as they walked across Putney Bridge. They were arrested.

At Bow Street Police Court, having committed the two men for trial at the Old Bailey, the Magistrate, Mr Fry, having heard Mr Child give evidence, told him, 'I don't think you ought to leave the box without my taking the opportunity to congratulate you on your courage and your presence of mind.'

On 3 May 1939, the men appeared before the Recorder of London, Sir Gerald Dodson KC, and both made statements from the dock. Browne told the court:

> Anything I have done, I have no regrets. I came over to England for the one reason that every Irishman comes here and that is to break the connection between Eire and England. Anything I have done has been done voluntarily. I have received no help from anyone. At the end of my sentence, whether it is 10, 20 or 40 years, I will endeavour to do the same thing

> again for a cause for which other men have given their lives and for which I can at least give a few years of mine.

Then it was Connell's turn:

> My father fought in the Boer War for the relief of an oppressed minority and in the Great War, for freedom. I fought for an oppressed minority in the six Northern counties. I am held on a charge of doing my duty in the cause of Irish liberty.

Having heard the evidence, the jury unsurprisingly did not need to retire to find both men guilty, and after Divisional Detective Inspector Clarke remarked, 'There is no doubt that Connell is the ringleader of this enterprise on which they went that night', the Recorder sentenced him to twenty years' penal servitude (which brought forth the shout, 'God save Ireland!' en route to the cells) and Browne to ten years. The latter shouted something in Gaelic which no one in the court was able to interpret.

The Recorder then called Mr Child before him and told him:

> It would not be right to allow this trial to conclude without some expression from the court, on behalf of the public whom you served so well, in appreciation of the service rendered by you. Unfortunately, it does not lie in my power in the circumstances to award you any tangible expression of the public's appreciation and regard, but at least I can offer you the congratulations of your fellow citizens and countrymen for your gallant behaviour and the thanks of the community for what you did.

One such member of the community was Mr H. Galway of Upper Berkley Street, W1, who wrote a fulsome tribute to Mr Child, via the editor of *The Times*, ending with the words, 'If any man ever earned the Albert Medal of the first-class, surely Mr Child has.'

Two days after the Recorder's remarks, Mr Child was awarded the Empire Gallantry Medal; instituted in 1923, only 130 were awarded, but following the George Cross being struck one year later, he became eligible to exchange his medal for the highest award for civilian gallantry the country could bestow. He attended Buckingham Palace on 25 October 1941 to receive the Cross from King George VI.

There's an interesting footnote to this story.

In August 1950, the Recorder received a letter from Connell in which he referred to the trial and the sentence and added, 'At the time, I felt that while it was all part of your duty, you had a certain reluctance or dislike for the job.' Connell wondered if he was correct in his surmise and ended his letter with the words, 'If you could settle it, my long-standing uncertainty would be resolved.'

Connell received a wonderfully diplomatic reply which read:

> I am instructed by the Recorder to say in reference to your letter that he never passes sentence on any fellow creature without a feeling of reluctance, and that your case was no exception to the rule.

Connell's co-conspirator asked nothing at all. Released from prison in 1947 and suffering from tuberculosis, Browne was dead within two months.

Chapter 10

An Overheard Conversation

On the night of 30 March, following the explosions at Hammersmith Bridge, there was a muffled explosion at a house at 12 Trafalgar Road, Moseley, Birmingham, and when the police arrived, a large quantity of explosives were found – 200 sticks of gelignite and 76lbs of potassium chlorate. The two Irish occupants of the premises were missing. One of them was Gerald Lyons but, as we shall see, like most unpleasant objects he rose to the surface again, this time in London, a few weeks later.

And shortly after midnight, there was an explosion in Bold Street, Liverpool; shop windows were shattered by a bomb affixed to a wire grille protecting an optician's window.

Back in London, during the early morning of Saturday, 1 April, there were a series of explosions: at 12.37am a bomb shattered the window of the *News Chronicle* at Chronicle House, Fleet Street. An hour later, at Gorf Couturier, Park Lane, there was damage to the shop front, and then at Heal & Son Ltd, Tottenham Court Road there were two explosions in quick succession at 3.02 and 3.04am which shattered five of the six concave windows, causing damage to the tune of £800. There were two more explosions, one at Messrs Barratts shoe shop in the Edgware Road and one at Messrs Coutts Bank in the Strand, but those can be left out, because it was Heal & Son that became the focus of interest.

One Samuel George Fluke aged twenty-seven, who described himself as a 'collector', was in the vicinity of Heal's when the bomb went off, and when he arrived at a coffee stall a few hundred yards away he was out of breath, according to an upholsterer named John Smart. Fluke got into conversation with some of the people there regarding the explosion.

'If I knew the bastards who dropped them, I'd hang them', remarked one of the clientele named Mr Chambers, and this caused Fluke to become agitated, saying, 'Who would you hang and who are you?'

He then wandered back towards the bombed store, whereupon Police Constable Banks, whose cards had been well and truly marked by an habitué of the coffee stall, told him, 'I'm a police officer.'

Whatever he was going to say next was interrupted by Fluke, who told him, 'You've got my pal Connell, so I suppose you want me.' Taken to a police car, he kicked and struggled, saying, 'If I get twenty years, there'll be others to follow me.' Banks was assisted by Police Constable Johnson, but once inside the police car Fluke raised both feet and kicked the driver, PC Banks, in the back, saying, 'I'll smash the car up – I'm not going without a struggle.'

At Tottenham Court Road police station, when Divisional Detective Inspector Peter Beveridge told him he would be put up for identification, Fluke said, 'What I did was for the good of the cause and if I get an opportunity, I'll do it again;' and when the sports coat that he was wearing was examined, there was found in the pockets a mixture of potassium chlorate and sugar. After he was charged, Fluke smiled and replied, 'That's about right.'

On his way to Marlborough Street Police Court he said, 'You've got my pal Connell, and now you've got me – but the fight will go on, just the same.' Noticing a news placard bearing the words, 'Seven London Explosions', he remarked, 'It's a pity it wasn't seventy.'

Charged with causing the explosion at Heal's, Fluke gave his address as Elmbank Gardens, Barnes which, by the oddest of coincidences, was the home address of Edward John Connell, who had been arrested for the Hammersmith Bridge bombing.

Appearing at the Old Bailey, Fluke denied any knowledge of the bombing or that he was in any way associated with the IRA. He was helped immeasurably by Edward Connell's parents; the father, John Connell, told the court that when Fluke had heard the sentences imposed on the Manchester bombers, he had stated virtuously, 'They deserved it. They can't expect to do things like that and get away with it.' And Mrs Catherine Connell stated that the jacket which Fluke had been wearing on the night of the bombing of Heal's – you know, the one on which traces of explosives were found – had been previously worn by her son. That was the son who had just been sentenced to twenty years' penal servitude. Are you keeping up with me? Good.

After just an hour's deliberations the jury acquitted Fluke, so the man who had bombed Heal's, and who was one of the other men in the car when Hammersmith Bridge had bombs planted on it, walked free. Fluke, who was allegedly a Loyalist, an Orangeman, was nevertheless hugged by Mrs Connell and had his hand enthusiastically shaken by Mr Connell and another of his sons, all of whom were staunch Republicans and who, it appeared, had embraced multiculturalism as long ago as 1939. Fluke returned to Ireland, where his claim that he was not a member of the IRA was disbelieved when he refused to account for his movements. He was sentenced to six months and interned thereafter.

* * *

But on the day following Fluke's arrest, Sunday, 2 April, police raided the address in Comeragh Road, West Kensington of John Leo Duignan and Peter Campbell and discovered ten bundles of 2oz sticks of gelignite, a 5lb pack of gelignite, 103 detonators, safety fuses and potassium chlorate.

Their arrest came about as a result of information and observation. On 29 March Duignan had arrived at Comeragh Road carrying two suitcases. On 1 April, police saw Campbell come to the address carrying a suitcase which appeared to be heavy. Police – they were apparently secreted in the front room of the house – overheard the conversation between the two men in Duignan's room.

Duignan asked, 'How much have you got?' and Campbell replied, 'I've got the lot. There's plenty of jelly for us here.'

'All right, put it under the bed', said Duignan. 'I'll meet you in half an hour's time at Hammersmith Broadway Station.'

After Campbell left the house he was stopped by police, and Divisional Detective Inspector Clarke entered the house, saw Duignan and found the case under the bed, put there by Campbell.

Asked if it was his property, Duignan replied, 'You have your orders, I have mine.'

A mackintosh was found, and the white stain on one of its sleeves turned out to be a composition of paraffin wax and potassium chlorate; in a pocket were traces of potassium chlorate, sugar and paraffin wax.

At Bow Street Police Court, after Detective Sergeant Williams gave evidence of the overheard conversation, the prisoners were asked if they wished to question him.

'I'm sorry to say, two thirds of your statement is ridiculous perjury', said Duignan, while Campbell expanded on this by remarking, 'The majority of your witnesses are all perjurors.'

Actually, this begs the question, how *did* the officers overhear the conversation? Walls that separated rooms in those solidly built terraced houses were far thicker and sturdier than in the new-build homes of today. Perhaps the conversation was overheard by lowering a microphone down the chimney of the room inhabited by the men – a practice sometimes adopted in those days – or perhaps the officers used the old-fashioned method of pressing a tumbler to the wall. Maybe they just had very acute hearing.

Nevertheless, despite the allegedly perjured evidence, the men were committed to stand their trial at the Old Bailey; having refused to plead, and while the jury were making up their minds whether or not the defendants were 'mute of malice', the prisoners solved the conundrum by speaking. Campbell told the court, 'English law and justice might be a fine thing in the eyes of Englishmen, but in Ireland, Palestine and India, it is a tyranny.'

On 19 May, found guilty of possessing explosives not for a lawful object, the Common Serjeant, Mr Cecil Whiteley KC, sentenced both of them to ten years' penal servitude.

'Up the Republic!' they chorused as they went down to the cells.

Chapter 11

More Bombings – and More Arrests

A rather battered figure appeared at Birmingham Police Court on 6 April. He was 36-year-old Lawrence Dunlea, and his head was heavily bandaged. Asked by Lord Ilkestone, the Stipendiary Magistrate, how the prisoner had come by his injuries, Superintendent Richardson replied simply and without a trace of regret, 'He put up a violent struggle and was hit on the head.'

Dunlea had been arrested during the evening of Wednesday, 5 April after he had been stopped in Newhall Street, Birmingham by police and had made an obvious movement towards the left pocket of his overcoat. Seized from behind by Detective Bannister, who pinioned his arms, Dunlea struggled and kicked, shouting, 'You're not taking me', and was only handcuffed after being bashed over the head with an officer's baton. The pocket which he had been trying to reach contained a Colt revolver with five rounds of flat-nosed 'dum-dum' ammunition.[1] In his jacket were six sticks of gelignite wrapped in copies of an IRA periodical, *Wolfe Tone Weekly*. Twelve rounds of ammunition suitable for the Colt were found in a jacket pocket, as well as fourteen rounds of .32 ammunition. Perhaps it was just as well that Dunlea had been clumped with the baton when he was; much more of his frenzied struggling could have resulted in his detonation. Additionally, twelve balloons and two sticks of gelignite were found at his lodgings.

'As a soldier of the Irish Republic, I refuse to ask any questions or make any statement at all', Dunlea told the court, and after the superintendent had informed the court that Dunlea's revolver had been fully loaded, he was remanded in custody.

At Birmingham Assizes on 14 July 1939 Dunlea stated, 'As a soldier of the Republic, I refuse to plead', but then went on to claim that the explosives had been planted on him by Birmingham CID. He added, 'I have been a soldier of the Irish

---

[1] A colloquial term for bullets which are manufactured – or modified – to expand on contact, thus producing a much larger wound.

Republican Army since before I was fifteen. Shoving us in British dumps for ten, twenty, thirty or forty years might break our heads, but it won't break our spirits.'

After Dunlea was found guilty, Superintendent Richardson was able to expand a little more on his activities, telling the court that he was a very dangerous and active member of the IRA who, at the time of his arrest, was the intelligence officer of the 4th Battalion[2] of the IRA in the Midlands. His job was to receive orders from his leaders and pass the instruction on to others, some of whom were now serving long sentences of penal servitude, to carry out explosions. The information that had led to the arrest of Dunlea in the first place was that he and others were planning to break into an ammunition dump in the Midlands to steal explosives. Mr Justice Singleton (one of the judges at the Court of Criminal Appeal who had released Gerald Wharton), after he was told that Dunlea was employed at Hams Hall power station at the time of the explosion on 16 January, sentenced him to twenty years' penal servitude.

Dunlea seemed to find the sentence to his liking. No patriotic shouts as he walked down the dock steps; he was smiling.

* * *

A man suspected – quite rightly – of being a member of the IRA was followed to a house in Stanley Road, Bootle in April 1939. This was the home of Rita McSweeney, who had come to live in Liverpool when she was ten. The daughter of a staunchly Republican family and a member of *Cumann na mBann*, with her newly acquired Scouse accent she made a perfect courier and supplier of arms and explosives. But now, fearing exposure and arrest, she fled and in June, using the alias of Barbara Jones, took lodgings with a Mrs Read at Clare Street, Cardiff. Mrs Read had helpfully carried Miss Jones' suitcase upstairs to her room and noticed that it was very light. Miss Jones told her landlady that she was living on the proceeds of a property left to her by an aunt and added that she passed the time by writing short stories. There she remained until 22 July, when she left, telling Mrs Read that she was going to London to visit her sister and that she would be away for a week. In her absence, Mrs Read cleared out her

---

[2] A battalion in the British Army represents a combat unit of some 500–800 soldiers. In an IRA battalion there were likely to be fewer than thirty combatants.

bedroom, and when she went to move her tenant's locked suitcase, she discovered that it was much heavier than before.

But Miss Jones hadn't gone to London. She was arrested the following day in Fishguard, Pembrokeshire, together with Richard Cohen, alias Michael O'Farrell, otherwise known as Richard Timmins. He was in possession of explosive substances which included electrical detonators and timing mechanisms; she was charged as an accessory.

She was remanded to Cardiff Gaol, and the suitcase from Clare Street soon arrived at the prison; after she had spoken to Gilbert Hare, the governor, who told her that he intended to hand the keys of the suitcase over to the police, she said, 'It's all up. The case is full of explosives' – and so it was. The reason for the increased weight of the suitcase, Mrs Read would be astonished to discover, was that it now contained four revolvers, seventy-nine rounds of ammunition and sixty-nine sticks of gelignite.

Following this revelation, Miss Jones appeared for committal purposes on 31 August at Cardiff Police Court, where there was a further surprise.

She was defended by a solicitor named Mr Sibbering Jones, and when the governor, Mr Hare, gave evidence about the keys to the suitcase being handed over, Mr Jones queried whether his conversation with Miss Jones was admissible, saying:

> Prison governors in this country are regarded as friends of prisoners (and rightly so) and prisoners often approach them for advice and information and on such occasions might make statements unknowingly which might be very damaging to them. It would be unfortunate if such conversations were given in evidence.

There must have been a simultaneous 'click!' as the jaws of the magistrates hit the top of the bench upon hearing this specious bollocks, but they recovered sufficiently to rule that the evidence of Mr Hare definitely was admissible and remanded Miss Jones back into his care at Cardiff Prison until she came to trial.

So, with the further charge added, Miss Jones appeared together with Cohen on 16 November 1939 at Carmarthen Assizes, where both refused to plead to the indictment. Cohen was convicted the following day, and Mr Justice Hawke told him:

> It looks to me as if you were a collector who was supplying these dangerous things to somebody else for dangerous purposes. Some of those who have already gone to penal servitude

> were, I am afraid, your confederates. I do not see that I have any alternative but to pass on you the heaviest sentence I am empowered to do.

He then sentenced Cohen to fourteen years' penal servitude and told Jones:

> I assume that you had been under the influence of Cohen and other people. I hope you will realize that you have done no good to your country by your actions.

She was then sentenced to concurrent terms of five years' penal servitude; following her release in 1943 she was deported.

Despite those arrests, the bombings continued, albeit slightly less frequently than before due to the depletion of the workforce.

* * *

Six explosions occurred early on the morning of 5 April. The first hint of what was to come was when a road-sweeper found a bomb in a refuse bin at Birmingham and then carried it a quarter of a mile to the local police station where, to the alarm of the personnel, he deposited it on the counter. It was quickly neutralized. An immediate search of all the area's rubbish bins commenced; a bomb exploded at Snow Hill, close to the Great Western Railway Station, and when Police Constable Bunt saw smoke coming from a bin in Congreve Street he went to find a fire extinguisher, but the bomb exploded. The third explosion occurred within 50 yards of the central police station – in a bin that had already been searched.

Two explosions in Liverpool were an attempt to disrupt the tramway system. In the first incident a bomb had been placed in shrubbery opposite the county cricket ground. Trees and foliage fell on to the tram tracks, although the service was not disrupted. The second explosion was of a bomb placed under a standard carrying overhead wires; a crater 1½ feet in diameter was blasted open in the road. A charge box at the base of the standard was blown into tiny pieces, some of which were found 75 yards away; it was fortunate that no one was passing by, since the razor-sharp slivers of metal could have caused fatal injuries.

A similar incident occurred in Bishop Street, Coventry, when a bomb which had been placed in a metal container on a standard exploded; although the tramway system was able to keep running, thirty windows in the Cranes Hotel opposite were blown in, and two doors were blown off their hinges.

A week of calm then went by. On 10 April, at a Republican demonstration held in Glasnevin Cemetery, Dublin to commemorate the Easter Rising, an astounding, hypocritical communiqué from the IRA Army Council was read out, stating that the operation groups of the IRA in England had carried out their tasks 'without causing casualties', the avoidance of which 'had been strictly ordered'. Mind you, they added, the order to avoid casualties could be countermanded, should Britain have recourse to extreme measures.

Then – following an empty threat to blow up Catford Bridge, Lewisham – during the evening of 12 April there were eleven explosions in public conveniences: six in London – at Hammersmith Broadway, Hyde Park Corner, Marble Arch, St Giles' Circus, Kilburn and the Elephant & Castle; four in Coventry; and one at Old Square, Birmingham. It appeared that a new chemical bomb had been used, employing carbide – a compound of carbon and metal used in the manufacture of cutting tools, lathe bits and saw blades – although fortunately, no one was injured. More conventional bombs, comprised of gelignite with unlighted fuses, were found in cubicles at Hammersmith and Hyde Park Corner.

On the evening of 13 April, two young men walked into the public bar of the Fox Hollies Hotel, Acocks Green, Birmingham, ordered a bottle of beer each, which they quickly drank, and left. There was then a small explosion, and heavy vapour came from a test tube which affected the eyes and noses of some of the patrons; two barmaids were seriously affected by the fumes, and a woman fainted. The local police tried to play down the incident, saying it was meant as a practical joke and there was no connection with the IRA, but they were wrong. Three weeks later, there would be several similar incidents, again in Birmingham and also in Liverpool and London.

Two nights later, a bomb exploded in a telephone kiosk in Jubilee Drive of the Kensington district, Liverpool – the second in four days. It was a tremendous blast, heard five miles away; the kiosk was blown to pieces, the concussion threw several people out of bed, and a woman in a nearby house was blown out her chair and had to be taken to the local infirmary. A man on a bicycle was seen riding away from the scene just prior to the detonation. At the same time, in Cricklewood, London, a night watchman discovered a brown paper parcel containing a bomb, which he duly immersed in a pail of water.

On the evening of 18 April, two bombs exploded in telephone boxes in London's Euston district. The first was in Hampstead Road, just before 11.00pm; the second occurred four minutes later, in Euston Road; two sides of the box and its roof were blown out, and a passing pedestrian was hit by splinters of glass and fragments of wood and steel, and was taken to hospital by ambulance. An immediate search was carried out of telephone kiosks in the vicinity, but the police had not been idle.

Earlier that day, Detective Inspector Whitehead had arrested John Joseph Keane after sugar, sulphuric acid and 1cwt of potassium chloride were found in his room at Camden Road, as was a hamper chock-full of explosives and a vase containing forty-four farthings for use with alarm clocks. The items had been found by Detective Hugh Scott, who was told by Keane, 'We don't care a damn. The worst you can do to us is shoot us. We don't mind what you do, because we figure our cause is right.' Later, in a calmer frame of mind, Keane had this to say:

> I would rather not say anything. Until I go into this thing thoroughly, I am not going to talk . . . I still prefer not to say anything. I am not making any statement at all and I am not interested where it was found. When I see the others, I will make a statement. This will be a statement of honour and I hope you people will treat it honourably. If I'd known you people were here, you would not have got me.

Having been charged, on his way to Bow Street Police Court he told police, 'For every one of us that is pulled in, twenty will step into the breach.'

More arrests were carried out on the same day. Two brothers, Joseph and Denis McGillycuddy of Burns Road, Harlesden, were arrested by Detective Inspector Cooper after their bedroom was searched and a Webley revolver and eight rounds of ammunition were found, as well as a suitcase containing a stick of gelignite with a fuse attached, a metal fuse with a lead attachment, a quantity of aluminium powder, a length of fuse and an alarm clock.

'I take full responsibility for all the property', said Joseph, while Denis remarked, 'I don't think there is any evidence against me' – but he was wrong.

A Mills hand grenade was found on top of a cupboard at the Richmond Gardens, Shepherd's Bush address of John Murrihy. The screw cap had been removed, and Murrihy told Detective Sergeant Cain, 'I've had it for some time. I didn't think there was anything wrong in that', but a Home Office explosives expert would later say that it could be filled with explosives by an amateur and used for its original purpose, so there was.

And if that were not enough, at 3.15 that morning, Detective Inspector Gerald Richardson paid a visit to Churchmead Road, Willesden, where he became acquainted with John Foley, who was in bed; underneath the bed was an attaché case containing ten bundles of 6oz gelignite with detonators and fuses attached, two boxes – one empty, one containing 5lbs of gelignite – 100 detonators, a bag of white powder, three detonators with fuses attached, four balloons, a roll of insulating tape, fourteen empty brown bags, a roll of string and a length of fuse.

Fifty minutes later, DI Richardson arrived at St Mary's Road, North Kensington, where he arrested a man who originally introduced himself as Patrick Healy but who was, in fact, Patrick Kelly. Told that he answered the description of a man calling himself Michael Griffin, who was wanted for being concerned with John Foley in possessing explosives at Churchmead Road, he replied, 'I've never been to Churchmead Road and I don't know where it is.'

His explanation started to come apart when he was picked out on an identification parade as being the man who used the name Michael Griffin and shared a room with Foley at Churchmead Road; and when it was discovered that a key found in his possession fitted the lock of the attaché case containing the explosives, his denial, which probably sounded a good idea to Kelly at the time, was in tatters.

At the Old Bailey on 17 May 1939, Joseph McGillycuddy stated, 'What I have done was my duty to my country and I have no regrets for it.' Having been told by Detective Inspector Cooper that the McGillycuddy brothers had associated with Michael O'Shea, recently convicted in connection with the activities of the 'S' Plan, the Common Serjeant sentenced both brothers to ten years' penal servitude.

John Murrihy heroically told the court, 'I'm an Irishman and proud of my country and am prepared to die for it', but the Common Serjeant refused to impose such a severe penalty; for possession of the Mills bomb he received five years' penal servitude.

The following day, Kelly and Foley appeared at the same court, in front of the same judge. Detective Inspector Richardson told the judge that both men were members of the IRA, had associated with the McGillycuddy brothers and that Kelly was a leading member of the organization. Sentenced to ten years' penal servitude, Kelly tried to climb over the front of the dock before he was restrained and led off to the cells. Foley, sentenced to five years' penal servitude and shouting 'Up the Republic!', also tried to escape from the dock; in his case, five warders discouraged him from that course of action.

On 28 June, John Joseph Keane was found guilty of possessing explosive substances and in a long, hypocritical harangue to the Old Bailey jury told them:

> The IRA have again been ordered to take up arms. We do not have any prejudice against the people of England but we hold it against the British Government which has suppressed our country for 750 years. That is why we are prepared to die in the morning for the cause we are fighting for.

Keane was a diehard terrorist. Detective Inspector Whitehead told the court that he had been a member of the IRA since 1913. In 1920 at Kilkenny he had been sentenced to six months' imprisonment for carrying dispatches. The following year, he was caught giving instruction in rifle drill to irregulars, and a drumhead court martial sentenced him to be shot. This was commuted to ten years' penal servitude, but after an amnesty he served just eighteen months of that sentence. Almost immediately after his release, he was sentenced to eighteen months' imprisonment for fighting against the Free State. Now, for the current offence, he was sentenced to ten years' penal servitude.

* * *

After 18 April, when a number of arrests had been carried out, once more there was a lull. On the day following the arrests, the remains were found of a home-made bomb which had exploded inside the Catesby tunnel railway line near Daventry, but no damage had been done. Two passengers on a bus at Meridian, Warwickshire discovered an attaché case under a seat which they handed to the conductor; opening it, he found a smoking bomb, which was defused when he threw it into a nearby brook.

During the early hours of 26 April there were five explosions in Liverpool, all within two hours. Devices pushed through letterboxes resulted in a door being blown across the street in School Lane and the front of a ships' instrument maker's being wrecked in Castle Street. A shoe shop and a hat shop were next, and when a bomb exploded at the printing establishment of the *Liverpool Daily Post* in Wood Street, its oak door was blown out and all the windows were shattered. More fortunate was the shop in South John Street belonging to a glass and china merchants. The company had lined their letterbox with sheet iron, and the bomb, which had burned fiercely for some time, did not penetrate the premises.

Rather worrying for taxi driver Mr Sydney Bourne was his discovery after he had taken two men from Congleton to Talke, Staffordshire. Having garaged his car, he did not use it until the following night, which was when he found a bomb on the back seat.

* * *

An oddity of a case was heard at Glasgow High Court on 9 May. It was not so much what Cormac McGarrigle had in his possession: four sticks of gelignite, seventeen rounds of ball ammunition, eight blank rounds of ammunition, thirty-two loaded cartridges, a fog signal, a box of percussion caps, a double-barrelled and a single-barrelled gun, thirty cartridge wads, a gunpowder flask and filler and 7lb 2oz of ball shot. That was damning enough, but it was the correspondence which accompanied it that was strange. There was a training manual, plus letters addressed to 'C. M'Garrigle, Adjutant, Glasgow Battalion, ICA' and 'C. M'Garrigle, Greenock Section, Glasgow Battalion, Irish Citizen Army'.

The Irish Citizen Army – *Arm Cathartha na hÉireann* – had been formed in 1913 (it would exist until 1947) as a paramilitary group of trade union workers established in Dublin for the defence of workers' demonstrations against the police.

It was explained to the presiding Judge, Lord Wark, that at that moment the ICA had not embarked on a campaign of terrorism and that they had no direct connection with the IRA; however, the IRA were in sympathy with the ICA's principles and had cooperated with them in the past.

This was sufficient for the court to be ringed with uniform and plain-clothes police, who scrutinized anyone entering the court, and to make Lord Wark extremely apprehensive about anyone, police or explosives experts, handling the exhibits. He said nervously, 'None of us want to be blown up!'

In any event, McGarrigle disclaimed any knowledge of the Irish Citizen Army, saying that he had come by the gelignite and the other explosives 'innocently' and that the correspondence had been given to him by a man – he had since disappeared – who had asked that letters coming to him might be addressed to McGarrigle's home address.

A very odd state of affairs, and McGarrigle was probably fortunate to be sentenced to just fifteen months' imprisonment.

Chapter 12

Cherchez la Femme!

The IRA scored an own goal on 3 May when there was an explosion at a house at 84 Cliff Rock Road, Rednal, Birmingham; it caused a great deal of damage and some injuries, and it led to four arrests.

The house was owned by 77-year-old Mary Ann Furlong, who lived there with her daughters Emily Mary Furlong, aged 38, and 28-year-old Evelyn Mary Furlong. The premises had been used by the IRA as a safe house for terrorists, one of whom was 26-year-old Martin Patrick Clarke, who had been injured in the explosion. It was the startled neighbours who telephoned the emergency services, not Mary Ann Furlong, who was living there under the name of Higgins. All three women were ardent republicans, and at the time of this incident their names were being circulated as 'wanted' in Northern Ireland.

As well as a safe house, the premises were also used as a headquarters in the Midlands for the manufacture of explosive and incendiary devices. Concealed in an armchair were fifty-one sticks of gelignite, and fuses, detonators, batteries and balloons were also found.

'I wish to take full responsibility for the stuff that was found', said the gallant Clarke, who had suffered burns to his face, arm and leg; and the three women denied all knowledge of the cache, saying that Clarke had merely called at the house and asked for lodgings.

An early attempt at breast implants was discovered after Emily Furlong was searched and two sticks of gelignite were found secreted in her brassière.

'I thought it was a sugar stick that my sister buys for my mother', she said artlessly, adding, 'It was certainly very, very like it, or I would not have put it on my person, knowing the danger.'

Her explanation caused some amusement at the Police Court, especially when the clerk of the court pointed out that the two items were clearly marked 'Gelignite'.

Matters became marginally less amusing when at Birmingham Assizes, on 14 July, she was sentenced to five years' penal servitude; she was deported in 1942. Her sister Evelyn was sentenced to two years, and Mr Justice Singleton told Mary Ann Furlong, 'I could wish I did not have someone of your age to deal with, but the public must be protected.' He sentenced her to three years' imprisonment.

Having been sentenced to twenty years' penal servitude, Martin Clarke became so exuberant, shouting, 'Up the Republic!', that it took three warders to restrain him.

At exactly the same time as the arrest of Clarke and the Furlong family, observations were underway in London which would bring a devastating blow to the IRA bombers.

* * *

During 1939, twenty-nine warrants to intercept telephone calls were granted by the Home Secretary, plus 973 warrants to open mail. Many of the latter, without doubt, were issued in respect of the IRA bombing campaign. Coupled with information from the security forces and elsewhere, plus that obtained from informants, it all resulted in widespread observations being carried out by Special Branch.

The training undergone by aids to CID (aspirants for the CID proper) in the art of surveillance during the 1920s and 1930s involved surreptitiously following their detective inspectors through the streets; if they were spotted by their senior officers, they would be rebuked with a clump round the ear and the admonition to 'do better next time'. A rugged apprenticeship, but one that paid dividends.

There used to be a saying in the Metropolitan Police regarding women officers carrying out observations in a busy shopping area: 'Put her in plain clothes, give her a shopping bag and no one will suspect her'; but the women used in this complicated and dangerous surveillance task – where crowds were minimal and shopping bags would be of no earthly use – had to be better prepared than that.

Margery Urquhart had been born in Patagonia in 1912, and she joined the Metropolitan Police in 1936. She served as a uniform officer on 'J' and 'K' (two of the outer Divisions), but her capabilities were soon noted and she was seconded to Special Branch.

Anne Winterbottom joined one year after Urquhart and served on 'A', 'W' and 'M' divisions before she, too, was snapped up by Special Branch.

The surveillance commenced at 6.20pm on 3 May and finished at 2 o'clock the following morning. The two women saw

Patrick Dower and Patrick Joseph McAleer leave their lodgings at Sidmouth Street, WC1 and followed them as they walked a mile to Great Portland Street Underground Station, where they met the third member of the gang, Gerard Bradford. From there, the three men travelled on to Baker Street Underground Station, where they met Timothy Murray plus Gerald Lyons and one other man, and where it appeared that Bradford was giving instructions to the others; from time to time during that evening, McAleer met up with various members of the gang. Shortly afterwards, the group split up – so did the watchers. Miss Urquhart followed Dower, Murray and the other man. At 11.35am, in the Euston Road, she saw Dower put something through the letterbox of George Newman & Co., motor car agents, at No. 369. Shortly afterwards, the men went to Com-Motors at No. 349, where Miss Urquhart saw Murray insert something into that company's letter box. The two men split up, so it was only Murray, whom she did not know, who was followed; he went alone to the Edgware Road, where he was seen speaking to two girls and some young men, after which he took the long route home to his lodgings at St Mary's Terrace, Paddington, arriving there at 1.00am. Fortunately, the two empty milk bottles that Miss Urquhart had put into her handbag for protection were not needed.

Meanwhile, Miss Winterbottom had followed Bradford and Lyons to the Aldwych, where at 12.30am outside the Aldwych Theatre she saw Bradford take something out of his coat pocket. Both men spent five minutes looking around them before walking off into Kingsway, where she saw them go to the shop premises of D. Gestetner Ltd. From there, the men walked and ran north to High Holborn, and when Miss Winterbottom was able to catch up to them she saw them walking away from the Crittall Manufacturing Co. Ltd. By now the streets were pretty well deserted, and it would have been foolish indeed for one woman to try to continue to follow two very dangerous individuals. It is more than probable that the two men were responsible for planting bombs at Tottenham Court Road and Charing Cross Road; they were already heading in that direction, up Denmark Street to Charing Cross Road, then north into Tottenham Court Road, before taking a leisurely stroll back to their lodgings at Acton Street. But if they did plant bombs, nobody saw them. The two men got home at 2.00am.

The women returned to the Yard to be debriefed, and one might have thought that officers would have been dispatched to the various premises that the gang had visited and the keyholders called out so that the premises might be searched; but for whatever reason, they were not. It has since been stated that 'the other man' with Dower and Murray was John Joseph Keane, but this, of course, is nonsense. As has already been seen, Keane was arrested with others on 18 April, two weeks prior to the surveillance operation, and remained in custody until he was later sentenced to ten years' penal servitude. So who was 'the other man' who was never caught? If he was a participating informant for Special Branch, this would explain why no action was taken to stop the bombs detonating, in order to prevent suspicion falling on him. It would also explain why the gang were able to be charged with planting the bombs at Tottenham Court Road and Charing Cross Road, even though none of the police officers saw them do it. All a bit bewildering, isn't it? Back, now, to the early hours of 4 May.

At 1.00am – and this would have been minutes after Miss Winterbottom saw the two men at Gestetner's – just by chance, patrolling Police Constable 164 'E' Blake found a parcel outside the premises which contained two balloons, one inside the other filled with liquid, and a stick of gelignite and a detonator. He put the parcel in a bucket of water and was later commended by the commissioner for his actions.

At 2.25am there were explosions where Dower and Murray had been seen at George Newman's in the Euston Road; the shop front was blown out and damage estimated at £90 was caused. Another explosion where Bradford and Lyons had been seen at Crittall's in High Holborn caused £125 of damage at 2.41am.

At 5.15am, and again just by chance – Police Constable 560 'C' Ernest Haywood discovered a brown-paper parcel in the doorway of the furnishing company Heal & Son Ltd, in Tottenham Court Road. Opening it, he found a balloon, a stick of gelignite and a fuse; after separating the gelignite from the balloon, he immersed the items in a bucket of water, which he then took to the police station. He was later awarded £15 from the Bow Street Reward Fund and awarded the King's Police Medal for gallantry.

Police Constable William Marshall was called to an explosion at Com-Motors – another place where Dower and Murray had been seen – which occurred at 8.45am and in which the shop front was blown out; 21-year-old Miss Amy Brand, standing at an adjoining tobacconist's kiosk, was taken to hospital having been injured by wood splinters. Edward Buckland, a timekeeper at Selmer & Co., musical instrument makers of Charing Cross Road, found a parcel inside the shop and, believing it had been delivered to the firm, placed it on a desk. When he picked it up at 9.15am, it exploded in his hands, and he threw it on the floor, whereupon it burst into flames. Curtains were thrown on to it, and while Mr Buckland was trying to stamp out the flames, there was a second explosion, and he and John Ivor Lloyd, a salesman, were thrown to the floor. Both men were taken to hospital, Mr Buckland suffering from leg injuries.

That morning, the bombers' three addresses were raided by a mixture of Special Branch men and CID officers, and the men were asked to account for their movements over the past few hours. Patrick Dower told Inspector Bridges that the case was a frame-up and that he had nothing further to say, then changed his mind and said, 'I'll take the lot. I'm standing up to my principles. I have nothing further to say.'

When Patrick McAleer was arrested, two detonators were found on him. 'I have nothing to say at all', he said. 'I think it's a frame-up by your people of the Special Branch. I have nothing to say at all; that's definite.'

Gerard Bradford told the arresting officers, 'I don't wish to make any statement'; Lyons said, 'As to my movements, I don't think that matters', and Murray made a signed statement.

Charged with conspiracy to cause explosions and with causing or attempting to cause explosions during 3/4 May, the men appeared at the Old Bailey before the Common Serjeant, who conducted an extremely fair trial of the terrorists. He ruled that there was no evidence to suggest that any of the defendants were guilty of the explosion in Charing Cross Road, or that McAleer, Bradford or Lyons were guilty of the explosions in Euston Road or the attempt at Tottenham Court Road. Additionally, he ruled there was no evidence to show that Dower, McAleer or Murray were responsible for the explosion at High Holborn or the attempt at Kingsway; nor could McAleer be connected with any explosion.

If the bombers were pleased at this dispensation of British justice, which they despised, they gave no indication of it, sitting sullenly in the dock and saying nothing.

When Dower had been found guilty of conspiracy to cause explosions, Inspector Bridges informed the court that he was a member of the IRA, a section commander and a trusted 'soldier of the Republic'. McAleer was a volunteer in the IRA, and when Inspector Bridges stated that he had been receiving treatment for tuberculosis, this caused him to bellow from the dock, 'I don't want sympathy from this court on account of my health!'

Bradford's arrest was, said Inspector Bridges, 'regarded by the police as of considerable importance'. His real name was Kirk and he had attended an IRA course on bomb-making in Ireland.

Murray was a member of the IRA and had for some time been closely associated with fellow Irishmen who had been causing explosions in London.

Sentenced to twenty years' penal servitude each, Dower, McAleer, Bradford and Murray all struggled violently in the dock with warders before being removed, McAleer shouting, 'Long live the Irish Republic!'

The identities of the two policewomen had not been disclosed in court; they were referred to simply as 'Miss A' and 'Miss B'. Now the Common Serjeant called them before him and told them:

> I think it right to express the appreciation of the court to you for the fine police work you did during all those hours and also for the way in which you both gave evidence in this trial. I hope the attention of the Commissioner of Police may be called to what I have said.

It was. While *Police Orders* reported that Inspector Bridges and seven other officers were commended by the commissioner 'for ability and persistence in a difficult case of conspiracy to cause explosions', a footnote added that 'two women police constables who were engaged in the above have been highly commended by the commissioner.' No names were given – the high commendation was appended to their personal records, although no details were disclosed – and both were appointed to Special Branch thereafter as women detective constables.

Back, now, to Gerald Lyons, who having been found guilty on the same charges as the others was brought back to the dock to face the charge of possessing explosive substances with intent to endanger life, plus possession of a revolver and ammunition for the same purpose.

The court heard that in February Lyons had rented a bedsit at Trafalgar Road, Moseley, Birmingham, under the name of Dunlop. On 30 March something evidently went wrong with an explosive device that was being manufactured; it had exploded, doors were torn from their hinges, a wardrobe and bedstead were smashed and a window was blown out. Mrs Annie Elizabeth Dunkley, who lived in a house opposite, saw Lyons and another man, both hatless, coatless and with dirty faces, run off down the road. It was suggested that the second man was either Pat McAleer or John Kearns, but if so, they were never charged. When the police arrived, they found two large drums of aluminium powder, 76lbs of potassium chlorate, 170 2oz cartridges of gelignite, 266 balloons, detonators, packages of mixed aluminium and iron oxide, lengths of safety fuse and other items all designed to make a complete bomb-making outfit. It was estimated that the unintentional explosion had been caused by two or three sticks of 2oz gelignite. Lyons' fingerprints were found on a bottle in the room, and after he was found guilty, Inspector Bridges informed the court that Lyons' real name was Gerard Anthony Dunlop. He had been connected with the IRA since 1937, and during that year he had been arrested in Belfast and sentenced to three months' imprisonment for being in possession of illegal documents relating to *Fianna na h'Eireann* (the youth organization of the IRA). In 1938 he had attended a course of instruction in explosives.

Asked if he had anything to say, Lyons said:

> I believe it is a just and Christian thing, trying to overcome tyranny. I believe it a Christian thing to strike at it and the British Government has tyrannised Ireland. While it exists it is the duty of every Irishman to try and overthrow this tyranny. I believe I have done my duty to my country.

And with that typically self-justifying jargon out of the way, Lyons, like his associates was sentenced to concurrent terms of twenty years' penal servitude.

Chapter 13

Another Own Goal – and More Arrests

On the day before the surveillance began in London, on 2 May, there was an explosion in a room at a house in Higher Temple Street, Manchester. Three Irishmen had been renting the rooms; one of them was Patrick Moriarty, who was not present at the time of the explosion. A man named Alfred Ruffles, who occupied the ground floor, rushed upstairs to find an IRA man who had correctly given his name as Bernard McGuinness when he rented the room, and who ran off. He took the first boat to Dublin and was never caught. Hot on his heels was the second man, who also escaped; his name was Joe Collins, although he also favoured the alias of Connor MacNessa, and he managed to take a few sticks of gelignite with him. When the police arrived and searched the room they discovered seventy balloons, sulphuric acid and sticks of gelignite.

The men who had escaped had been slightly injured, and their descriptions were circulated and hospitals and doctors were alerted. Then a suitcase containing acid and inflammatory materials was found by a cleaner at the Manchester Corporation omnibus depot under the seat of a bus and was immediately plunged into water. The two incidents were connected.

On 12 May, bombs were put through the letterboxes of five premises in Market Street and Piccadilly, Manchester, and police investigations into those offences, plus the explosion at Higher Temple Street, led them to a house at Dunstal Road, Wythenshawe, where they found Patrick Moriarty in bed with John Duggan, who shared the house with his sister, Mary Duggan.

'I don't know what to say', she said when 4lb of potassium chlorate, two sticks of gelignite, a detonator, two pieces of powder fuse and eleven balloons were found under the bed.

'I never knew anything about it', said Moriarty, while John Duggan told Detective Inspector Forster, 'It's all my property and nobody knowed it was there, bar myself.'

Additionally, a house at Clifford Street, Chorlton-on-Medlock, Manchester was visited by police, and there the escapee from

Higher Temple Street, 31-year-old Connor MacNessa, was arrested for being in possession of 261 sticks of gelignite, two sticks of Saxonite, a paper bag containing potassium chlorate, four pieces of powder fuse, one fuse detonator, nine rounds of revolver ammunition, a paper bag containing twenty-nine balloons and a number of street maps of Manchester, Salford and Liverpool and a map of England and Wales.

Inspector Forster told the Police Court at Manchester that when he was charged, MacNessa had replied, 'What I did, I did for Ireland', although this was denied by MacNessa, who whimpered to the magistrate, 'I was beaten in the police station, last night.' But that, and MacNessa's denial, had no effect, and he, together with everybody else, was remanded in custody.

At a later appearance, Mary Duggan was granted bail; that was a mistake, because she left for Ireland and was never seen by the mainland authorities again. Moriarty and MacNessa were picked out on identification parades as having been in the room at Higher Temple Street where the explosion had occurred.

At Manchester Assizes, where the case was tried by Mr Justice Stable, Moriarty was legally represented and gave evidence saying that he was not a member of the IRA, had never knowingly had explosives in his possession and had not conspired to cause explosions. When a detective sergeant gave evidence regarding incriminating items found on a suit which belonged to Moriarty, Duggan broke his self-imposed silence, jumped to his feet and shouted, 'Paddy Moriarty is not responsible for that stuff on those clothes! I often wore them; he had nothing whatever to do with the IRA at all.'

Summing up, Mr Justice Stable told the jury:

> For Heaven's sake, let us approach each one of these cases with the same sense of completely detached, unruffled fairness as we approach every other criminal case. Don't let it be said that because of these explosions we approach a case of this kind in any other atmosphere than that in which we habitually approach a criminal trial . . .

At that point, the Judge was interrupted by MacNessa, who stood up and exclaimed:

> I want to state I am not a criminal; I am a prisoner of war. I demand the treatment due to a prisoner of war. In this case, I do not care what sentence you pass on me; if I come out of

> gaol alive, I will come out as I go in, a soldier of Ireland. If then, there are only half a dozen men with walking sticks fighting for Ireland, I shall join them.

'I thought you wanted to make some statement of fact regarding someone's evidence', said the Judge. 'I am not going to listen to you making a political speech.'

'You refuse to let me speak?' challenged MacNessa, to which the Judge coldly replied, 'Sit down' – and he did.

After an hour's deliberations, the jury found Moriarty (who was married to Mary Duggan) not guilty, and he was discharged; the other two were convicted.

'I should be wasting perhaps valuable time if I said anything to you', said the Judge, who by now was probably quite fed up with listening to terrorists' rhetoric, and he sentenced both Duggan and MacNessa to twenty years' penal servitude. Inevitably, they both shouted, 'God save Ireland!' as they also inevitably struggled with warders on their inevitable way to the cells.

* * *

At the same time as the Duggans and MacNessa were being rounded up in Manchester, some active investigations were being carried out 214 miles to the north by the police in Glasgow. Headed by the no-nonsense Chief Constable, Percy Sillitoe (later Sir Percy Sillitoe KBE, DL and Director General of MI5), a raid was carried out on the Celtic Literary Society in an assembly hall at 132 Trongate after a number of Irishmen had begun to congregate there. Under the concert platform of the hall were found 540 sticks of gelignite, a quantity of cable fuse, wire and an alarm clock, and eight men were arrested.

Glaswegian police were famed for being very big, very tough and even less inclined than their London Flying Squad counterparts, to take 'no' for an answer, and they soon discovered that Edward Gill Jr. had, on 10 May 1939, broken into the Grangard Brick & Sand Company at 470 Grangard Road, Glasgow and stolen 156 sticks of gelignite, 514 detonators, 60 feet of white tape fuse, a metal canister, a pair of fuse cutters and detonator nippers. The majority of those items were discovered at his father's address at 21 Beechgrove Street, Glasgow. It was just as well there had been no experimentation with the 'white tape fuse'. It was not of the usual slow-burning variety; this was instant fuse, which burnt at the rate of 3 feet per second.

Five of the men who were originally arrested had the charges against them dropped; apart from Gill, two others remained in custody, 60-year-old James O'Hara and John Carson, aged 20.

O'Hara had made a classic mistake which would help lead to his conviction. He had conveyed a cheap brown suitcase containing 150 sticks of stolen gelignite to the IRA's branch headquarters in Liverpool and had rather carelessly wrapped some of the explosive in a piece of torn brown paper with part of an address written on it. But the IRA agent in Liverpool believed – wrongly as it turned out – that he was being followed, so he dumped the suitcase in Paxton Street, near Liverpool's Exchange Station. When it was found and examined, on 14 May, Liverpool CID found the incriminating partial address: 'Miss J. Gardner, 37 Duke Street …'

Every Duke Street in every borough, town and city was checked out, until it was established that the Duke Street referred to was the one in Glasgow – which was also O'Hara's address.

During the men's appearances at Glasgow Police Court, security was paramount, as it was at the High Court, Glasgow on 8 August 1939; credentials were demanded from those who attended the court, many of whom were turned away. Found guilty, Gill was asked by Lord Russell if he had anything to say before being sentenced. He had:

> That paid agent of British imperialism has branded me as a criminal. I wish to say here and now that I don't consider myself a criminal. If it is a crime to love Ireland and hate British rule in Ireland, then I am a criminal and will always be a criminal. God bless the IRA!

But the sentence of ten years' penal servitude appeared to shock Gill. He turned pale and merely muttered, 'God save Ireland', before he was led away.

The following day, O'Hara and Carson were found guilty. O'Hara had nothing to say and what Carson said was of little relevance:

> There is no connection between the Celtic Literary Society and the IRA. The IRA is a military organization and the Celtic Literary Society a social movement. Most of what the witnesses said was irrelevant. There will never be any peace in Ireland until the British garrison has been cleared out.

With that, both men were sentenced to ten years' penal servitude.

Chapter 14

Lavatories, Hotels and Cinemas

Meanwhile, back down in London, there were three explosions at Underground station lavatories on the night of 13 May 1939. The first, at 8.00pm at Marble Arch, replicated the previous explosion of 12 April. There were hundreds of pedestrians near the Marble Arch subway at the time, and glass and masonry were blown on to the pavement and roadway. Five minutes later, there was an explosion at Harrow Road which fortunately caused only minor damage, but at 8.20pm a bomb – fashioned with gelignite like the other two – exploded at Hammersmith, where one had detonated a month previously. An attendant bravely but unsuccessfully tried to smother the bomb, and although he was unhurt, one of the cubicles was almost wrecked.

These incidents went in waves of similar types. The next was a series of incendiary devices planted in seven hotels, throughout the country, on 19 May.

There was an explosion at the Grand Hotel, Morecambe, and a broken bottle which had contained paraffin and acid was found in a room which had been booked by a man with an Irish accent who had provided a false address in Birmingham and had left prior to the incident.

At the Victoria Hotel, Southport a man booked a bedroom in which a fire occurred, and at the Carlton Hotel, Blackpool a man 'of a foreign appearance' disappeared after a fire broke out in his room. At the Imperial Hotel, Eastbourne a man with an Irish brogue who arrived on the London train vanished after the bedroom he had booked caught fire. As in all of the previous cases, false addresses in Birmingham were given.

A balloon partially destroyed by acid was found in a bedroom at the North-Eastern Hotel, Harrogate, and a man with an Irish accent asked for a room for the weekend at the Kingscliffe Hall Hotel, Margate. He took a large attaché case to his room on the second floor, consumed dinner and three glasses of whiskey, then left without paying at 8 o'clock. In his wake a fire broke out in his wardrobe, fed by clothing which had been saturated with paraffin.

Much the same happened at the Hotel Victoria, Southend, where the guest, described as 'a slouching Irishman', and with an unreliable address in Cardiff, had not been seen since he took a suitcase to his room. The suitcase was found burning close to a bed which had been soaked in paraffin.

So those were the lavatory and hotel campaigns out of the way – the next targets were cinemas.

* * *

In early May, tear gas bombs had exploded simultaneously at the Trocadero and Paramount cinemas in Liverpool which were only 20 yards apart. Fifteen people were taken to the Royal Infirmary – two of them were detained – and a number of police officers who entered the Trocadero were overcome by the fumes and received first aid.

Exactly the same type of device – a cylindrical object with a screw cap, worked by a detonator – was left at a news cinema in Church Street, Liverpool on 29 May by a man who ran out of the cinema. There was a hissing sound, followed by a sheet of flame, and the building was filled with tear gas fumes. It was initially feared that the cinema would catch fire, but George Potter, the chief operator, grabbed a fire extinguisher and put out the smouldering bomb. An attendant called for calm, all of the exits were thrown open and the 200 patrons staggered outside, coughing and with tears streaming down their faces. Among the twenty people taken to hospital were the five girl attendants, who had stoically remained at their posts until everyone vacated the cinema.

The same night, four magnesium bombs exploded at the Paramount Cinema, New Street, Birmingham. The audience of 300 had their panic allayed by a man who stood up and good-humouredly shouted, 'Don't worry, keep calm – it's only the Irish again!'

A search of Birmingham cinemas was carried out that evening; an unexploded magnesium bomb was discovered in the Gaumont Cinema, Steeplehouse Lane, but the following night a bomb, thought to have been left overnight, exploded in the West End Cinema in Suffolk Street.

The day after the West End Cinema explosion, there was another at 9.00pm in one of the toilet cubicles at the New Victoria Cinema, Vauxhall Bridge Road, London. Joseph Malone emerged from the cubicle in a state of shock, his hand badly burnt. Tear gas fumes percolated into the cinema, where there were 1,700 people, and a dozen of them had to leave. Several people who entered the area were overcome by the fumes – the chief of staff at the cinema, Mr Albert William George Dean, was particularly affected, suffering chest pain, coupled with coughing and sneezing – and police officers wearing gas masks attended and found the bomb; the cap had come off the top of it.

Taken to hospital to have his burns treated, Malone was seen by Divisional Detective Inspector Haywood and told him, 'I want you thoroughly to understand I am alone in this. I'll tell you all about it. The thing went off in my hand a bit too quick.'

In common with many other criminals who have experienced a traumatic experience at the time of their arrest, once Malone started talking he couldn't stop. In a written statement he said:

> This afternoon, I was in Hyde Park and put together a gas bomb . . . I took a balloon containing a bomb into the New Victoria picture house. After half an hour, I squeezed the bulb which is waxed and it should have gone off a quarter of an hour after. I squeezed it too hard and it went off in my hand. It knocked me out. I was not unconscious but I was dazed . . . It is me alone who is responsible for the bomb exploding in the cinema. I did it as a member of the IRA, of which I am a soldier and I would gladly do it again if I had the chance.

The following day, while he was being conveyed in a police car, Malone asked Detective Sergeant Frank Gibbon, 'Was there any other excitement in town last night? Another half a dozen should have gone off. I suppose the fucking yellow rats funked it.' This comment was later denied.

Evidence was given at Bow Street Police Court by 60-year-old Frederick Harold Dupré MBE, FCS, chemical adviser to the Home Office, who stated that the item was a Stokes Bomb which liberated tear gas. Asked if the gases were dangerous, Mr Dupré replied that they were noxious and would completely disable a person for a time. They would not cause permanent injury providing the victim was removed from the affected area; the danger in a crowd, said Mr Dupré, was panic.

Appearing at the Old Bailey on 28 June 1939, Malone was found guilty of maliciously causing an irritant gas to be taken by Mr Dean with intent to annoy; and having been told that Malone had been actively associated with members of the IRA, both on the mainland and in Ulster, the Common Serjeant handed down five years' penal servitude; Malone died two and a half years later at the early age of twenty-five in Parkhurst Prison.

Actually, the 'yellow rats' referred to by Malone may not have been as dilatory as he initially thought; the day after his arrest, an unexploded tear gas bomb was found in the Empire Cinema, Leicester Square, after the audience had left.

* * *

Time for a change of game plan by the bombers; now, on 9 June, sixty incendiary devices were sent to Post Office sorting offices.

The first bomb exploded at 8.20pm in the Wimpole Street post office, causing burns to the handler; an immediate search of the office was carried out, resulting in the discovery of four more bombs. When another bomb exploded at Broadwick Street sorting office, the Yard sent out a call to all the police stations in the Metropolitan Police District, asking officials to search all sorting offices and pillar boxes in their areas, and fourteen more devices were found, all of which ignited; just after 10.00pm, a pillar box was found to be on fire in Kentish Town.

At 7.55pm a mailbag on the Birmingham to London express was seen smouldering; it was noticed by a guard, who flung it from a window as the train neared Northampton. Several workers sorting night mail on trains suffered burns to their hands and faces, and bombs were now exploding in sorting offices in Manchester, fifteen in Lincoln, twelve in Leicester and four in Birmingham; eight employees were treated for burns.

As a mail train from Glasgow reached London, a mailbag was found to be smouldering, and a fire broke out in a pillar box in Streatham. When a parcel exploded at the West Central Post Office in Hyde Street, the Metropolitan Police cancelled all leave, and special constables were posted to all public works.

With such an increased police presence there was, naturally, a lull in proceedings; it lasted in London for two weeks – then came the sustained attack in central London on 24 June which is described in this book's prologue.

Chapter 15

Railway Stations and More Arrests

On the morning of 2 July there were seven explosions at London, Midland and Scottish railway stations, all in the Midlands. The first incident was at Derby, where a 63-year-old cloakroom attendant noticed a blue flame coming from a suitcase and made a dash for the door. He had only just got outside when the explosion occurred, injuring him, and he was taken to hospital. At Leicester, a wooden structure in the main booking hall was shattered and a 61-year-old ticket collector received injuries to his left arm, legs and face; a hundred windows in the vicinity were blown out, with the explosion being heard four miles away. An hour later, the cloakroom at Birmingham New Street was extensively damaged; an attendant noticed flames amongst the parcels and ran out of the office to sound the fire alarm. As he ran along the platform, so the bomb detonated. Part of the roof caved in, parcels and bags were scattered all over the floor and station officials were lucky not to be hit by the flying debris. The glass in the cloakroom was blown out on to the platform, and the blast wave caused the windows in a train standing opposite to shatter.

There were explosions at Nottingham and at Coventry, and luggage was damaged by the blast. A junior parcels porter at Stafford station saw smoke coming from one of the cases and reached the door just as the bomb exploded; a hole was blown in the floor, sections of the glass roof were shattered, the ceiling of the control office caved in and window frames and glass flew into the roadway. A fire followed an explosion at Leamington Spa which wrecked the bookings and parcels office.

* * *

But three days after those explosions, the police were at work again, carrying out arrests. Detective Inspector Whitehead had been keeping observation on a group of men in Harrow Road; they were arrested, and as they were conveyed by police van to Harrow Road police station, one of the men, 19-year-old Thomas Nelson, was seen trying to hide a piece of newspaper upon which he had written the names and addresses of banks and post offices in the Kilburn district which had been mentioned in the 'S' Plan. The lodgings at Craven Park, Harlesden, of a second member of the group, Patrick Donaghy, were searched, and on top of a wardrobe a burnt suitcase stained with acid was found, together with a roll of electrician's tape and pieces of wax containing chlorate. The other four men in their group were released through lack of evidence, but there was sufficient to tie in Nelson and Donaghy with Michael O'Shea and others who had been sentenced in March for conspiracy to cause explosions.

Nelson was picked out on an identification parade as being the person responsible for putting a package in a pillar box opposite Madame Tussaud's on 24 June; he had then jumped on to a passing bus shortly before the pillar box exploded. The two men were committed to the Old Bailey, where Nelson stated that he was nowhere near the pillar box on the night in question but was unable to call witnesses to say where he was since, sadly, they had all been deported. When Donaghy was found guilty, Detective Inspector Whitehead told the Common Serjeant that he was 'a very willing tool of the IRA and would do anything for them', and that Nelson 'devoted his entire time to the IRA and had been used as a connecting link between different sections operating in London.' On 21 September, both men were sentenced to twenty years' penal servitude at the Old Bailey.

* * *

During June and July 1939, the Special Branch surveillance teams were kept at full stretch. John Charles Woods, his wife, Ella May, and also Gary Jones and Ann and Rose Conway were seen carrying heavy packages and visiting five different addresses – this was both prior to and following the explosions at Piccadilly Circus. Not only were the surveillance squads working flat out, with intercepted telephone calls and mail providing valuable intelligence, so were the Special Branch informants. And there was another source of information: the British public. They were becoming thoroughly sick and tired of these dangerous explosions disrupting their daily lives; even those who were not directly affected knew others who were – commuters, Post Office and railway workers – and they wanted to help. Immensely helpful were landladies, hotel workers, letting agents and simply nosy neighbours; because the terrorists had been warned about keeping away from predominantly Irish communities, some of them stuck out like sore thumbs. Comings and goings at odd hours, clandestine meetings with others who appeared as furtive as themselves, carrying attaché cases, suitcases or parcels – this all provoked suspicions, which were often passed on the police.

And now the net was tightening; it resulted in Detective Inspector Whitehead keeping observation, in rather cramped conditions for over seven hours, on 11 July, on a house in Tavistock Square. When he saw 25-year-old Ann Conway enter the premises he followed her into a room on the first floor. In a wardrobe he found a woman's blue dressing case, which Miss Conway said was hers; it contained forty-four sticks of 2oz gelignite, ten detonators, eighteen wax cylindrical containers and a quantity of other explosive substances. Asked if she wished to account for these items being in her possession, she replied, 'No. That's your job to find out.' She then pointed to a bottle of liquid, the cork of which was burnt, and told the inspector, 'It's a good job you called, as there would have been a nice blaze in about an hour.'

At that point, Gary Jones arrived and asked for Conway; initially he said he was her brother but then admitted his identity. He was told that he had been seen in her company on a number of occasions and that he would be charged with being concerned with her.

'I don't know what you're talking about', said Jones, although, of course, he did.

When Conway was charged that afternoon, she replied, 'The stuff was in my possession and not in Gary Jones's.'

On the same day, Detective Sergeant Cain and other officers went to a house at Tudor Court South, Wembley, the home of Mr and Mrs Woods. In the garden shed the officers found a revolver, cleaned and oiled. 'You're not going to take that!' protested 41-year-old Ella Woods. 'I prize it. It did good work in 1921/22.'

Sergeant Cain noticed that part of the back garden had recently been turned over. The officers dug down and about one foot under the surface they found two jars containing wax and a lump of wax shaped like a tumbler. Under a heap of grass and manure Cain also found an electric battery. Rubber gloves were found, and the powder on them turned out to be a mixture of potassium chlorate and sugar. Underneath a chair cushion in the kitchen was found a copy of the supplement to the 'IRA Proclamation', dated 5 April 1939.

When he was charged with conspiracy to cause explosions and possessing a firearm without a certificate, John Woods replied with regard to the second charge, 'That's quite all right', but added, 'I didn't see any explosives.'

Mrs Woods said, 'I had nothing at all, I am absolutely certain.'

The following day, at midday, Inspector Whitehead returned to Tavistock Square, where 22-year-old Rose Conway, the sister of Ann, had been detained. He told her, 'I understand that you entered this room at 11.45am with this case which is full of explosive substances.'

Amongst the case's contents were 100 sticks of gelignite and fourteen detonators; asked if she wished to offer an explanation as to how they had come into her possession, she replied, 'No'. Told that she would be detained, she replied, 'I've been expecting this for some time', and after she was charged at Bow Street police station, she responded, 'I have nothing to say.' However, when the inspector asked her occupation, she replied, 'I don't get paid for working for the IRA; I do it voluntarily.'

During the remands at Bow Street Police Court, Mr Vincent Evans for the Director of Public Prosecutions outlined the facts; when it came to the wax found in the Woods' garden, he told the court that bombers would mould wax into the shape of small tumblers (as, in fact, some had been), into which sulphuric acid was poured. It was then placed in a balloon, which was laid on top of a mixture of sugar and potassium chlorate. The wax containers, sealed at both ends, prevented the acid from getting to the explosive substance, but at the required moment, when the wax was smashed, the acid burned its way through the balloon and 'a severe conflagration' took place on contact with the mixture of sugar and potassium chlorate.

Sergeant Cain described finding badges and cards referring to Sir Roger Casement who, the officer helpfully told the court, 'was executed as a traitor to this country'.

'He was a born Irishman, so he cannot be a traitor to this country', protested Mrs Woods. 'No Irishman can be a traitor to this country. I know some dead men are very powerful men like Sir Roger Casement, for instance.' She then went on to complain that the police had dug up vegetables from her garden 'in spite of the fact that we may be needing food so badly in a day or two'.

Precisely what this rhetoric was expected to achieve, particularly the claim that Mrs Woods had been deprived of sustenance from her vegetable garden, was unclear, but it failed to move Sir Rollo Graham-Campbell, that very affable Magistrate, to any clemency, and all five prisoners were committed to stand their trial at the Old Bailey.

The Conway sisters and Gary Jones all predictably refused to plead when they appeared at the Old Bailey before the Common Serjeant, Mr Cecil Whiteley KC. However, John Woods pleaded not guilty, as did his wife; the reason for this was that if she, a diehard Republican, refused to plead, it would suggest by imputation that she was just as culpable as the others, as was her husband, who must by the fact of their marriage have known what was going on.

He was represented by Bernard Gillis (later to become a High Court Judge), and responding to questions from his counsel, 43-year-old John Woods said:

> Until I saw them at the police court, I had no knowledge of explosive substances and I had never before seen a suitcase said to have been found at my house . . . I am not Irish. I'm a Londoner and know no members of the IRA . . . My wife is Irish and on one occasion, I went with her to an Irish social and dancing club . . . I'm an engine driver on the LMS Railway and I'm often away from home for long periods.

Questioned by the Common Serjeant, Woods said that he was surprised when the police dug up 'certain articles' from his garden and found the Irish documents in the house which belonged to his wife; he told the Judge that he thought the IRA explosions were 'terrible things'.

Asked by prosecuting counsel if his wife was interested in the IRA, Woods replied, 'I don't know', adding, 'I'm finding out a lot since I've been attending court.'

'Would you like, in your own interest, to say what you have found out?' asked the Judge, to which Woods sorrowfully replied, 'No. I don't want to make it worse' – and that completed the picture of a man who, it appeared, had become enmeshed without his knowledge in events completely beyond his control and had been utterly duped.

That was the conclusion that the jury obviously came to, having deliberated for two hours on 21 September; John Woods was acquitted of all charges and he kissed his wife as he left the dock. His freedom was short-lived. Arrests are not allowed to be made within the precincts of the Old Bailey, so the Special Branch officers waited until he had left and was walking along the street, before taking him off to Cannon Row police station where he was detained, pending proceedings under the Emergency Powers Act.

Back in No. 1 Court, the other four defendants had been found guilty, and the court learnt from Detective Inspector Whitehead that Mrs Woods was a member of the Roger Casement Club and had been seen on many occasions in London meeting active members of the IRA.

Gary Jones – he was also known as Gray and referred to as 'Halfpenny' – had been under observation for months. As officer commanding the IRA in London, he had played an active role behind the scenes in the IRA and had organized outrages.

The Conway sisters had left Liverpool in April, saying they had been recalled to Éire; in fact, that was a ruse. They had come to London and at the time of their arrest they were negotiating for a house in Sussex, which was intended as a store for explosives, in order to avoid the active scrutiny of the police in London.

Ann Conway's real name, said the inspector, was Moira (or Mary) McSweeney. She was the leader of the women's section of the IRA, had sixteen girls in her charge and had been responsible for posting the IRA proclamation prior to the outrages in January.

Rose Conway – or McSweeney – had associated in Liverpool with John Joseph Hannon, who had recently been sentenced to seven years' penal servitude during the Manchester trials. 'Anything I have done or supposed to have done, I did for my country and am proud of it!' cried Rose from the dock, and as the Judge sentenced the four of them, each to ten years' penal servitude, she shouted, 'Up the Republic!' and Jones chimed in with, 'God save Ireland!'

Chapter 16

Murder, Arrests and New Legislation

When there was an explosion in a house at Bury New Road, Salford on 13 July and two men were seen running away, Manchester police, who found explosives there, had a pretty good idea as to the identity of at least one of them.

John McCabe, a 21-year-old engine driver, was traced to an address at Trafford Road, Eccles, where he was found to be in possession of a quantity of oxide of iron, powdered aluminium, potassium chlorate, two glass funnels, a map and the agenda of a meeting with an IRA district committee. When he appeared at Salford Police Court, in a very surly tone of voice he unoriginally claimed that 'the stuff's been planted on me'.

Charged with conspiring with others to cause explosives, he appeared at Manchester Assizes and refused to plead; after Mr Justice Cassels warned the jury to avoid prejudice, he was found guilty on 23 November. Inspector Howarth told the court, 'Since his arrest, he has boasted of his connection with IRA activities and at the time of his arrest he was one of the principal officers of the Lancashire and Midland districts.'

Did the prisoner wish to say anything? The prisoner did not. Twenty years' penal servitude.

* * *

The day following McCabe's arrest, there was another, rather thrilling arrest at Southleigh Gardens, Leeds. Chief Inspector William Chester led the search of the house – two women were present at the time – and in the upstairs bedroom the officers found a parcel containing 5lbs of gelignite, plus a suitcase containing a further 15lbs of the explosive. When William Sheridan walked into the house and was informed of the find, he punched Chief Inspector Chester, and a struggle ensued.

As he was taken to a police car, Sheridan suddenly shouted, 'Look out, they've got me!' – and at that moment, the occupier of the house, John Patrick Jones, turned the corner.

'Look out, they've got me – get away!' shouted Sheridan, but Jones didn't – he walked into the house and said, 'I don't know anything about it.' He and the two women who were arrested had the case against them thrown out at the Police Court.

Not so James Morgan who, when he arrived at the house, initially told the officers his name was Casey. However, when he was taken to the room where the gelignite had been found, he said:

> I should like to take all responsibility for it. I brought it here a few weeks ago. Don't ask me where I got it from. I expect you can guess the rest. I'm the bloke you're looking for. It's a dangerous game we're in. It's all right if we win but it's a fucker if we lose.

He went on to admit being a member of the IRA for the past seven years, and when he was formally charged he replied, 'My real name is Shamus McCann and my address is Belfast. As a soldier of the Irish Republican Army I am proud that anything I have done or am charged with is for Ireland.'

Sheridan protested his innocence, said he had never been a member of the IRA, had no knowledge of the gelignite and had only struggled because he was unaware that the men were police officers.

At Leeds Assizes on 28 November, Sheridan's case was dismissed on the directions of the Judge, Mr Justice Oliver, but Morgan was sentenced to twelve years' penal servitude.

* * *

One of the worst IRA outrages took place on 26 July 1939. Just before 2 o'clock in the afternoon, there was a terrific explosion from a sulphuric acid bomb in the cloakroom at King's Cross LNER terminus. An inspector, a sergeant and two constables from the railway police rushed into the affected area and, groping their way through the thick smoke, pulled out the injured.

The shock was felt throughout the station buildings as well as by pedestrians 150 yards away; an attendant at the controlled pedestrian crossing on the main road was thrown from the box in which he was sitting, but he was one of the fortunate ones.

The bomb had been placed under the receiving counter where packages for early callers were stored, and splinters of wood and glass were sent flying in all directions. Dr Donald Campbell aged thirty-six of Edinburgh, who had just returned from the continent with his wife, took the full force of the blast; both his legs were blown off and he was taken to St Pancras Hospital, before being transferred to the Royal Free Hospital, where he died three hours later. Mrs Jessie Campbell and four of the cloakroom attendants were also taken to hospital, one of them in a serious condition.

Then at 9.30 that evening there was another explosion, this time at Victoria Station, of a time bomb in a suitcase in the cloakroom; three cloakroom attendants and two porters were taken to hospital. The heavy shutters above the counter were forced down and buckled out of shape, and a train standing at platform 15, opposite the cloakroom, had its windows shattered. There was pandemonium; people in a nearby news theatre got to their feet in alarm, and hundreds of others rushed to the station to see if they could help, only to be met by panicking people exiting from the station.

Security was doubled, then trebled at important buildings, public utilities, railway bridges and stations. Houses where known IRA sympathizers were known to meet were turned over by the police, who checked the movements of suspects; those unable to satisfactorily account for their movements were hauled in and interviewed, and while some were released – because despite suspicion, there was nothing else that could be done with them – others were put up for identification.

Anyone who brought packages and suitcases to be deposited at main line stations was asked to open them. Those who refused to do so were politely informed that the item could not be accepted (and this refusal was accompanied by a hurried phone call to the police). Detectives were posted at the London stations, and at King's Cross and Euston a special watch was kept on passengers boarding for Liverpool and other northern towns. Officials in trains who travelled regularly between London and the ports of embarkation for Ireland were questioned to see if they could provide any information regarding recent arrivals to this country from across the Irish Sea.

So while the police were busy, searching suspect premises and making arrests, what on earth were the Government doing? Apart from insisting on being even more closely guarded than usual, they were dragging their heels, that's what.

* * *

As well as introducing the Street Playground Act on to the statute book during this period, it apparently seemed important for the Government to inform the police that the intricacies of the Motor Vehicle (Authorisation of Speed Types) Order (No. 1) 1937,

Amendment (No. 2) Order 1939 should be the focus of their attention, rather than the catching of terrorists.

On the same day as the murder of Dr Campbell, the matter was debated (not for the first time) in the House of Commons. Fears were expressed that 'the innocent might suffer' as a result of the proposed legislation; the Opposition wetly suggested that persons against whom expulsion orders were made should have the opportunity to appear before a High Court Judge. The Home Secretary, Sir Samuel Hoare, declared bluntly that if a judicial procedure such as that were introduced, the Bill would be useless against IRA outrages.

He bolstered his argument with a list of impressive statistics: between January and July 1939 there had been 127 attacks by the IRA, one person had been killed and fifty-five injured. Those convicted of IRA offences amounted to sixty-six, and 1,500 sticks of gelignite had been seized by the police as well as 1,000 detonators, two tons of potassium chlorate and ferrous oxide, seven gallons of sulphuric acid and 4cwt of aluminium powder.

He added that the IRA campaign had been monitored by 'foreign organizations', and although he failed to name names he was referring, firstly, to Germany – he had, of course, been briefed by the security services that the author of the 'S' Plan, Jim O'Donovan, had travelled there to set up contacts and that agents of the Nazi intelligence agency, the Abwehr, were in contact with the IRA. The other organization was *Clan na Gael*, the Irish-American lobby who had financed practically the whole of the 'S' Plan, and Sir Samuel certainly didn't want to mention them. In the summer of 1939, as war with Germany was looming, the British Government wanted the United States as an ally, rather than risk alienating them by mentioning something unpleasant that had already happened, albeit with help from a minuscule faction of their population.

Sir Donald Somervell pointed out that the latest outrage was proof that ordinary methods were insufficient to deal with the IRA, and that there were cases where the police were satisfied that complicity in plots existed but in which it would not be possible to obtain evidence to gain convictions. The sources of police information could not be revealed for fear that the lives of their informants would be in jeopardy if their identities became known. The amendment proposed by the opposition was defeated by 212 votes to 123, the committee stage was over and, although some members of the Opposition whimpered, the House agreed to forgo the Report Stage and proceed to the third reading, when the bill was passed with a substantial 218 votes to 17. The Prevention of Violence (Temporary Provisions) Act received royal assent on 28 July 1939 and came into force on the following day; the police now had additional powers of search and were able to arrest, without warrant, any person who they reasonably suspected of committing an offence under the act and to detain them for up to five days. It also gave the Home Secretary the power to exclude and deport persons who he was satisfied were connected with the IRA.

As far as the police were concerned, it was about time. Between then and the end of the IRA campaign, 119 suspects were expelled from Britain, thirteen were prohibited from entering and twenty-one had to register with the police.

Chapter 17

A Password – and a Nunnery

At 11.45am on 27 July, Detective Inspector Charles Allen went to a house in Brunswick Square, where he saw John O'Regan, a servant at that address. Upon searching the basement, the police found two attaché cases and a paper bag containing 87 detonators, 608 balloons, 30 wax containers and 17 packets of potassium chlorate and sugar.

O'Regan told the officer, 'Two men brought them here last Saturday and asked me to hand them over to a man who would call today.' He added that he was unaware that the cases contained explosives and that when the man called he would give the password 'Billy Brennan'.

The police then secreted themselves; and when Herbert Moore knocked on the door at 3.10pm and gave O'Regan the password, he was admitted and, pointing to the cases, asked 'Is that the stuff there?' Both men were detained, but later, the occupier of the house, Mr Wilson, saw a certain Edward Stapleton descend into the basement area carrying an attaché case and leave without it. Mr Wilson telephoned Scotland Yard and then followed Stapleton until he met a policeman, who arrested him. An examination of Stapleton's discarded attaché case revealed six detonators, sulphuric acid, nine packets of potassium chlorate and sugar, balloons, fuses, insulating tape, adhesive plaster and wire. In addition, when he was searched, Stapleton was found to have in his possession a piece of paper on which was written the telephone number of the Brunswick Square address, plus the words 'Billy Brennan'.

At Bow Street Police Court, after the Magistrate, Mr McKenna, was told that O'Regan's mother had applied for her son to receive legal aid, he rather aggressively asked him, 'Do you want legal aid at the expense of this country? Are you without means and cannot pay for it?'

But he granted aid after O'Regan replied simply, 'I haven't got a cent.'

At the Old Bailey, before the Common Serjeant, on 22 September, when the three men pleaded not guilty to conspiracy to cause explosions, Stapleton stated that O'Regan was not and never had been a member of the IRA, but that he had been used, without his knowledge, as a dupe in forwarding their aims and objects. He rather spoilt his spirited defence of O'Regan when the prosecuting counsel tried to question him, whereupon Stapleton replied, 'I am a member of the IRA and I am not answering any questions.'

The three men were found guilty, and while Stapleton and Moore were both sentenced to ten years' penal servitude, sentence on O'Regan was postponed until the October sessions, when he was mercifully bound over for two years to keep the peace.

* * *

Sticks of gelignite were pushed through the letter box of Mount Pleasant post office in Liverpool; the front of the building was blown out, the letter box was propelled 10 yards across the road and the roadway was littered with broken glass and timber. Just 25 yards away, flames shot out of a pillar box, and residents poured water into it prior to the arrival of the Fire Brigade.

The Leeds–Liverpool canal was completely blocked at Green Lane, Maghull, near Liverpool, when a wooden swing bridge was blown up and windows in nearby houses were shattered. On the same day that Inspector Allen was carrying out his arrests, two farm labourers discovered seventy-four sticks of gelignite attached to a pylon carrying electricity grid wires in a field at Downholland, near Ormskirk, Lancashire. They had made their discovery at 11.00am; the gelignite was connected with wires to a battery and an alarm clock, timed to go off at 1.00pm. With great presence of mind (and quite considerable courage) they disconnected the wires, then ran to inform their employer.

This led to the arrests of 19-year-old Christopher Kenneally, who was charged with placing the explosives on the pylon, and of Terence O'Hanlon and John Carney; the three of them were charged with committing malicious damage to the swing bridge at Maghull. When they arrived, handcuffed to detectives, at a special court at Ormskirk which was guarded by armed police, only the press, police and court officials were admitted. When their names were called, they sprang smartly to attention.

Whilst they were on remand, on Saturday, 26 August, at 11.10pm, George Whittaker was seen strolling along Renshaw Street, Liverpool, five minutes after a bomb had blown out the front of a sub-post office in Lodge Lane. It was the latest of four explosions which had occurred in Liverpool that weekend. He was seen to be fumbling in his coat pocket, which had caught alight; smoke and flames were coming from it. He was carrying a mackintosh, which he threw down, and there was a loud explosion. Whittaker was chased by a militiaman who was returning to camp and a railway policeman; at that moment, crowds of people returning home from the cinema and theatre joined in the chase, and he was caught in Newington, a blind alley, and put in a police van, but not before throwing away a parcel containing thirteen sticks of gelignite, a detonator and a balloon containing acid. The crowds hammered on the sides of the van shouting, 'Lynch him!' and as the van was driven off down the narrow street, they did their level best to overturn it.

Taken without further incident to the local police station, with a large hole burnt in his right-hand jacket pocket and his clothes smouldering, Whittaker, much like his contemporary, Joseph Malone, who had been treated to some of his own medicine when the bomb he was priming in the cinema suddenly exploded, started talking:

> I cannot say much, except that I am a member of the IRA for some years. I did not expect the bomb to go off until 2.00am but one of the balloons must have been a weak one. I cannot answer any questions. We are not supposed to make any statement until after the end of our trial. Of course, I believe in the cause of a united Ireland, and we will go on until we bring it about and we *will* bring it about.

As an afterthought, he later added, 'I cannot say anything that might incriminate me' – although so far, he had done quite well in achieving just that.

Whittaker's lodgings were kept under observation, and a couple who gave their names as Mr and Mrs James Smith were followed back to their lodgings in Prescott Road, Rainhill, Lancashire. In fact, they were Vincent Crompton and 19-year-old Margaret McDonnell – who also gave her name as Jean Dobson. They separated, and Dobson was later arrested, as was Crompton, although not before detonating a bomb at their address in Prescott Road on 30 August. In fact, the damage was minimal, but it did leave a large quantity of explosives plus a treasure trove of forensic evidence to connect Crompton to a series of explosions.

They appeared at Liverpool Assizes, and on 27 October 1939 all of them – with the exception of Terrence O'Hanlon, who had all the charges against him dismissed – were found guilty of conspiracy and causing explosions.

Carney said from the dock that the prosecution had not proved that he had conspired to commit any of the acts in the charges, although this was rather pointless, because the jury had clearly thought otherwise.

Crompton stated that he wanted to clear Dobson, whom he had used for the purposes of the IRA, and he stated that he had been responsible for giving Whittaker the explosives 'that nearly cost him his life'. He went on to say:

> All those jobs in Liverpool in that last couple of weeks, I did myself. I'm not just saying this to look big in court and to look a decent fellow trying to get the others off. I'm not pleading for any leniency. I know what I'm going to get, before I get it.

Whittaker wanted to be helpful as well, saying that he had not received any bombs from Dobson and that she was 'quite innocent of anything in the nature of bombs', although he was, of course, proud to have been associated with the campaign in England to attempt to force the withdrawal of troops from Northern Ireland.

The court was told that Crompton was not Irish but had been born in Manchester. He had served in the United States Army, the British Army and the International Brigade in Spain. Sentencing Crompton to twenty years' penal servitude, Mr Justice Stable told him:

> You are not even Irish; for what motive you embarked on the series of abominable crimes of violence of which you are apparently rather proud, I do not know. Your appreciation of the situation is rotten.

Carney and Whittaker were each sentenced to seven years' penal servitude, and Kenneally was sent to a Borstal Institution for three years.

Telling Dobson that she would come up for sentence the following week, Mr Justice Stable said, 'I had better talk to your father if I can, and I want to see the priest who lives in your parish and the probation officer.'

Her home surroundings were described as being 'extremely satisfactory', and Dobson's father, John McDonnell, said that he had done his best to end her association with Crompton; for a week he had succeeded, before she ran off again. The probation officer concurred that she had undoubtedly come

The Instigators of the 'S' Plan

Above left: Seán Russell.

Above right: James O'Donovan.

Dominic Adams – murderer.

Above left: The Noah's Ark public house, Southwark, following the explosion on 16 January 1939.

Above right: The Thames Embankment Rescue Mission, Southwark, following the explosion on 16 January 1939.

Newton Street, Manchester, where Albert Ross was killed on 16 January 1939.

Newton Street, Manchester, 16 January 1939.

Whitworth Street at the junction with Princess Street, Manchester, 16 January 1939.

The Midland Bank, Park Lane, London after the explosion on 25 June 1939.

The Grand Union Canal after the explosion on 3 September 1939.

The wrecked luggage office at King's Cross railway station, where Dr Donald Campbell was killed on 26 July 1939.

The aftermath of the King's Cross explosion, 26 July 1939.

Above left: Mr Justice Singleton.

Above right: The Recorder of London, Sir Gerald Dodson KC.

Above left: The Common Serjeant, George Cecil Whiteley KC, MA, DL, JP.

Above right: Mr Justice Humphreys.

Above left: Detective Superintendent Robert Fabian KPM.

Above right: Maurice Childs GC.

Margery Urquhart OBE, with her brother and sister at the time of receiving her award.

Crowds outside Manchester City Police Court, 10 February 1939.

Hammersmith Bridge following the explosion on 28 March 1939.

An IRA flyer printed in 1938.

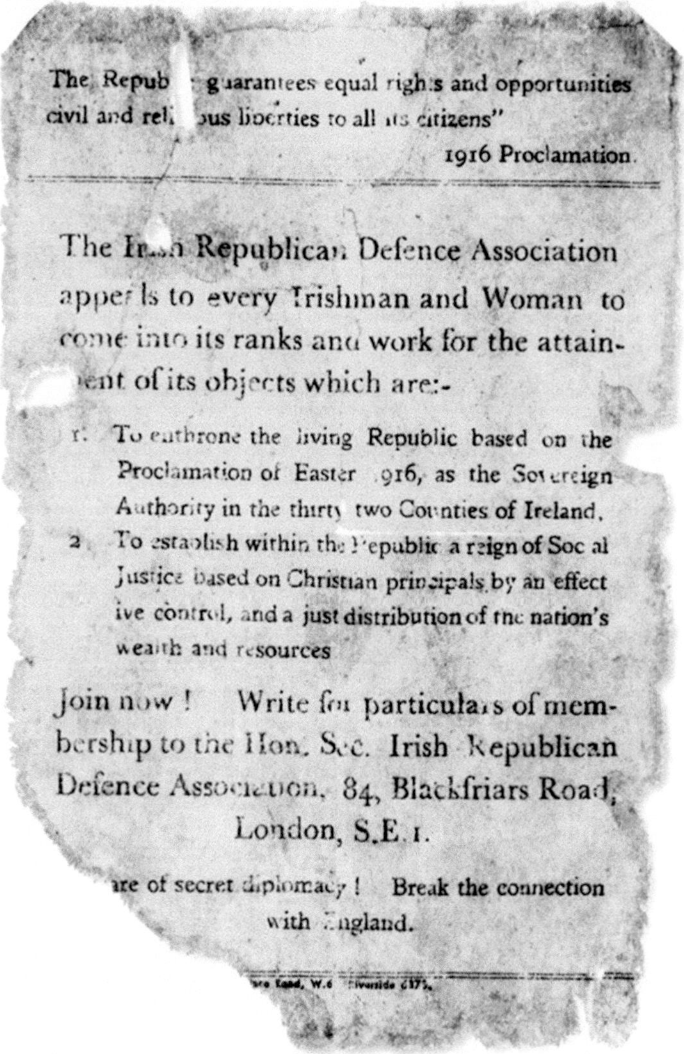

"The Repub[lic] guarantees equal rights and opportunities civil and reli[gi]ous liberties to all its citizens"

1916 Proclamation.

The Irish Republican Defence Association appeals to every Irishman and Woman to come into its ranks and work for the attainment of its objects which are:-

1. To enthrone the living Republic based on the Proclamation of Easter 1916, as the Sovereign Authority in the thirty two Counties of Ireland.
2. To establish within the Republic a reign of Social Justice based on Christian principals by an effective control, and a just distribution of the nation's wealth and resources

Join now ! Write for particulars of membership to the Hon. Sec. Irish Republican Defence Association, 84, Blackfriars Road, London, S.E.1.

[Bew]are of secret diplomacy ! Break the connection with England.

...Road, W.6 Riverside 617...

Part of a bomb at Piccadilly on 24 June 1939.

HARRISONS OPTICIANS

LAST EDITION

The Midland Daily Telegraph

HOGARTH CYCLES
COVENTRY MADE
FOLESHILL RD.

FRIDAY, AUGUST 25, 1939

ONE PENNY

BROADGATE WRECKED BY EXPLOSION

Like a Miniature Battlefield

Four Dead, Ten Seriously Injured and Forty Treated at Hospital

CITY CENTRE SCENE OF DEVASTATION

Shopfronts Shattered Over Wide Area

STREET STREWN WITH CASUALTIES AND DEBRIS

The Dead and Injured

LATEST ABOUT THE CRISIS

LATE NEWS

COVENTRY EXPLOSION

MOVING THE INJURED

MORE SHOP WRECKAGE

Newspaper headlines, Coventry, 25 August 1939.

Broadgate, where five people were killed and seventy-two injured on 25 August 1939.

Above and below: Broadgate.

Above and below: Broadgate.

Broadgate – showing part of the bicycle used to transport the bomb.

The remains of the bicycle used to transport the bomb.

Two of the Broadgate murderers

Above left: James Richards.

Above right: Peter Barnes.

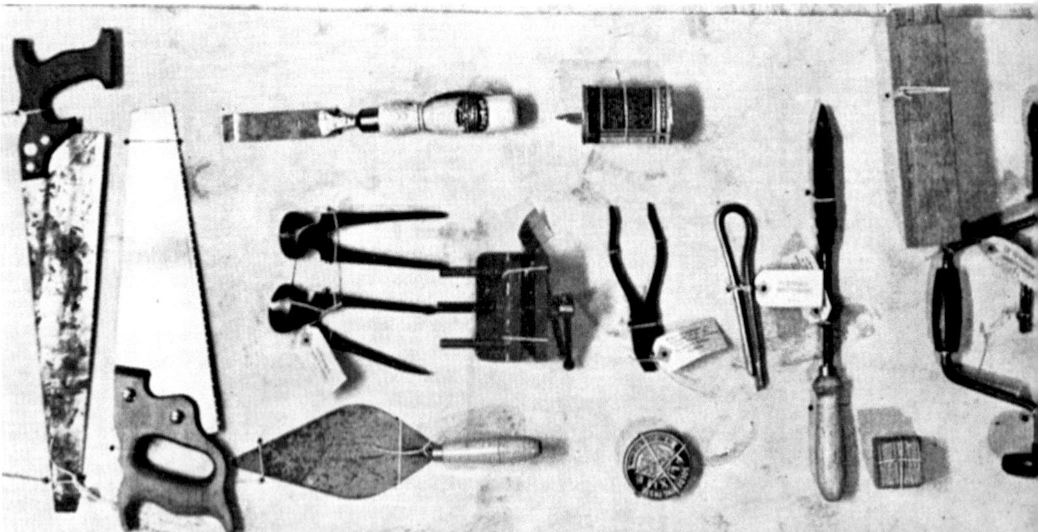

Tools used for the construction of the Broadgate bomb.

Above left: Brendan Behan.

Above right: Éamon de Valera.

Aftermath of the bombing in Birmingham, 1940.

A police constable guards the wrecked entrance of the Midland Bank, Park Lane, London following the explosion on 25 June 1939.

under Crompton's influence, and Dobson assured the Judge that she would not associate with anyone connected with 'this sort of political violence'.

Mr Justice Stable told her that if she broke her promise she would be liable to a heavy prison sentence, before binding her over for two years on condition that she went to a training home, under the care of nuns.

Chapter 18

A Dreadful Conspiracy

Despite the increased police presence, on the night of 28 July telephone wires were cut at six kiosks in Piccadilly, Leicester Square and the Euston Road. There were half a dozen explosions in letter boxes in Blackburn, Preston, Bradford and Halifax, and one in a mail bag at Huddersfield railway station.

But there were no incidents at Euston railway station, or on the trains leaving there for Holyhead. Following the new emergency legislation, the night mail that evening was packed to the gunwales with folk en route to Ireland. All the seats had been taken, passengers were standing in the corridors and some in the vans. The exodus continued over the next few days; Special Branch detectives were on duty at Euston, ready to arrest IRA men who were circulated as wanted, but those who were merely suspected or were IRA sympathizers were allowed to go on their way – they would not, however, be allowed back.

The Houses of Parliament were closed to the public until further notice by order of the Lord Great Chamberlain, the official responsible for organizing ceremonial activities such as the State Opening of Parliament. Special constables were drafted in and police river patrols increased, to ensure the safety of public buildings and bridges.

When the Lord Mayor and Lady Mayoress, together with members of the City Corporation, left Victoria Station to visit Zurich, in connection with the Swiss National Exhibition, extra police were on duty to keep the platform clear for the Lord Mayor's official coach, and barriers were put in place to prevent the public getting too close.

Letters were received at Essex County Hall and the Chelmsford head post office which read:

> If you value your lives, you are advised to take sick leave. Your damned police don't know of the Irish patriots. In a few days, we will show you. We have the bombs and we know where to plant them. The county hall will look a pretty sick mess by this time next week. If lives are lost, it will be your own

> fault. You have been warned. God save Ireland and to hell with England.
>
> (Signed): Adjutant, IRA

In fact, nothing happened in Chelmsford. There were, however, forty cases of malicious damage to telephone kiosks in London and three cases of incendiarism to the mails in Birmingham. A woman with an Irish accent booked into the North Euston Hotel, Fleetwood, Lancashire, deposited her suitcase in her room on the top floor and left. Six hours later, there was a loud explosion, the room was set on fire and fragments of glass from the shattered window were blown on to the promenade, 20 yards away. The second incident occurred in the Sandringham Hotel at Southport after a couple, both with Irish accents, left their second-floor bedroom and an explosion occurred in a wardrobe drawer; in both cases, metal canisters had been used.

It was said that the IRA were planning reprisals to mark their displeasure at the new legislation which an insolent British Government had dared to bring to the statute book – on 3 August they announced that the campaign against Britain would continue for another two and a half years, and this was underlined on 19 August, when three incendiary devices exploded in Birmingham, causing damage to the mail. But a fourth unexploded bomb was found, containing potassium chlorate, sugar, a balloon and sulphuric acid. It was addressed to the Secretary of the Admiralty and the handwriting was attributed to one Patrick M'Brine, a 57-year-old labourer. He and his stepson, 27-year-old Stanley Joseph Rice, were arrested, as was 23-year-old William Bradley, who like his companions was a labourer, and all were charged with conspiracy and possessing explosives.

All refused to plead when they appeared at Birmingham Assizes on 15 December 1939, but inevitably they were found guilty; Mr Justice Singleton sentenced M'Brine to fifteen years' penal servitude and told Rice and Bradley, 'because of your ages, you will only be sentenced to ten years' penal servitude.'

Several hundred sticks of gelignite were found in a pile in the grounds of Newton Lodge, Potter Newton, Leeds, and it was thought that the person(s) who had abandoned them had done so believing that their discovery was imminent. It was thought that members of the IRA were responsible, but had the IRA chiefs in Dublin been asked, the suggestion would have been haughtily repudiated. The explosives had been dumped next to a quarry widely known to be a children's playground, and the IRA's belief in the sanctity of human life was indisputable; they had repeatedly said so.

In addition, the Home Secretary had issued eighty-six orders, seventy-nine of which were expulsions and seven were prohibition orders. What with that, plus the number of terrorists locked up, either on remand or serving sentences, it appeared that members of the IRA were pretty thin on the ground.

But they were nevertheless present in sufficient numbers to organize some impressive acts of terrorism, the first of which was in London.

* * *

Detectives come in all shapes and sizes, and so do informants or 'snouts'. Some informants walk straight in off the streets unannounced – these have to be treated with a great deal of caution. Usually, snouts are recruited by detectives in one of a number of ways: a kind word to the magistrate or perhaps the watering-down of charges, coercion (not necessarily to be recommended), blackmail (*definitely* not to be recommended!) or permitting bail – in exchange for the provision of information.

Detective Sergeant John Gosling of the Flying Squad received an enormous amount of information from snouts because they genuinely liked him, and he them. He was the antithesis of his partner, Detective Sergeant Matt Brinnand. Tall and thin, Brinnand hated criminals, but they came to him with pertinent information because they were too frightened not to. In particular, Brinnand loathed ponces (and they were terrified of him), and therefore prostitutes who were badly treated by their pimps knew that they had, if not a friend, at least an ally in Brinnand.

On 21 August Brinnand received information from a prostitute that Irish terrorists planned to detonate explosives simultaneously at New Scotland Yard, Westminster Abbey and the Bank of England. Usually such information would have been jealously guarded by the Squad so that they could act on it and claim all the credit; on this occasion, commonsense demanded that the intelligence be shared with Special Branch to mount a joint operation.

On 24 and 25 August, observation was kept on a flat at 32 Leinster Gardens, Bayswater. On the second day officers followed Jack Gibson and John Evans to Hackney, where they took delivery of two items: Gibson was seen pushing a bicycle with a carrier attached and Evans, a box-tricycle, and they were followed back to the Leinster Gardens address, where there was another box-tricycle. This had previously been delivered by a Daniel Crotty, who had left the area.

Gibson and Evans were quietly arrested; the police then entered the premises. On the first-floor landing they heard a ticking sound, and Detective Sergeant Leonard Crawford of the Flying Squad found a hatbox containing two sticks of gelignite plus 28lbs of potassium chlorate and paraffin wax attached to a detonator, a battery and an alarm clock timed to explode at 2.30. By now, it was past noon, so there was no time to spare. Crawford with cool efficiency cut the wires and removed the gelignite; it would later earn him a commissioner's high commendation and a £10 cheque from the Bow Street Reward Fund. Two other hatboxes containing bombs of considerable size, three alarm clocks and some batteries were also found. All could be neatly fitted into the box-tricycle or the cycle carrier.

Searching the flat, Crawford smashed a panel in the locked bathroom door, behind which was James O'Regan. He escaped on to the roof, where he attempted to hide behind a water tank. Crawford grabbed hold of him, and after a desperate struggle, 50 feet above street level, he pushed O'Regan through the bathroom window, where he was seized by other officers. Daniel Jordan also struggled violently but was overpowered.

Pointing to the bombs, Jordan said, 'There's nothing to worry about for a bit. We're all soldiers of the IRA and are righting the wrong your country has done.'

The Assistant Commissioner (Crime), Ronald Howe, was present. Having been awarded a Military Cross for making a hazardous reconnaissance during heavy shellfire in the First World War, he was no stranger to potentially explosive confrontations. Regarding the terrorists, he later noted:

> When they were bundled down six flights of stairs, ending up in a somewhat sorry condition, I did not feel it incumbent on me to make a report to the Home Secretary as to any excessive zeal shown by the detectives concerned.

At the Old Bailey, where the men refused to plead to the indictment, Mr Frederick Dupré stated that had Crawford's disabled bomb detonated it would have produced a very violent explosion.

'Supposing it had gone off in this court?' asked the Common Serjeant.

'Almost certainly, everybody in court would have been killed', replied Mr Dupré, adding, 'and probably the whole building wrecked.'

Found guilty, the four men were each sentenced to twenty years' penal servitude on 17 October, and five weeks later,

Daniel Crotty was arrested. He, too, refused to plead but on 12 January 1940 was found guilty at the Old Bailey; although Detective Inspector Bucknill believed that he was the brains behind the conspiracy, the Common Serjeant sentenced him to ten years' penal servitude.

So back at Scotland Yard on 25 August, the detectives felt pretty pleased with themselves, as well they might have. Four prisoners were locked up, and the three bombs which were timed to detonate at 2.30 had been neutralized. Had they been aware – as their four prisoners were certainly aware – that there was a fourth bomb, similarly timed to explode at 2.30, that would have seriously dampened their spirits.

But they didn't know; and at almost precisely that time, 97 miles away in Coventry, that bomb, also placed in a carrier cycle, did explode, with dreadful consequences.

Chapter 19

Broadgate

Coventry was no stranger to IRA bombs; since the commencement of the campaign, the city had suffered twenty explosions, and miscellaneous unexploded items of ordnance had also been found there.

The last explosion to occur in Coventry's city centre happened on 25 August 1939. A carrier cycle with a bomb weighing 5lbs in its basket was left propped up by the kerb at about 1.45pm in Broadgate, a busy shopping centre, outside a shop named Astley's. There were plenty of shoppers in the area; it was a market day. There were also people returning to their places of work following a late lunch break. One of those people was 21-year-old Elsie Ansell, who paused in front of H. Samuels jeweller's shop; she was due to be married in a fortnight's time. The glittering array of jewellery was the last thing she saw. At 2.32pm the bomb on the carrier cycle exploded.

Miss Ansell's body was found outside Burton's, the tailor's shop next door to Astley's. She lay there, on her left hand side, with her knees drawn up. Her right hip and buttock were partly blown away, her right knee and leg were pulverised and her right foot was torn and shattered. Her right shoulder had been torn almost completely off, and the lower part of her right hand and wrist were badly shattered; the little and ring fingers had been blown off. Her face had been torn away and the exposed front portion of her skull revealed her lacerated brain. There were many other wounds, as well as debris which was later removed from her body.

Her employer, William Charles Beck, was called to the mortuary but was unable to identify her body. The best he could do was to identify the few fragments of clothing that were left and the engagement ring on her left hand.

She had been due to be married at St Barbara's Church on 9 September; instead, she was buried there in her wedding dress on 30 August. Her fiancé, Harry Davies, left a spray of cream roses on top of her coffin, with a card that read: 'With everlasting love and remembrance from your husband to be, Harry'. Following Elsie's death, her mother, Laura, was cared for by Harry Davies' mother. She never recovered from the shock of her daughter's death and died at the age of forty-nine, six months later.

Miss Ansell's body was found next to that of James Clay, an 81-year-old widower and a grandfather. His death had been caused by shock and internal bleeding after being struck in the abdomen by metal projectiles; they caused a wound three inches in diameter.

It was initially thought that the third victim was Mr Hollander of Coundon Road, because a bill with that name and address was found in the victim's pocket. That was understandable; due to the devastating effect the explosion had had on the body, it was difficult to ascertain that the victim was in fact 15-year-old John Corbett Arnott, a paperboy for W. H. Smith, who was about to make a delivery to his customer, Mr Hollander. On the day after her son's burial, Mrs Arnott had the following letter published in the *Midland Daily Telegraph* on 30 August which is heartbreaking in its simplicity:

> Dear Mr Editor,
>
> Will you please print my thanks where you will, but I feel I would like to put into print my thoughts as well. The doctors and nurses tried to save my boy's life but God said 'No'.
>
> The kind thoughts of the people go to help me bear my cross. We all have a cross to bear, and when I look at others' plight, I feel my cross is only light.
>
> To the kind nurses who took me to kiss him 'Good-bye' thanks, and I'll always remember the youngest nurse's sweet face. God gave me these words in the loneliness of the night when his little sister was sleeping by my side. Once again thanks for all your kindness, I'll never forget.

By coincidence, the fourth victim, Rex Gentle, was a 30-year-old trainee manager with W. H. Smith who lodged with the Arnott family. He had changed his lunch hour so that he and John could eat at the same time, in order that John's mother would not have to prepare two separate meals. His twin brother Jack fainted before he could make an identification; it was left to his sister-in-law Ruth to identify him, purely by the shape of his mouth. Before the injuries which Rex had sustained were recounted at the inquest, Jack left the room; Ruth stayed. The details were so horrific that she never divulged a word of them to her husband – or to anybody else.

The final victim was 50-year-old Gwilym Rowlands, a road-sweeper who was working on the pavement outside Astley's when the bomb exploded; he was identified a few hours later by his wife. This must have been almost impossible; he had sustained multiple puncture wounds to his face, skull, chest, arms and legs. Amongst the many other injuries, there were deep puncture wounds on the right side of his chest, one of which was four inches deep and which had penetrated his heart.

Alexander Ballinger was the manager of Astley's shop and was standing about two yards away from the shop's front window when the bomb exploded. The whole frontage of the shop was blown in on him, together with the woodwork, blinds and doorway; the glass from the window was blown 60 feet into the shop. Mr Ballinger was blown backwards and was lucky to sustain only a total of nine lacerations to his body; he was one of seventy-two people injured, twelve of them seriously – including 14-year-old Muriel Timms, who had a piece of metal removed from her leg and walked with a limp for the rest of her life – most of whom were treated at the Coventry and Warwickshire Hospital. The services of twelve blood donors were requested, and provided – they were much needed.

The whole area was a scene of devastation; forty-three business premises in Broadgate and the surrounding streets were extensively damaged, the worst-affected being Astley's, and Montague Burton and Mansfield on either side of it. Sketchley's, directly opposite Astley's, was also badly damaged, and both buildings had to be shored up. Smithford Street and Hertford Street which led off the Broadgate, 120 yards away, sustained damage, and pieces of metal flew over the top of the 60ft high National Provincial Bank and landed in Greyfriars Lane, 200–300 yards away.

In the immediate aftermath, amid the dust and the smoke, onlookers who crunched through the broken glass were understandably frightened, shocked and confused. They simply could not comprehend what had happened. Just prior to the explosion, an aircraft had passed overhead. With rumours of imminent war with Germany, some thought that the war had actually commenced and what had occurred had been an air-raid. Others had seen lorries, which they believed were carrying TNT, driving through the area and thought that one of them had exploded.

It was not too long before realization had set in that this had been the IRA's twenty-first (and final) attack on the city of Coventry. In fact, three men were seen running from the scene; interpreting this as a tacit admission of guilt, a crowd gave chase shouting, 'Lynch them!' The men were stopped by the police, after which it was established that they were simply passers-by fleeing in horror from the carnage they had just witnessed.

Two IRA men had been responsible for the actual planting of the bomb. The first was Joseph B. – known as Joby – O'Sullivan. He was never named by his accomplices and he died, years later, in a psychiatric institution.

The other was 23-year-old Dominic Adams and he, like O'Sullivan, made good his escape, although not back to his native Belfast – he sought the sanctuary of Éire. Adams became Chief of Staff of the IRA during the Second World War. Coincidentally, his nephew is Gerry Adams, the former president of Sinn Féin, who has stated on numerous occasions that he is not and never has been a member of the IRA.

But there were others involved – and now the hunt was on to find them.

Chapter 20

The Hunt for the Murderers

Everybody wanted to help, and the police set to work with a will. What had been speculation, rumour and gossip was now regarded by the furious locals as fact; the suppositions might not necessarily have been true, but each of the leads had to be followed up, and they were. Eventually, it appeared that the sequence of events which led up to the atrocity was as follows.

Joseph and Mary Hewitt were married in Belfast in August 1935, and in the November of that year Joseph Hewitt came to Coventry to find work; his wife and his mother-in-law, Brigid O'Hara, followed a week later. A baby was born in 1938, and they first rented a house in Meadow Street, Spon End, where they took in lodgers, at least two of whom were members of the IRA and heavily involved in the mainland bombings. They were never arrested, although they were later interned. After these two left, another lodger arrived who gave his name as James Richards and who agreed to pay 23s 0d per week for bed and breakfast. On 12 June 1939, the Hewitt family, Mrs O'Hara and Richards moved into 25 Clara Street, Stoke, a mid-terraced house which they rented from Loveitt & Sons. At the rear of the premises there was a garden and a passage, known locally as a 'jetty'; it was also overlooked by the neighbouring properties.

Joseph Hewitt was a semi-skilled labourer and he worked as a tinsmith's mate. His wife had taken a job as a shop assistant, and Mrs O'Hara ran the house and looked after her 15-month-old grandchild.

The oddity was James Richards; he had no job – he had signed on at the local labour exchange but had not attempted to seek work – although he appeared to have plenty of money. He got up late, hung about the house, went to the cinema and entertained a number of visitors at the house during June – all men. When Mrs O'Hara asked him if he was going to find work, he replied that he already had a job; he was an Operations Officer from Dublin. This, said Mrs O'Hara later, meant nothing to her; Richards gave a vague explanation, saying that it was his job to contact other fellows in the town and they gave him money.

But the 29-year-old was not as idle as all that; Richards' real name was James McCormick and, like Hewitt's previous lodgers, he was a hard-working and fanatical member of the IRA.

Richards – he will be referred to thus in this narrative – had begun to store explosives (particularly potassium chlorate) at the house. This in itself was a sound plan, because it was a quiet, respectable area, but after the passing of the Prevention of Violence Act Richards became concerned that his cache might be discovered. In fact, within a few days of the Act becoming law, over 400 homes in the Coventry area were searched.

He therefore hit on a reckless plan; he decided to dig a hole in the floor of the cupboard under the stairs and secrete the explosives there. It was two feet deep, eighteen inches wide and twenty-two inches long. But the problem, as many tunnellers would find in the years that followed in German PoW camps, was where to get rid of the soil which had been dug out? Bury it in the garden, that's where; this was also the perfect place to mix the cement to line the walls of the pit, something Richards was well able to do, since he had previously worked as a plasterer's labourer. Unfortunately, Richards was seen doing this by a neighbour, Mrs Margaret Riley. Another neighbour, Mrs Dove Gibbons, saw three, sometimes four men in the garden at weekends carrying stuff in buckets and shovels. This activity continued until about a week before the explosion at Broadgate. Joseph Hewitt helped Richards make a concrete cover for the pit, and they were seen mixing cement in the back garden. When a neighbour, a Mrs Howard, walked into the house she saw Richards in the pit, and Mrs O'Hara exclaimed, 'What in the name of God are you doing?'

'This', he replied, 'is for a bit of a dump.' Nowadays, that expression is a colloquial one to describe the evacuation of one's bowels; then it was used in the context of a cache of explosives. However, the pit was never used.

What only became known later was this. In October 1938, a man had received permission to build a large wooden shed on a Coventry Corporation allotment near Bell Green Road. He gave his name as 'Norman', but in reality he was Dominic Adams and he had volunteered to take part in the bombing campaign.

In March 1939, Adams obtained lodgings in Meadow Street – the street where the Hewitt family lived – and the shed was ordered and constructed at the allotment. It was used to store explosives, and three men were frequently seen visiting it; some attempt was made to cultivate the allotment, but most of their time was spent inside the shed. On Sunday, 13 August at 4.45pm there was a tremendous explosion. The floor of the shed had been littered with grains of potassium chlorate, and Richards had carelessly dropped a lighted cigarette. The grains ignited and Richards tried unsuccessfully to stamp out the flames, but realizing that time was running out, Richards and – according to eye-witnesses – one other man, plus two girls, took to their heels before an explosion littered the surrounding 20 yards with grains of the chemical and fragments of balloons and metal. Windows were broken over a wide area, a dense cloud of smoke hung over the scene for some time, and in the confusion the men boarded a tramcar in Stoney Stanton Road and escaped. The girls, initially thought to be connected with the men, were nothing of the sort. They were teenagers whom the fleeing men rushed past in order to escape. Who was the other man? Was it Joby O'Sullivan? Maybe.

But whatever the case, Richards was now bereft of explosives so more needed to be acquired. Enter Peter Barnes – let's hear a bit more about him.

* * *

At the beginning of August Peter Barnes, another IRA man, arrived in London from Ireland via Liverpool. Barnes stayed in London with his fiancée, Sarah Anne Keane, although he also took a room in a boarding house at 176 Westbourne Grove. He travelled about the country, to Coventry on several occasions, and to Liverpool and Glasgow; his job was to convey explosives from a central dump to operatives in those cities, one of whom was Richards.

Barnes arrived on Monday, 21 August at Clara Street, and after some conversation with Richards, Mrs O'Hara was asked by Richards to go and purchase a suitcase for Barnes and to be sure to obtain a receipt. This was because the IRA demanded a degree of accountability in the expenditure of their funds.

While Mrs O'Hara was carrying out her errand, Mrs Hewitt was asked to go out and purchase two flour sacks. She did so but because she considered the price – two shillings – too high, she also asked for a receipt. The suitcase purchased by Mrs O'Hara for 7s 6d, complete with receipt, was suitable; the flour sacks were not. The mesh of the sacks was too coarse to contain potassium chlorate, and Barnes said, 'These aren't right, they aren't the right ones', whereupon Mrs Hewitt, accompanied by her mother, returned the items to the shop. She asked for finer, white calico bags, but the shop did not stock them and Mrs Hewitt's two shillings were returned to her. The shop staff did not ask for the receipt, so that, together with the suitcase and its receipt, returned to London with Barnes that evening.

The following day, Richards and another man went to the Halford Cycle Company at 29 Smithfield Street, and while Richards waited outside, the other man paid a £5 deposit on a 'Karriwell' carrier cycle. The purchaser gave his name as Mr Norman and his address as 56 Grayswood Avenue, Allesley Old Road, Coventry and agreed to return in a few days to pay the outstanding balance of 19s 6d and take delivery of the cycle. The name and address were, of course, false; the buyer was Dominic Adams. He was known to Mrs O'Hara and her daughter, as was confirmed when Mrs O'Hara asked Richards where he had been and he replied, 'I've been with Adams to buy a bicycle. We left it at the shop and I'm fetching it on Friday.'

On Thursday, 24 August, someone described by the Hewitts as 'the strange man' arrived at Clara Street. This was Joby O'Sullivan. He had brought some tools with him and he worked at manufacturing a bomb in the front sitting room during the day and again in the evening. At about 7.00pm Barnes arrived, carrying his suitcase and a parcel which appeared to be heavy and was full of potassium chlorate. Richards took the parcel into the scullery. Barnes left, saying he had to catch a train at half past eight. Mrs O'Hara went into the scullery and saw Richards opening the parcel; it contained white powder. Shortly afterwards, the two women left the house pushing the baby in a pram; this gave rise to a certain amount of conversation among the neighbours, especially since they did not return until 11 o'clock that night. Richards and Hewitt were in the scullery; the parcel had been placed under the sink, now tied up in brown paper.

The Hewitts left for work on the morning of Friday, 25 August; O'Sullivan returned and he and Richards completed making the bomb. Now all was ready, and at 12.30pm Richards went to Halford's shop, where he paid the balance and took possession of the carrier cycle No. V 2615.

He left it in the 'jetty' at the back of the house, then O'Sullivan placed the explosive parcel in the carrier and cycled off, with the alarm clock set for 2.30pm. He left it outside Astley's in plenty of time to escape before it went off.

Later – and by that I mean seventy years later – in a published newspaper interview, O'Sullivan stated that the bomb had been intended for the police station but the cycle 'kept getting stuck in the tram lines'. If that were so, he passed three turn-offs for the police station before making his escape via the railway station.

On the afternoon of 25 August, and following the explosion, Mrs O'Hara went into town for some shopping and, learning of the outrage, returned home and showed Richards the brief report in the newspapers.

'Look at the paper', she said, to which Richards replied, 'It must have gone off very quick.'

'My God, it's terrible!' she exclaimed. 'All these people killed and wounded – that's the bomb you made!'

Richards simply kept on reading the paper, and Mrs O'Hara added, 'We'll soon have the police here!' to which Richards replied, 'The police will never find us here.'

However, Mrs O'Hara, her daughter and son-in-law would tell a rather different story when they were first confronted by the police.

Forty-one-year-old Chief Inspector Cyril George Boneham of the Coventry City Police led the investigation, but at that stage he knew nothing of Barnes or Richards, or of 25 Clara Street. The previous day, Barnes had returned to London from Coventry and into the outstretched welcoming arms of Miss Sarah Anne Keane in her lodgings at 115 Warwick Avenue.

Help for Chief Inspector Boneham came from London on the evening of the Coventry bombing, when at 8.50pm Barnes walked into his attic room on the fourth floor at 176 Westbourne Terrace, Paddington.

There he was greeted, rather less amorously than he had been by Miss Keane, by Detective Sergeant William Hughes of the Special Branch.

* * *

Barnes – or some of his chums – may have been keeping dubious company; but following the Coventry explosion, the prostitute who was Brinnand's informant contacted the Yard again and provided Brinnand with Barnes' name and address. One thousand pounds is a tidy sum for an informant to receive nowadays; over eighty years ago it was astronomical, but that was the ex-gratia payment handed to Paddington's Painted Princess, who promptly set sail for warmer climes, just in time to evade the fury of the IRA and the onslaught of the Second World War.

So since it was Brinnand's information, why was it not he who carried out the arrest? The answer is simply this: if it was thought that a suspect could make a connection between the detective carrying out the arrest and the source of the information, the job was given to a detective from another area (or in this case, a different department).

Therefore, it was Sergeant Hughes who had arrived an hour before Barnes and been admitted to his room by the landlord. A search revealed three packets of white powder; analysis revealed that it was a mixture of potassium chlorate and sodium carbonate, with some scent. He also found some dungarees with a small amount of potassium chlorate on them. A raincoat had a considerable amount of that compound in it, and an examination of a hat revealed more potassium chlorate than that found on the raincoat.

Barnes admitted that all of those items were his and added, 'I bought the packets from a woman in Oxford Street; they are shampoos.'

Hughes told him that he and his associates were police officers and said, 'We have reason to suspect you of being in possession of explosives and being concerned in causing explosions in Coventry.'

Taken into custody, Barnes replied, 'Yes, I have been in Coventry, but coincidences can happen, can't they?'

It was a smart remark and one that he undoubtedly regretted making; certainly it would be the last cocky utterance that he would give vent to in what remained of his thirty-two years.

Hughes searched him; in his outside jacket pocket he found a letter marked, 'For Jim Kelly', and as Hughes started to read the letter, Barnes told him, 'That's just a letter I wrote to a friend.' Dated 24/8/39, and with all its misspellings and grammatical mistakes, this was what was written:

> Dear Jim,
>
> I am sure your wondering why I did not write but I no you will understand how tings are. I am still here in London I am very lookey so far T.G. I got it very hard after coming over. I did not meet the man I was to meet. He was gone so I had to go to Liverpool the next day and I did not meet anyone there either so I was a week and did not meet one. I was nearly mad so then I met one and he told me all was gone but himself so I had to fix up things for myself. We got over a few then and got things fixed up what I am on. I go from one place to the other and bring the S – believe me it is hard but I got way well so far. I am after coming back from Coventry tonight 11.30 so by the time you get this the Paper should have some news. Of course I do not when I will be picked up. I am sure you can see by the papers how things are. I would not advise you to think of coming over now and it looks very like war. It may be good for us. Some of the boys think that anyway but don't no. Well Jim I do hope your kid is all right by now and I do hope

> you were able to get the money fixed up alright as I am all right for money so far. If I don't luse them after this job then I will be fixed very bad for it cost me 5/6 a night for bed and breakfast and I grub out for the day, so it costs some to stay here. Well Jim I will say no more this time for it is very late and I have to be out very erely in the morning. You no I cant give you any address. Tell Kenny I was asken for him an I could not write to him. I may be going over to Dublin soon. There may be a letter there from you. I got one the day I left so no more. I will write you agen if I can. I would love to get a letter from you but I cant.
>
> So, cheers for R
> from your old Pal.
> Dixon.

Barnes also had train times from Euston to Liverpool written on a piece of paper. He was taken to Cannon Row police station.

Police paid a call on Miss Keane; she had in her possession the receipts for the flour sacks and the suitcase that Barnes had left with her.

Barnes was initially charged with the same offences as James O'Regan and co. and appeared at Bow Street police court; it was not too long before those charges were dropped against Barnes and he found himself on the way up to Liverpool.

Prior to that, others had made their way to that city: a small team from the Metropolitan Police Special Branch, which included Detective Inspector Sydney Barnes and Detective Sergeants William Hughes and Arthur Cain. There was also another detective, but unlike his fellow officers he was not a member of Special Branch. His name was William George Parker and he was a detective chief inspector at Scotland Yard's C1 Department, which housed the Flying Squad and also what was colloquially known as the 'Murder Squad'. He had joined the police in 1919 and after appointment to the CID had been commended and rewarded on eleven occasions for smart police work. Within days of arriving in Liverpool he had been highly commended by the commissioner for 'promptitude and ability in a difficult case of manslaughter'.

Special Branch officers knew little about murder, and officers from C1 Department knew as much about terrorism; Parker was sent because he was a brilliant murder investigator. He was used to presenting well-written reports to the Director of Public Prosecutions exploring every aspect of a murder investigation, and now he would cobble all of the evidence in this case together and eventually present a compelling case at Warwick Assizes.

Chapter 21

Arrests for the Broadgate Bombing

Detective Inspector Barnes and Chief Inspector Boneham were two of the police officers who paid a visit to 25 Clara Street at midday on 28 August; present were Mrs O'Hara and James Richards. Having established that the tenants were Mrs O'Hara's daughter and son-in-law, a search was carried out. On a sideboard was a woman's handbag – this belonged to Mary Hewitt – and inside was a leaflet saying, 'Break connections with England' and a card which read, 'Hearty congratulations long life and happiness from officers and members of the Betsy Grey Branch'.[1] It was signed *Cumann-na-mban* – the name given to the women's organization of the IRA – with a signature, Besl Feippde.

Inside a cupboard in the scullery was a quantity of tools: a wood chisel, two pairs of pincers, a bench vice, flux material used for soldering, a pair of pliers and cleaning acid, also used for soldering, a piece of solder, a soldering iron, three pieces of oak, a brace, two twist drills, the braces for use with a smaller drill and a trowel. There was also a quantity of screws and bolts, insulating tape, pieces of paper torn from a 4½ volt dry cell battery and a strip of paper which had to be torn off before the battery could be used.

A new, untarnished brass setter was found, used to set the hands of an alarm clock, but it did not fit any clock in the house. In the coal store was found a suitcase.

At 1 o'clock Mary Hewitt entered the house, and Barnes spoke to Mrs O'Hara, telling her that she answered the description of one of two women who had purchased two flour bags at Celia's, a shop in Walsgrave Road. This was her reply:

> On 21st August at about 2.00pm in the afternoon, I sent my daughter Mary to Celia's, Walsgrave Road, to buy two flour sacks. She brought back two bags wrapped in newspaper with the receipt for 2s. which she had paid for the bags. I wanted linen bags to make sheets for my daughter's baby's cot. When

---

[1] Betsy Grey was decapitated in 1798 following the battle of Ballynahinch, and her heroism resonated with Irish patriots; a fan club in her honour still exists.

> I opened the parcel, I found that they had sent coarse sacks which were not suitable so I and my daughter Mary took them back to Celia's and the woman in the shop took the bags and gave me back my 2s. I did not hand back the receipt to the woman but I think I left it on my mantelshelf in my back room on the ground floor of my house.

However, quite apart from the fact that she omitted Barnes and Richards from that account, there was no baby's cot in the house; in fact, the child slept in her pram.

Mary Hewitt later made a statement at Coventry police station. In part, it read: 'At about 2.45pm that day, my mother sent me to buy two flour bags which she wanted to make sheets with . . .'

One of the other officers present was a local officer, Detective Constable (later Inspector) William Sykes, who searched Richards and in his trouser pocket found a setter for an alarm clock – a different one than that previously found.

'What do you use this for?' asked the officer, to which Richards replied, 'Oh, that! The kiddie has been playing with it and I suppose I must have picked it up.'

Richards also made a statement at the police station, giving an account of his movements. Regarding the day of the bombing, he said:

> On Friday, 25th August, I got up about 1.00pm. I had a cup of tea and a wash and shave. I shaved in the back kitchen near the window when the man next door called to me and told me there had been an explosion on Broadgate. Some time about 3.00pm Mrs O'Hara went down town. I stayed in until about 8.00pm, when I went out with all of them. We had a walk down to Broadgate where the explosion had been. We were saying what a terrible thing it was and Hewitt was saying he did not agree with it at all . . .

Joseph Hewitt made a statement. At the time of the explosion, it was verified that he was at work. Shown some of the items found at his address, he said, 'I have never seen the clock keys before. I know nothing about the electric batteries or the glass tubes. That is my soldering kit but I have never used it.'

In fact, the soldering kit had been used, and when Richards was shown the same items, he replied, 'I know nothing about those things; I am only the lodger.'

That was that for Monday, 28 August – and the occupants of 25 Clara Street returned home.

* * *

But the following day, Chief Inspector Boneham and his officers made a return trip to the premises and a further search was carried out, in the presence of all the occupants. Under the stairs Boneham saw that the tiles were uneven and that there was new cement covering them. William Rollins, a service layer with the Coventry Gas Department and a person familiar with the laying of concrete and cement, was sent for. He came to the conclusion that the tiles had been there ever since the house was built and that the cement on the tiles which had been removed was about 3-4 days old. Underneath the tiles was a cement slab and underneath that, the pit, which had been cemented. On the top of the slab were the imprints of blue bricks from the causeway in the back garden, and it was Mr Rollins' opinion that the slab had been made in the garden, on top of the blue bricks. In fact, when he went into the garden, he found cement adhering to those bricks which was similar to that found under the stairs, and at the top of the garden he found a dry cement bag of recent origin with some cement still in it. By the coal house door the ground had been recently dug.

What did the occupants of 25 Clara Street have to say about this? Boneham certainly wanted to know and he asked Joseph Hewitt, 'What is this pit used for?'

'I have never seen it before', he replied.

'But you and Richards have been seen mixing cement and making concrete slabs', said Boneham.

Hewitt was persistent in his denial: 'There has been no cementing done here since we came.'

Richards concurred, saying, 'I have never done any cementing.'

Mrs O'Hara stoutly backed up her son-in-law, saying, 'There has been no cementing done since we came to live here', and her daughter agreed, saying, 'That is right, inspector.'

But as well as Mr Rollins' expert opinion, this was not the conclusion reached by Thomas Henry Brown, the clerk to the letting agents, who had inspected the house prior to letting it to Hewitt. The pit was not there then, he said, and in consequence it could not have been present when William Henry Lewis had been the tenant of the house until April 1939. Mr Lewis denied mixing cement in the back garden during his tenure of the house, and indeed he had not; but as neighbours would testify, they had seen Richards doing just that.

The four occupants were released until detention orders were applied for, and on 2 September they were all arrested under the provisions of the Prevention of Violence Act.

The following day, 26-year-old Detective Constable Charles Ronald Gibson, who had previously taken photographs of the devastation at Broadgate, was on duty at Coventry police station with Policewoman Kathleen Mary Rowe, when Mrs O'Hara suddenly said, 'Can I see the inspector? I am going to tell the truth. I do not see why I should shield anyone.' Then, pointing to DC Gibson, she said, 'I call on this officer as a witness of what I have said.'

Miss Rowe informed Chief Inspector Parker of Mrs O'Hara's request, but it was followed by a further revelation when Mary Hewitt asked the same officer, 'Has my mother told you that I want to see the inspector?'

'Do you wish to speak to the officer in charge of the case?' he asked Miss Rowe, and was told, 'Yes, please.'

And what mother and daughter had to say to the police was very different from what they had told them previously.

* * *

Now Mrs O'Hara had a great deal to say, which was set out in great detail in a written statement under caution, in which she stated, 'To show that I fully understand the nature of the caution, I sign my name.'

She mentioned the callers at the house to see Richards, who took them into the front room and shut the door so that she could not hear their conversation. But Richards did tell Mrs O'Hara that one of the callers had been sent to prison.

'His name is Jones or Halfpenny', Richards had said, and that was true; Gary Jones, alias Gray, the London OC, had been arrested and in due course would be sentenced to ten years' penal servitude.

Mrs O'Hara described the digging of the pit and said that cement was delivered to the house by lorry and that her son-in-law assisted Richards. Prior to the pit being dug, the suitcase which was found by police in the coal shed had been placed in the cupboard under the stairs; it was full, said Mrs O'Hara, of white powder.

Now for the first time she mentioned Barnes and said that it was he, not she, who had sent her daughter for the flour bags; she detailed the events of the evening prior to the explosion in Broadgate, including the arrival of 'the strange young man'. Most importantly, she recounted the conversation on the morning of the bombing between him – Joby O'Sullivan – and Richards about acquiring the carrier cycle. Importantly, she mentioned that

Richards had told her that when Dominic Adams had ordered the carrier cycle he had worn spectacles, so that the shopkeeper would not know him again.

She finished the statement with these words:

> As I can see it now, I can see what has happened in the house at 25 Clara Street. I was only a lodger and if I had known what Richards and the other men who came to see him were planning to do, I would not have stopped there one minute nor would I have allowed my daughter and the baby to stay there. I think it is terrible that those poor people should have been killed in Broadgate through the wickedness of these men and I am anxious to do all I can to help you.

Then it was the turn of Mary Hewitt, who told the chief inspector, 'I want to tell you the truth as to what has been happening at our house for the sake of my baby', and she, too, made a lengthy written statement.

She described how 'strange men' would come to visit Richards, frequently bringing suitcases with them, and on one occasion she saw Richards take white powder out of a suitcase and make it into a paper parcel. The suitcase remained in the scullery for two weeks – she tried to lift it, but it was too heavy – and then it was put in the cupboard under the stairs. She described seeing Richards take white powder out of it and make it into parcels, until the suitcase was empty, at which point it was placed in the coal house.

Mrs Hewitt told her husband that she thought the powder was explosives and that he should get rid of Richards; and that if she was sure that the powder was explosives, she would not stay in the house at night. She went on to say:

> Joe warned me not to go messages for Richards or any of the men if they called. He told me I could go home to Ireland, but that he couldn't come with me. He said you are innocent and if there should be any trouble he would take responsibility. When we were alone and talking I have pleaded with my husband to have nothing to do with Richards. He used to get annoyed with me and told me to go home to Ireland and he would allow me £1 a week. I also told him that if anything happened I would never shield him. Soon after I first saw the suitcase in the cupboard under the stairs, Jim Richards started digging a hole in the floor where the suitcase stood. I told my husband to stop the hole from being dug but he would not listen to me and I was afraid to say anything more in case he turned me and my child and mother out.

Mrs Hewitt described the flour bag errand at the behest of Barnes and then, on the day before the Broadgate bombing, seeing 'the strange man' – O'Sullivan – her husband and Richards all drinking beer and with new tools which she had never seen before. On the day of the bombing, she returned home for lunch at about 12.15pm. Richards and O'Sullivan were in her bedroom working with the tools on a wooden box; Richards was dealing with some white powder, both in a box and in a white bag. She demanded to know what they were doing in her room; they replied that they would not be very long.

After Richards told her that he was going out to get a cycle, O'Sullivan appeared very agitated and said, 'Isn't Richards a long while?' She went upstairs to her bedroom and then, in the words of her statement:

> I went upstairs to see what they had been doing in my room. I saw a parcel wrapped in brown paper and tied with string lying on the floor in the centre of the room. The tools had been cleared away. I did not go near the parcel. I was upset as I knew what they had done and were going to make an explosion, but I did not know where. I was upset because they had used my bedroom. I left my bedroom and went out of my house and returned to work at about a quarter-past one o'clock. I left Richards and the strange man in my bedroom. About a quarter to four, a girl in my workplace told me that a terrible explosion had happened in Broadgate. I was terribly upset when I heard that people had been killed and I wished that I had been the young girl that was killed by the bomb. If I had known for sure what Richards and the other man were doing that morning and where the bomb was going to be placed I would have surely told the police. I was afraid to come to the police for my husband's sake. I remember one evening, I cannot say whether it was just before or just after the explosion in Broadgate, I saw my husband and Jim Richards mixing some cement in the yard, which they put over the hole which had been made under the stairs. After they had put the top on they put the tiles back.

Mother and daughter were two obviously frightened people. Having told a pack of lies to start off with, they now needed to try to extricate themselves from the mess they had got themselves into. Of course, this knocked Richards' story of not getting up until 1 o'clock and then having a shave on the day of the bombing into a cocked hat – nor did it do any good to Joseph Hewitt's story of not carrying out any digging and cementing.

But the fact of the matter was that by these admissions both women had also placed themselves right in the middle of a very unpleasant conspiracy.

All of the evidence was placed before the Attorney General. The evidence against Richards and Barnes was fairly clear-cut. Joseph Hewitt certainly had a case to answer. But what of the women? Although (according to the law at that time) Mrs Hewitt was neither competent nor could be compelled to give evidence against her husband, should she (and Mrs O'Hara) be called as prosecution witnesses against Richards and Barnes? If they were, and if on the day of the trial they recanted their confessions, probably the worst that could happen would be that they were imprisoned for contempt of court (and not for very long, either). And if they were to stand trial, the matter contained in their statements – as the Judge would tell the jury – was only evidence against the person making that statement. The Judge would also tell the jury to disregard anything mentioned in those statements regarding any other defendant.

But of course, the jury *would* have heard that evidence; and even if they tried their hardest to ignore it, being human, they might well not.

That being so, the Attorney General thought it best to charge the lot and leave it to the court to sort out.

On 4 September, Chief Inspector Parker told Joseph Hewitt and Richards that they would later be charged with possessing explosives for an unlawful object; and while Richards made no reply, Hewitt said, 'I have nothing to say to you about it.'

The following day, Chief Inspector Boneham charged Joseph Hewitt and Richards with possessing explosive substances. Richards replied, 'You did not find any potassium chlorate on me', while Hewitt said, 'I have nothing to say; that charge is a frame-up against me.'

On 8 September both women were similarly charged, to which Mrs O'Hara made no reply and Mary Hewitt said, 'I do not know what to do.'

But on 27 September all of the prisoners – now including Barnes – were charged by Chief Inspector Parker with the five murders, to which Barnes replied, 'I was in London on that day.'

Joseph Hewitt replied, 'I am not guilty; my wife and her mother is innocent. I was working that day.'

Richards said, 'I know nothing about it, neither does Mrs Hewitt or her mother or Joe Hewitt.'

Mrs O'Hara made no reply, while her daughter said, 'I was working that day, inspector.'

Further charged with conspiracy to cause explosions, Barnes replied, 'I do not know anything about it', Joseph Hewitt said, 'Not guilty, not my wife or her mother' and Barnes chimed in with, 'Neither am I guilty', while none of the others made any reply.

On 30 September the statements of both women were served on the male prisoners; Barnes replied 'All right', Hewitt, 'OK' and Richards made no reply. On the same day, the same statements were served on mother and daughter. Mary Hewitt simply replied, 'Thank you, Sir', while Mrs O'Hara started to say, 'It is terrible . . . ' before she was stopped and cautioned by Inspector Barnes, after which she continued, 'It is all right. What my daughter told you is the truth.'

And there we shall leave matters for the time being. In the five weeks between the explosion at Broadgate and the charging of the prisoners there had been many other incidents, and it's time to bring the reader up to date with them.

Chapter 22

Dirty work at Dartmoor – and War

Nowadays, Dartmoor prison at Princetown, Devon has a Category 'C' security classification and houses among its 640 inmates white-collar, non-violent criminals, plus a number of sex offenders, some of whom apply for treatment programmes to persuade anyone who might be interested that they really do realize their past behaviour has been unacceptable. In this way they can convince any credulous members of a parole board that they are rehabilitated and can qualify for early release – in the hope that they can get out into the community and offend some more.

This liberal regime was not always in force at Dartmoor.

Three years' in the building, it was completed in 1809 to house French prisoners from the Napoleonic wars, followed three years later by Americans taken in the war of 1812. Within its granite walls the conditions were so terrible and the overcrowding so acute that by 1815, out of the 6,000 prisoners, 1,470 had died.

A riot in 1815 resulted in troops being called in; seven prisoners were shot dead and sixty wounded. From 1920 the prison housed some of society's worst offenders, and in 1932 there was an outbreak of violence which resulted in thirty-two of the inmates being charged with inflicting grievous bodily harm, riotous conduct and malicious damage; many were given heavy additional sentences to those they were already serving.

Discipline was draconian; offences ranged from talking to insolence to fighting. However, attacking a warder or incitement to mutiny was punishable with a flogging with the cat-o'-nine-tails. Number one punishment diet consisted of bread and water; the time limit for that was fifteen days. However, number two punishment diet was bread, porridge and potatoes – certainly more nourishing than number one, but it could be imposed for up to forty-two days.

By 1939, although a few prisoners were military personnel serving sentences after having been convicted at courts martial, the majority of the inmates were serving sentences of penal servitude. The Penal Servitude Act 1857 had replaced transportation; its sole purpose was not to try to reform but to punish the prisoner. It covered terms of imprisonment from three years to life, and the prisoners were employed on public works, usually in quarries, digging drainage ditches or repairing drystone walls.

When the Act first came into force, the first few months of an offender's regime was spent in solitary confinement, and leg-irons were imposed on recalcitrant prisoners. A contraction of 'leg-irons' became 'laggings', and this was used to denote penal servitude; hence the expression 'old lags' to describe those who had served those sentences – or 'journeys', as they were commonly known.

With some exceptions, the prisoners serving penal servitude had been convicted of violent offences; often their lives had followed the whole penal route from approved school and borstal to prison (with and without hard labour), often accompanied by corporal punishments such as caning, strapping, birching and flogging. Some had received previous sentences of penal servitude, and these punishments, coupled with hard work in the quarries, made them physically as hard as nails and mentally bitter and resentful.

When members of the IRA were sentenced to penal servitude, many of them for twenty years, for some this was the first time they had been incarcerated and they were quite unprepared for the rigours to follow. Inmates who had used explosives to blow open safes were well respected in the pecking order of the prison, because if anyone was at risk, it was the safe-blower himself, not members of the public; however, those who used explosives to terrorize, maim and kill members of the public were held in low esteem, and the common or garden prison inmates had their own rules and ethics regarding them.

Therefore, on 28 August 1939, when eleven convicted IRA terrorists were shipped in to Dartmoor to bring the numbers housed there up to 365, they would have been well advised to keep their mouths well and truly shut; it was the height of recklessness for them to openly and loudly praise those responsible for the bombing at Broadgate three days previously.

At tally point – when a head count was made of the prisoners marching out to, or returning from work parties – emotions boiled over, and before the warders could intervene, every one of those eleven IRA men had the living shit smashed out of them by the other prisoners. John Healy, sentenced to ten years' penal servitude for distributing explosives to other terrorists, came off worst of all and was one of three terrorists to be hospitalized. Suffering from pneumonia, it was initially thought that he was going to die, and he refused to provide information to the detective inspector who had been deputed to investigate the fracas. On 23 October he was returned from Plymouth hospital to recommence his interrupted penal servitude, but this time less loquaciously than before.

* * *

On 27 August, the first of four bombs exploded at 3 o'clock in the morning outside the main entrance to the Town Hall in Blackpool; a car was seen being driven at high speed in the vicinity just prior to the explosion. Two more bombs were found in a dustbin outside Woolworths; one was extinguished by the fire brigade, the other was put into a bucket of water by two night watchmen. The fourth bomb was found in the grounds of the central police station in Albert Road. Twelve sticks of gelignite had been placed between the offices of the chief constable and the superintendent; that, too, was neutralized.

The seventh explosion in three days occurred in Liverpool on 29 August, when a bomb was thrown from a car, close to the corporation's tramway; the lights were turned off and the car sped away. The explosion smashed the windows in a telephone box, but the tramway track was not damaged and no passers-by were hurt.

The people of Shotts, Lanarkshire were pleased that a bomb under the rails of the LMS main Glasgow to Edinburgh line failed to explode when it was discovered on 3 September, but most people in Britain had more pressing concerns, because that was the day that Britain declared war on Germany.

As the sonorous tones of Neville Chamberlain, the man who had been an inventive Chancellor of the Exchequer in 1931 and an utterly disastrous Prime Minister since 1937, echoed from the public's radio sets, the country readied itself – for the second time in twenty-one years – to engage in a massive global conflict.

Not that the police were unprepared. The Metropolitan Police Commissioner, Sir Philip Game, was now sixty-four, in poor health and had been considering retirement, but he patriotically decided to remain in post until the end of the war. Three days before the declaration of war, 1,764 police pensioners and special constables were recruited by the Metropolitan Police to form a War Reserve for the duration. They would soon number 27,000, and many other constabularies followed suit. They would be much needed, not only to perform often heroic duties in the six years of war that would follow, but also to combat the menace of the IRA.

It had been stated in the IRA's 'S' Plan that their offensive against Britain should not coincide with a war against any other foreign country. This, together with their assertion that injuries should not be inflicted on the general public – indeed, authorization was given to abort any operation where ordinary people's lives might be put at risk – was hypocritical rubbish.

Between the declaration of war and the conclusion of the IRA's bombing offensive, six months later, there were five disruptions to trains on railway lines, telephone wires were severed on eight occasions and forty-eight incendiary devices exploded. Twenty-one explosive devices were defused, but the same number exploded, causing severe injuries to passers-by.

And now, it's time to return to Coventry.

CHAPTER 23

Ill feelings in Coventry

There was a backlash against Irish people who lived and worked in Coventry, over 2,000 of them; understandable perhaps, given human nature, but quite wrong.

However, public opinion being what it was, threats were made, there was a call for all Irish workers employed in the city to be sacked and a demand for Irish tenants to be evicted, although some voluntarily left before harm could befall them. It is possible that any who held strong republican views may have changed their minds; or at any rate were less reckless in openly voicing their opinions than the eleven prisoners in Dartmoor had been.

There was a march through the city by 2,000 workers at the Armstrong Whitworth Company; when they reached Pool Meadow they protested against 'cooperating with Irish labour', and the march then continued until they reached the Market Square. There they urged the general population to join them, another 1,000 did so and a deputation met up with the Lord Mayor, Sidney Stringer. Fortunately, Stringer managed to defuse the situation, accurately pointing out that the majority of Irish people in the city were as appalled at the atrocity as anybody else. He also set up a relief fund for those affected by the outrage, and a month later, this had reached the not inconsiderable sum of £800, or £52,640 in today's money.

The Catholic churches in the city were unanimous in their condemnation of the attack, reminding their parishioners that the penalty for belonging to the IRA and plotting to overthrow the church or state was excommunication. Some of the Irish population suggested forming an 'Irish Union', in which they would pledge to inform the authorities regarding any IRA activities.

But anti-Irish feeling continued for long after the bomb outrage. Clive Bishop was a youngster who attended the Catholic All Saints School in Coventry. He and his brother desired to join the local scout group, and when they applied, it appeared that the local scoutmaster would be only too glad to enrol them – until, that is, he was told the name of the applicants' school.

'You Catholics then?' he gasped.

Upon being told that the brothers were indeed of that faith, he roared, 'Get out, you murdering little bastards and never let me see you again!'

The boys ran home in tears, and their parents had to explain to them the foolish and irrational prejudices that some Coventry folk were unable to relinquish.

A nonsensical rumour started circulating about the ethnic origins of the City's Chief Constable, Captain S. A. Hector, who found it necessary to state:

> Stupid rumours have reached me that I am of Irish extraction. I am a Somerset man. I am not Irish and had had no Irish connections and have never even been in Ireland.

That seemed to put the rumours to rest, and in fact, as a result of his leadership during the later air raids, he was awarded the King's Police Medal.

Following the explosion, a great deal of newspaper coverage concerned Dominic Adams, whom the police desired to interview, but of course, he and his fellow murderer Joby O'Sullivan had scuttled back to the sanctuary of Éire.

That left Barnes, Richards, Mrs O'Hara and the Hewitts to face the music; and it was little use for any of them to put forward the defence, 'I didn't put the bomb in the basket of the cycle, so I can't be guilty of murder.' It would never be disputed that none of them had physically placed the bomb in the basket, but under the Explosive Substances Act, 1883, it was ruled that:

> Any person who unlawfully and maliciously causes by an explosive substance an explosion likely to endanger life or to cause serious injury to property shall be guilty of felony.

Well, that was clear enough; and so was the following section:

> Any person who does any act with intent to cause by an explosive substance, an explosion likely to endanger life or to cause serious injury to property and any person who has in his possession or under his control any explosive substance of that character is by law, guilty of felony.

Now we turn to Section 5 of the Act, which reads:

> Any person who, within or without Her Majesty's Dominions, by the supply or solicitation of money, the providing of premises, the supply of materials, or in any manner whatsoever

procures, counsels, aids, abets or is accessory to the commission of any crime under this Act, shall be guilty of felony and shall be liable to be tried and punished for that crime as if he had been guilty as a principal.

Therefore, anybody who caused death in pursuance of a felony was, in English law, guilty of murder. In those days, in a charge of murder, naming only one person was preferred; and in this case the victim chosen was Elsie Ansell.

So that was the charge brought against the five defendants when they appeared at Warwick Assizes on Monday, 11 December 1939, a charge to which all of them pleaded not guilty.

Chapter 24

The Broadgate Trial

Legal aid could be provided by the IRA to anyone charged with a capital offence, but if it was offered to any of the defendants – and due to a lack of funds, it might not have been – the offer was not taken up. All had instructed Coventry and Birmingham firms of solicitors and were defended as 'poor persons'; and what was more, none of them refused to plead, as was the norm with IRA prisoners. Had any of them done so – or had been found to have received legal aid courtesy of the IRA – it could have proved highly detrimental in the eyes of the jury.

The prosecution was led by Richard O'Sullivan KC, KSG, who was then fifty-one years of age. Born in Cork, he had served with the Royal Artillery during the First World War, and he developed and expounded his ideas on the Christian origin of the common law of England.

After the jury was sworn, an application was made by Douglas Jenkins on behalf of Barnes and Richards for separate trials, an application that was echoed by Mr A. M. Lyons KC, MP for Joseph Hewitt. The reason was clear; had those applications been successful, the evidence in the statements of Brigid O'Hara and Mary Hewitt would not be heard. However, counsel for the two women, Mr T. H. Winning, *definitely* wanted those statements to be heard.

The application for separate trials was refused by the Judge, Mr Justice Singleton, and Mr O'Sullivan opened the case for the Crown. It was a long, detailed opening, in which he stated in part:

> One might perhaps gauge the iniquity of this massacre of the innocent by reflecting that no civilised state has, or has even claimed, the right of the power to decree the death of an innocent person. Even in a time of war, the taking of innocent lives – the lives of women and children and non-combatants generally – is forbidden.

Then the first witnesses who appear in any major trial – photographers and a plan-drawer – gave their evidence, which was not disputed.

An engineer named Alfred Joseph Mazengarb saw the arrival of the tradesman's cycle at about 1.30pm and noticed on the back of the machine the words 'Keep tyres hard'. He had a good look at the rider and on 15 September he attended an identification parade in which Joseph Hewitt, Barnes and Richards participated; Mazengarb was able to say that the rider of the cycle was not present, which of course he was not. He could have been shown a series of photographs including one of Joby O'Sullivan had the police known his identity, but those who knew that the cyclist was O'Sullivan kept that information to themselves. Mr Mazengarb saw the cycle again at 2.15pm, exactly where it had been left, outside Astley's, and recalled that the parcel in the carrier was box-shaped.

Ronald Johnson, a compositor, also noticed the wording on the rear mudguard of the cycle; he stayed close to it, looking in Burton's window for about half an hour before, like Mr Mazengarb, fortunately leaving the area at 2.15pm.

Joseph Osborn Grove was not so lucky; he, too, saw the cycle and was standing opposite Samuel's shop when the explosion occurred, receiving four wounds to his legs. Robert Kevin Kinsella did not have the opportunity to see the cycle; as he approached Astley's, the bomb exploded and he was thrown to the ground. He saw several people lying on the ground, one of whom was James Clay, who was dying and whom he picked up. He was then taken to the hospital, having sustained wounds to his shoulder, feet, stomach and leg.

More fortunate was John Worth, a road-sweeper who, at the time of the explosion, was behind a blue saloon car in Broadgate. He did not see the remains of the cycle which struck the car but he was knocked to the ground by the force of the blast, sustaining injuries to his thigh and both arms.

Police Constable Harry Cecil Cooper celebrated his thirty-ninth birthday on the day that he gave evidence, that he was on duty in the Broadgate at the time of the explosion; he was too far away to be injured, noted the dead bodies and also the number of cycle – V 2615 – which was covered in white powder and which lay by the car.

There followed a procession of witnesses who saw the murdered victims, who described their injuries and who identified the bodies. When the horrific injuries to Elsie Ansell's body were described, Mr Justice Singleton said quietly, 'I think that is enough.'

The fragments of the cycle were gathered; there was no doubt that it was the one purchased from Halford's. The next witness to be called was 39-year-old Charles Woodroffe Ede, who after twenty years service with the Royal Garrison Artillery had retired in 1934 with the rank of captain. He had been immediately appointed as one of His Majesty's Inspector of Explosives at the Home Office, and he had visited Broadgate within four hours of the explosion. Mr Ede knew what he was talking about; he concluded that not less than 5lbs of explosive had been used and that it had been sited under the handlebars of the cycle. Queried by the Judge as to how he had come to this conclusion, and how he could tell the explosion had not occurred at ground level, Mr Ede replied:

> If it had been on the ground, one would have found a crater in the ground and the explosive, if it was lying on the ground, would have blown away some of the roadway. There was no crater there . . . the splash marks I saw on the road were obviously caused by a number of small splinters being shot down on the roadway.

Then came the neighbours in Clara Street, all of whom could tell stories of the mysterious comings and goings of male visitors to the Hewitts' address, and of one occasion when five of them entered the premises at 11.15 at night. There were those who told of digging in the garden and the sound of a report and blue flashes coming from the house during the evenings. It is never a good idea for defence barristers to try to belittle witnesses, particularly in a case as sensitive as this one, so for Jenkins, on behalf of Richards and Barnes, to sneeringly suggest to Mrs Florence Abbott that the blue flashes she had seen were due to a bout of indigestion was distinctly counterproductive.

Sarah Ann Keane appeared in the witness box stating that she was Barnes' fiancée and told of how he had given her three packets which he claimed he had purchased from a woman in Oxford Street and which, he said, contained toothpaste, powder and bath salts. She was familiar with bath salts – they were crystals, she said – but what was in the packets was white powder. They were scented, and she told Barnes to put them in a drawer 'to make his clothes smell nice'. Miss Keane also mentioned that Barnes had given her the two receipts and that she had seen him write a letter – it was suggested to her that he copied it out, something that Miss Keane was unaware of. All she could say was that on the evening of Friday, 25 August he left her lodgings – as far as she was concerned – to post the letter.

Three weeks after the explosion, Mrs Ethel Grose attended an identification parade at which she identified Peter Barnes as the man she saw on 24 August during the lunch hour entering 25 Clara Street carrying a brown suitcase. Queried as to the accuracy of her identification, she told the Judge, 'I have no doubt at all', and on that note, the first day's evidence concluded.

Three employees of Halford's took the stand the following day; one could not identify anyone who on either occasion had entered the shop to purchase the carrier cycle; another identified Richards, who had picked the cycle up after the balance had been paid, and a third who similarly identified Richards also identified Barnes as being present when the cycle was first ordered. Barnes would state that he was in London on that day, although the witness, Frank MacRobb Andrews, gave evidence to the contrary.

Evidence was given by the police of the searches, the gathering of evidence and the arrests, and then there was discussion regarding points of law as to whether or not the statements made by the two women should be allowed in evidence – they were – and statements taken from Richards and Joseph Hewitt to account for their movements were read.

Now it was the turn of Alan George Raine Whitehouse, a staff chemist at the West Midland Forensic Science Laboratory, Birmingham. He had examined the front part of the frame of the cycle (which, he said, had been subjected to an explosion), as well as the suitcase found at Clara Street, the trench coat belonging to Joseph Hewitt and a tea chest; all contained traces of potassium chlorate.

The defence got Mr Whitehouse to admit that potassium chlorate could be used as a disinfectant, that it was used in schools for research and that it had been used for toothpaste; but on re-examination he agreed it would have been 'unusual' for a suitcase to be used for disinfectant purposes. A rather more positive witness for the prosecution was Frederick Dupré, who was now working at Woolwich Arsenal.

The three items allegedly containing toothpaste powder and bath salts had been tested by Mr Dupré, and having established that all of them were a mixture of potassium chlorate and sodium carbonate with some scent (an unusual composition of chemical elements), he was able to say:

> It is not a bath salt because it does not soften the water as bath salt is supposed to do. It is not a hair wash because it contains no soap and forms no lather. This particular mixture has a very disagreeable taste and would not make a good tooth powder.

Having also established that various items of clothing found at Barnes' lodgings contained potassium chlorate, and having agreed that he had considerable experience in examining home-made bombs, he also agreed that a delayed-action bomb could be constructed by using an alarm clock; indeed, it had recently been done frequently.

He was asked to describe what tools were necessary to construct a clock bomb. Having been shown the tools found at Clara Street, of which Joseph Hewitt claimed ownership, Mr Dupré replied:

> I have seen those tools and there is sufficient there to convert an ordinary alarm clock into a time switch and practically every tool would be used. The saw is required to make the wooden block; the chisel would be for cleaning the cut when you have finished sawing; the twist drill and the brace are for boring the holes through the wooden block and to the back of the clock, so these bolts can be used to attach the wood to the back of the clock; also for boring the disc, which in this case is a coin; there is a hole bored through there, and the twist drill and brace would be required for that; while you are boring or sawing the coin or the brace strip for the springs or the wooden block, they will be held in the vice. The wires are soldered to the strips and you require a soldering iron to solder and one of the fluxes. They are both soldering fluxes. The pliers would be used to hold the brace strips whilst soldering. They get too hot to hold in the fingers so you should hold them with pliers. The pincers could be used for fixing the nuts. Very likely the back of the nut would have to be screwed while you are holding the nut in front. The insulating tape is very much used to hold things together when connecting them. That only leaves out one saw and the drill; everything else is used.

He examined the two setters for an alarm clock, one of which had been found in Richards' pocket; both came from the same clock. The metal strip on the dry battery was suitable for the contact which would feel the pressure of the coin when it was rotated.

Asked if he had experience of fine sacks or pillow cases being used to hold potassium chlorate, Mr Dupré replied, 'Pillow cases have been used on several occasions for this fine powder. It is very fine and would get through any material not of a very fine weave.'

'What sort of thing is a bomb made of?' asked the Judge. 'Where is it put in relation to the clock bomb?'

'It is a mass of powder – the one I am thinking about – contained in a pillow case which contains a detonator', explained Mr Dupré.

'The clock goes on top of the sack outside, away from the powder and the whole is placed in some convenient receptacle. The clock has no relevance except to set it off . . . brown paper would do, anything to keep it together. The ones I have seen recently have been put in ladies' hatboxes.'

Asked by the defence about the result of putting a handful of potassium chlorate on a fire, Mr Dupré said there would be a violent burst of flame but that it would probably do no harm.

But in re-examination, the evidence of the neighbours seeing blue flashes was mentioned and Mr Dupré was asked if this could be related at all to any experimentation made with any of the materials.

To this he replied, 'If potassium chlorate was set on fire it would make a bright, violent flame, and a description I heard yesterday would fit that quite well.'

And having nullified Mr Jenkins' ridiculous suggestion that indigestion on the part of a witness was the cause of the blue flashes, the case for the prosecution was closed.

Each of the prisoners had said at the Police Court, 'I am not guilty, I reserve my defence.'

Now it was their turn.

Chapter 25

The Defence for Barnes

To start the second day's proceedings, Mr Winning made an application to the Judge (in the absence of the jury) that there was no case to answer in respect of the two women, saying that in the case of Mrs Hewitt there was no evidence that she had any right to control the powder, the vice or other implements found in the house, saying:

> There is evidence that Mary Hewitt was sent out, or did in fact go to a shop to buy bags. It is quite clear she did not know for what purpose they were to be used, because she bought something decidedly unfitted for the purpose. There is evidence that Brigid O'Hara took those bags back at the request of somebody in the house, and got bags of a finer mesh.

'It goes a little further than that', remarked Mr Justice Singleton.

'And there is evidence', said Mr Winning, 'that a bag might be useful in the making of a bomb.'

'It is a little further than that', said the Judge.

'With respect, no', said Mr Winning firmly.

Just as firmly, Mr Justice Singleton said:

> You and I have to face it, either way. Is it not this, that Mary Hewitt went out to get two bags, that those which she brought back were not suitable, but stayed outside while her mother went in; that thereafter the receipt which she had obtained for the 2s 0d she paid is traced to the man Barnes in London. Then you have the evidence of the other witnesses as to the possible use of bags. Is there not some evidence at least of conspiracy, I am not saying it is conclusive evidence, but is there no evidence with regards to that? It is not purely possession; it is a little more than that, possibly.

There were more legal arguments between Mr Winning and the Judge, with interjections from Mr O'Sullivan, but eventually, having exhausted all the possibilities, the Judge declared that the case against the two women was one for the jury.

Peter Barnes then took the witness stand.

Led by Mr Jenkins, he told the jury that he had lived in Offaly, Ireland, had arrived in London with his savings of £13 at the beginning of August, taken lodgings at Westbourne Terrace and met up with his fiancée, Miss Keane, at Warwick Avenue; he also described the alleged purchase of the three packets of powder in Oxford Street.

He then went on to say that by chance he had met a man named MacMahon, whom he previously knew from Dublin, in Hyde Park. They discussed finding work, and MacMahon told him that he knew a man named Norman, who lived at 25 Clara Street, Coventry and who, if Barnes went there on Monday, 21 August, would be able to fix him up with a job.

MacMahon then asked Barnes to lend him a suitcase, which he did, and MacMahon, giving him ten shillings, told him, 'Buy your case anywhere you like and you can give it back anywhere, but I can have yours. I will meet you on Thursday at two o'clock at your digs.'

Having completed this extraordinary transaction, off went Barnes to 25 Clara Street, where for the first time he met Richards, who told him he had no knowledge of anyone named Norman but offered him a cup of tea and introduced him to Mrs O'Hara. It was she who Barnes asked to purchase him a suitcase – 'About two feet, a good one' – and gave her ten shillings. She returned with the suitcase, gave him a receipt for 7s 6d and the change of 2s 6d.

Had there been any conversation about flour sacks? There had not.

Barnes then returned to London the same day and met MacMahon, as arranged. He handed over the suitcase and his change, and MacMahon returned Barnes' suitcase, together with a letter for Norman who, he felt sure, would now be at Clara Street.

Back went Barnes to Coventry, taking with him the suitcase he had loaned to MacMahon, into which he had put an overcoat, a hat and a suit of pyjamas, plus the letter to Norman. But Richards confirmed that no one by that name was at Clara Street, so back to London went Barnes, where at Euston at about 10.00pm he met MacMahon, as arranged, who wanted to know how Barnes had got on. He apologised about Norman; he had sent Barnes to the wrong address.

Barnes declared he was fed up and he decided to return to Ireland on the Saturday. MacMahon asked him if he would take a letter with him to give to a Jim Kelly at 45 Parnell Square, Dublin.

He told Barnes, 'I will write it on a few pages of notebook and you can copy it out on a sheet of paper and put it in an envelope and deliver it.'

Overlooking the fact that Barnes' home at Offaly was sixty miles from Dublin, and that if he posted the letter himself it would arrive far quicker than Barnes could personally deliver it, MacMahon wrote on five or six pages from a notebook and handed them to Barnes – and that concluded matters for Thursday, 24 August.

The next day, he went to Miss Keane's address, copied out the deeply incriminating 'Dear Jim' letter, which was signed 'Dixon' – he remembered, now, that that was a nickname used by MacMahon – threw thc original notes on to the fire and put the envelope in his pocket; it was there that the police found it that evening.

Can you see the way things were going? I can. Time for a bit of cross-examination by Mr O'Sullivan.

* * *

Barnes agreed with Mr O'Sullivan that the explosion at Broadgate was 'an inhuman crime' and stated that he was not a member of the IRA, nor did he agree with their acts.

He denied bringing potassium chlorate to Clara Street, but with regard to traces of that chemical being found on his hat, dungarees and trench coat, well, that must have come from the suitcase that MacMahon had borrowed; and he added, 'Perhaps he may have used my case for carrying powder – I do not know.' But in any event, it was that suitcase into which he bundled those items when he went to Coventry on 24 August, and concerning the packages he had purchased from the girl in Oxford Street, he knew nothing about them containing potassium chlorate.

Also in his room was a map of London and a guidebook containing a map of Glasgow. These, Barnes said, had been given to him by a man by the name of MacVitie, whom he met on the boat from Ireland, not that he had ever been to Glasgow or ever intended to, and what was more, he had never been to Liverpool either. Then why, asked Mr O'Sullivan, did you write train times down on the piece of paper found at his lodgings headed 'Eust' and 'L'po'?

To start off with, Barnes did not think that was his handwriting; then he admitted it was.

'When you noted down those times, what were they for?' asked Mr O'Sullivan.

'They must have been when I was at the station waiting', replied Barnes. 'I had to wait an hour at Coventry.'

'What were they for?'

'I used to take down the times trains would come and go. I had no interest in them.'

It was a feeble answer and an unconvincing one, rather like his explanation of the potassium chlorate found in his possession.

Barnes' explanation of purchasing the suitcase for MacMahon was bizarre; why not buy him a suitcase in London? Why buy him a suitcase at all? Was MacMahon incapable of buying his own suitcase? When Barnes had gone to Coventry on the Monday he did not have a suitcase with him; when he made the repeat journey on the Thursday he did – the one allegedly borrowed by MacMahon – but why? He knew that he intended to return to London that night and that he intended to spend the night at Miss Keane's lodgings, about 500–600 yards away from his own address – why take that suitcase to Coventry at all? 'It was convenient to bring the case', was Barnes' explanation.

He agreed that on both occasions he had gone to Coventry to see a man named Norman – that the first person he met was Richards – and that Norman was the name used by Richards when the carrier cycle was used. 'He told me he did not know him, anyway', said Barnes.

Now Barnes was asked if he had requested that Mrs O'Hara should purchase some sacks for him, and this Barnes denied. The questions came thick and fast.

'Did you ask anyone in that house on the Monday to go and get you some flour sacks?'

'I did not.'

'Did Richards in your presence ask anyone to go and get some flour sacks?'

'Not that I heard.'

'If a conversation took place in the front room of that house – and it is a small room – you could not fail to hear if it had been said?'

'If it was said in my presence, I could not fail to hear.'

'Did you open the parcel containing the sacks that day when it came back?'

'No.'

'Were you there when that parcel was opened?'

'No, I did not see any parcel at all.'

'Did you say, "These are not right; they are not the right ones"?'

'No, I did not.'

'Did you ask Mrs O'Hara if she would take them back and change them for white calico bags?'

'I did not.'

After admitting asking Mrs O'Hara to purchase the suitcase for him, Barnes was asked, 'You told us you got receipts for the suitcase and the sacks – two receipts?'

'I got the receipt for the suitcase. I do not know nothing about the receipt for the sacks.'

'Did you in fact have the receipt for the sacks as well, whether you knew it or not?'

'I was not aware that I had.'

'Did you in fact have it?'

Bearing in mind that Barnes had given both receipts to Miss Keane, he was obliged to answer, 'Yes, I must have.'

'Did you in fact get back from Mrs O'Hara the two shillings for the sacks which she had paid for them?'

'No, I did not hear anything about the sacks at all.'

Mr O'Sullivan dealt with the scenario of MacMahon writing the 'Dear Jim' notes, standing late at night in Warwick Avenue.

'Did you ever say to the police that this was a letter which a gentleman whom you knew years ago in Dublin had invited you to copy out and send for him to an address in Dublin?' asked Mr O'Sullivan.

'After I had been arrested, I heard no more about the matter until I was charged in Birmingham or Coventry at a court', replied Barnes.

Barnes said that he did not know the Jim Kelly who was the subject of this letter; he did know another Jim Kelly, to whom he had written three or four times since his arrest.

'Look at the letter, Exhibit 26. This says "For Jim Kelly" on the envelope', said Mr O'Sullivan. 'Did you tell the police officer when you were arrested that this was only a letter you had written to a friend?'

'Yes', replied Barnes.

'Was that true?'

'No. I did not think it was necessary for me to explain to him.'

'Did you explain?'

'I just said simply, to a friend.'

'You heard the officer give his evidence and he was not challenged about it', said Mr O'Sullivan and then took Barnes through the letter, sentence by sentence.

'"So I had to go to Liverpool the next day",' read Mr O'Sullivan. 'Is that why you had in your possession in your writing the trains, to and from Euston and Liverpool?'

'I know nothing about Liverpool', replied Barnes.

"'And I did not meet anyone there either so I was a week and did not meet one" – can you understand that?'

'I do not know.'

"'Believe me it is hard but I got away well so far. I am after coming back from Coventry tonight 11.30" – that was true?'

'Yes.'

There were questions raised as to the other items in the letter written on behalf of MacMahon – the MacMahon whom Miss Keane had never seen, nor to the best of Barnes' knowledge had Richards, the Hewitts or Mrs O'Hara, the MacMahon whom Barnes had made no attempts to trace. However, then Barnes was asked, 'When you came to the passage "I am after coming back to Coventry tonight" was that the first time that you knew Mr MacMahon had been in Coventry that day?'

Barnes could only answer, 'Yes.'

He denied that MacMahon did not exist, and then Mr Justice Singleton had a number of questions to put to him regarding MacMahon which included, 'He had not been to Coventry, had he?'

'I do not know whether he had or not.'

'He was a friend of yours, or you were friendly with him? If he was going to Coventry that day there was no reason why you should not go together?'

'No.'

'He told you to go, you say, and he would meet you when you came back?'

'Yes, that night.'

'So you knew he was not at Coventry?'

'Yes, as far as my knowledge went.'

'And it was he, you say, who asked you to write the letter saying, "I am after coming back from Coventry tonight 11.30"?'

'Yes.'

It is fair to say that Barnes' account of the letter, and just about everything else, was in tatters.

Chapter 26

The Defence for Richards

When James Richards gave evidence he confirmed that he had met Barnes for the first time at Clara Street and stated that it was he who sent Mrs Hewitt for the flour bags when they were in the kitchen; Barnes, he said, was in the sitting room. On the second occasion he saw Barnes, he brought with him a small suitcase, which was left unopened in the hallway. Richards described meeting and staying with the Hewitts, and then this astonishing exchange followed.

'On Tuesday, 22 August, you and somebody else went to order a bicycle?'

'Yes.'

'Who was that?'

'I refuse to give his name but it was not Peter Barnes.'

'What sort of clothing was he wearing?'

'He was wearing a sports coat and flannel pants and a grey pullover, and he was wearing spectacles.'

'To your knowledge, is that man in this country now?'

'He is not.'

'Who bought the bicycle?'

'He bought the bicycle. I was standing outside while he was buying it.'

'Was the bicycle collected on Friday the 25th?'

'Yes, I collected it.'

'What was it to be used for?'

'I do not know. The orders I got was to collect the bicycle and give it to the man in 25 Clara Street.'

'Who gave you the orders?'

'The man that purchased the bicycle.'

'You brought the bicycle to the house?'

'Yes, I left it at the back of 25 Clara Street.'

'Who took it away?'

'It was a man that was in the house, came to 25 Clara Street on Thursday with a parcel.'

'Was that the man who bought the bicycle?'

'No, it was another man.'

'Did you see a bomb?'

'Yes, I did.'

'Did you make a bomb?'

'No, I do not know how to make a bomb.'

'When did you see the bomb or the parts of the bomb?'

'On the Friday.'

'Did anybody fit it together?'

'Yes, this man that called on the Thursday, called on the Friday and fitted it together. The man that made the bomb took it away. He is not the man that ordered the bike.'

'Is that man in this country now?'

'I do not think so. I never seen him since. He was to call back for his tools that he left there, but he never came back.'

'Did you see him take the bomb away?'

'Yes.'

'What time was that?'

'On the Friday about ten after one.'

'Did you know where he was going to take it?'

'No.'

'Did you know when it was timed to go off?'

'No.'

'Would you have been any willing party to it being taken to Broadgate?'

'No, I would not, not to Broadgate, not in the middle of the day.'

'Would you have been a willing party to the bomb being let off in Broadgate in the middle of the day?'

'No.'

'Or anywhere in the middle of the day?'

'No.'

'Would you have been a willing party to anybody's life being endangered?'

'No, sir, I would not, because it is the instructions from the Irish Republican Army that no lives are to be endangered.'

'Are you a member of what is known as the IRA?'

'I am, yes.'

* * *

Well, that was the cat out of the bag – if the jury hadn't guessed it already – and what Richards was saying was, yes, I knew there was a bomb but I didn't make it, I didn't know it was going to be detonated in Broadgate and I'm not going to tell you who was responsible.

Cross-examined, Richards stated that he had supplied the 'white powder' for the making of the bomb and when he was unable to get a white sack of fine enough mesh he handed it over to the unknown man in a paper bag.

'For the purpose of making the bomb?' asked Mr Justice Singleton.

'No, for the purpose of holding the powder', replied Richards, and since he had just admitted supplying the potassium chlorate for the purpose of bomb-making, it's difficult to say whether Richards was deliberately trying to distance himself from actually being a party to constructing a bomb that killed five people, or whether he was just being a smart-arse.

Richards admitted keeping the explosives and distributing them to anyone who called, but refused to reveal the provenance of those materials. In fact, he refused to admit quite a lot.

'Were you in fact an organizer?' asked Mr O'Sullivan.

'No.'

'Were you an operating officer?'

'I refuse to answer the question.'

'Did you tell Mrs O'Hara that you were an operating officer?'

'No.'

'If you told her you were an operating officer, was that the truth?'

'I refuse to answer that.'

When Mr O' Sullivan asked who had paid him, Richards replied, 'I refuse to tell you who paid me', and at this point, Mr Justice Singleton interjected, with:

> Listen to me. You appreciate this, do you not? The jury are charged with the duty of trying you. You appreciate, do you not, if you are asked a question and you say every now and again, "I refuse to answer", it will not help you much. You appreciate that?

To this, Richards replied, 'I do', and having made his point, the Judge said, 'Very well, I will say no more.'

But Richards had plenty more to say, mentioning the digging of the pit, the appearance of 'the strange man' whose name he knew but refused to divulge and seeing the construction of the bomb.

'Are you inviting the jury to believe that you were not interested in what was being done?' asked Mr O'Sullivan.

'No', replied Richards, 'the only thing I was interested in was giving him the powder that he asked for.'

'And for what purpose did you give him the powder?'

'Well, it was not for me to know his purpose.'

'Do you tell my lord and the members of the jury you did not know what use was being made of the powder?'

'I knew it would make a bomb.'

'You did?'

'Yes', replied Richards and then contradicted himself in a particularly asinine fashion by adding, 'I did not know if he wanted to make one or not. I know potassium chlorate is for the purpose of making a bomb. It was my duty when him or any other man belonging to the Irish Republican Army called for powder to give it to them, and that is all I know about it.'

So it went on, admission followed by retraction. When it was mentioned that Mrs O'Hara had shown him the newspaper reports of the explosion, Richards said, 'I was very much surprised because I did not think it was made for to go off in the middle of the day.'

'Did you say to her, "Look at the paper. It must have gone off very quickly"?'

'Yes, and that was my reason for saying that because I thought I was told it was to go off at night time.'

After saying that he was unaware of where the bomb was going to be detonated, Richards was asked, 'Did Mrs O'Hara say, when you read the paper, "My God, it is terrible to have all these people killed and wounded! That is the bomb you made"?'

'No', replied Richards. 'She said, "My God, it is terrible that all these people have been killed!"' But then he added, 'She did not mention anything about the bomb we made.'

Once more, Richards had accepted being a party to the bomb-making, but when he was asked if he had said to Mrs O'Hara that the police would never find the address at Clara Street, his response was one of jaw-dropping stupidity:

> I told her that I did not think that was the bomb that that man had in the house; I did not think that that was the bomb that went off in Broadgate and I told her not to worry about the police, that they would not it find there.

Having established from Richards that there was no other distributor of IRA explosives in Coventry, Mr O'Sullivan went on to question him regarding the statement he had made to the police as to his background and whereabouts since coming to England.

This he airily dismissed, saying, 'I think they had no right to cross-examine me when I was not charged, so I just gave them any statement.'

He was taken through his statement, admitting some parts were true and some partly true, while also saying that he had not mentioned pertinent occurrences and that sections of the statement were quite untrue.

'Why did you tell them untruths?' asked Mr O'Sullivan.

'Well, that was to suit myself', replied Richards.

What was quite clear was that Richards was a stranger to the truth.

Chapter 27

The Defence – the Hewitts and O'Hara

Joseph Hewitt, surly and not the sharpest knife in the drawer, was next to take the witness stand.

Having established that not only was he a person of good character, but not a member of (or owing any allegiance to) the IRA, he described how he, his wife and baby and mother-in-law had come to live, together with their lodger, Richards, at 25 Clara Street. It was clear that he was a hard-working manual labourer. Hewitt said he knew nothing of explosives in his house, and when it was suggested that there had been flashes or burnings there, his reply was, 'No, it is a lie.'

Shown Exhibit 27 – the card bearing the words 'Break Connection with England' and 'Undo the Conquest' – which had been found in his bedroom, plus the card which read 'From officers and members of the Betsy Grey branch, *Cumann-na-mban*', Hewitt admitted that that organization was 'the Ladies Auxiliary of the IRA, or something'. The card was given to his wife at a place where she went dancing together with a present when they were married, and when he was shown an IRA song commencing with the words, 'Ireland is calling her children, defend me, serve me or die' he was unable to say how that got into the house.

Regarding Richards' digging of the pit under the stairs, he said he knew nothing about it until it was finished; when his wife mentioned it, he complained to Richards.

'Did you hear the witness, Dove Gibbons, say that she saw men emptying buckets at the back door and that sometimes there were three men and sometimes four?' asked Mr O'Sullivan.

'The witness was quite wrong', replied Hewitt.

'The witness said it was done at weekends, is that quite wrong, too?'

'Yes.'

'You would be at home at weekends?'

'I would. The witness in Coventry got in the witness box and said the man next door helped make that pit too and he carried buckets of stuff. That woman did not say that in this box, but she said it in Coventry so that shows you that the woman is making up a fake.'

Having said that the charge against him was a frame-up, Hewitt was asked if he had a soldering set and he replied, 'No.'

'There was a soldering set found in your house', said Mr O'Sullivan. 'Did you say to the police officers when you were asked about this matter, "The soldering set is mine"?'

Hewitt replied, 'I said, "The tools belong to me".'

'Did you say to the officers on 28 August, "I have never seen the clock keys before. I know nothing about electric batteries"?'

'I did', replied Hewitt.

'Did you say, "That is my soldering kit but I have never used it"?'

'I said, "Them tools belong to me".'

'Look at Exhibit 44. Is that signed by you?'

'Yes.'

'Is the last sentence above your signature, "That is my soldering kit but I have never used it"?'

'If I said that, I have been a bit upset at the time and I have made a mistake.'

'Did you say that?'

'I must have said that. It is wrote down.'

'You signed your name immediately below that sentence?'

'Yes.'

'Was it read over to you before you signed it?'

'Yes.'

A little later, Hewitt was asked, 'When did you first become aware that white powder, potassium chlorate, was in your house?'

'I could not exactly tell you the date nor the day, but my wife got at me about it. She thought there was powder in a case and she thought it was explosives. I said it could not be explosives if it was powder.'

'Did she tell you that you ought to get rid of Jim Richards?'

'She did.'

'Did she say she would not stay in the house at night if she was sure it was explosives?'

'She did.'

'Did you warn her not to go on messages for Richards or for any men who might call?'

'Yes.'

'Had men been calling?'

'As far as I heard.'

'Why did you warn your wife not to go messages for the men that called?'

'Well, when my wife started to tell me about the bag with powder in it I had a bit of suspicion and of course I passed it off.'

Hewitt agreed that he had told his wife that she could return to Ireland without him, but then he was asked, 'Did you tell your wife, "You are innocent and if there is any trouble, I will take responsibility"?'

'My wife has made a mistake in that. I said to my wife when she told me about the suitcase and the powder that if it was explosives and the police came here that she would be innocent and I would be taking responsibility for having them in the house.' He then added, 'That is, if they were explosives.'

Asked why he had never asked Richards if the white powder was explosives, Hewitt replied, 'Well, it did not concern me.'

It appears there were frequent arguments between Hewitt and his wife regarding the presence of Richards, and when Mr O'Sullivan asked, 'Did she tell you if anything happened she would never shield you?' Hewitt replied, 'Yes.'

He admitted making a slab for the pit under the stairs and having filled it in, at about 9.00pm on Thursday, 24 August. But although he admitted seeing 'the strange man' he denied emphatically that it was on the night of 24 August, when others had said he arrived at Clara Street. He said that man arrived on the Tuesday or Wednesday, and that on the Thursday night, when Mrs Hewitt and Mrs O'Hara took the baby out in the pram and then returned to see Hewitt, Richards and 'the strange man' together, he was in bed. 'My wife has got confused there on account of the trouble she has been in, and she has mixed me up with him, or something round about that. She says things there that are quite wrong.'

Hewitt was unable to account for the potassium chlorate found in the pocket of his trench coat, saying, 'I might have picked them up off the floor and put them in my pocket but I could not say how they got there.'

'I suggest you were aware that explosives were being stored in your house?' said Mr O'Sullivan.

'No.'

'I suggest you were aware and cooperating on the night of 24 August when the preparations were being made?'

'No.'

'And that you allowed your soldering set to be used for the making of the bomb that was in preparation?'

'I have no soldering set, so I could not allow anything I have not got to be used to make anything. There was never no bomb made at my house to my knowledge, and I have never had anything to do with the making of a bomb.'

And that was the case for Joseph Hewitt.

* * *

Brigid O'Hara was next. With Mr Winning leading her through her evidence, she described the family arrangements (which included Jim Richards) at Clare Street, and she recalled that when she had raised a query regarding the pit dug out underneath the stairs, he had told her, 'It's for a bit of a dump.'

She described meeting Barnes for the first time on Monday, 21 August, when he came to the house and asked her to buy a suitcase for him and get it wrapped up in brown paper, which she did, handing him the 2s 6d in change, plus the receipt.

She also described the incident of returning the flour bags her daughter had purchased, of giving the refund to Barnes and how, the following day, Richards had gone with Dominic Adams to buy a bicycle and mentioned the conversation when Richards returned.

More importantly, she gave evidence that on the Thursday, Barnes returned to the house carrying a small suitcase and that later he, Richards and her son-in-law all examined an open parcel: 'It was like a white powder in it, like salt.'

On the following day, she described seeing 'the stranger', whom she had seen for the first time the previous evening, arrive at the house carrying a brown paper parcel. When Richards left later that morning to collect the bicycle and she asked him what he wanted it for, he had replied, 'You will know later.'

Whilst waiting for Richards to return with the bicycle, the stranger appeared flustered, asked the time and said, 'I wonder what is keeping Richards; he is very long.' When he did return, the men had a parcel 'like a boot box' which they were working on before it was tied up, and the stranger left with it.

Following the explosion at Broadgate, when Mrs O'Hara brought the newspapers home and mentioned the outrage to Richards, his alleged reply was, 'That is the bomb we made up in the front bedroom and it went off on time.'

If that was correct, it was one of the most damning pieces of evidence in the trial. However, when it came to cross-examination, Mrs O'Hara was a complete disaster. She contradicted herself ludicrously, time and again, and whether this was because she was panicking, imagining a noose being slipped around her 49-year-old neck, because of stupidity or because of a desire to stretch the truth to its limits in order to treat the jury to the version of events that she wanted them to believe, it's difficult to say.

Her testimony could have been regarded as comical, if not downright hilarious, had it not been for the fact that Brigid O'Hara, together with the other four defendants was facing a capital charge – she and all of them were fighting for their lives.

The first to cross-examine her was Mr Jenkins, who appeared for Barnes and Richards.

'In your statement you never said that you saw the three men, Jim Richards, Peter Barnes and Joe Hewitt examining the parcel, did you?' he asked.

'Yes, I did', she replied.

'Is this what you said: "After Barnes had gone I went into the scullery to get a drink and saw Richards opening the parcel"?'

'That is incorrect. That was later on in the night, but earlier in the night the three men were there.'

'You said that you saw Richards opening the parcel?'

'No, the three men opened the parcel.'

'Why did you say, "After Barnes had gone I went into the scullery to get a drink and saw Richards opening the parcel"? Why did you not say at that time, "I saw the three men examining the parcel"?'

'I swear I saw the three men examining the parcel.'

'Why did you not say that in your statement?'

'I did say that in the statement.'

'You have heard this statement read at least twice. Do you recollect what you said?'

'I know what I said.'

'Let us see what else you said. On the Friday, did you say this: "Before going he [Richards] said to me, 'I am going for the bicycle which Adams ordered'?" Did you say that?'

'No. He did not say that.'

'Why did you put that in the statement?'

'I did not put it in the statement.'

'Can you read the statement?'

'I cannot read very well.'

'I am reading to you what you said at the time: "Before going, he said to me, 'I am going for the bicycle which Adams ordered'." You say he did not say that?'

'No, not to me.'

And so it went on, with Mrs O'Hara continually contradicting herself; she was a complete nightmare to her own counsel, the prosecuting counsel and the other defence barristers.

Cross-examined by Mr Lyons, who appeared for Joseph Hewitt and needed to distance his client from the assertion, 'That is the bomb *we* made', the inconsistencies and denials continued, and then she was asked, 'According to this statement, this is what you said: "I realized the position and said to him, 'My God, it is terrible to have all these people killed and wounded; it is the bomb you made'." According to this statement, that is what you said to Richards? That is wrong?'

In a moment of deliberate misunderstanding or complete imbecility, Mrs O'Hara replied, 'Well, I hardly made a bomb. I would hardly go and say I made a bomb when I did not make it.'

Wearily, Mr Justice Singleton asked, 'Do you follow what learned counsel means?' to which Mrs O'Hara replied, 'No, I do not.'

'He shows you that in the statement which you signed, you told the police that you said to Richards, "My God, it is terrible to have all these people killed and wounded, that is the bomb you made"?'

'How could I say that when I did not know he had made a bomb?'

'It appears that you said that to the police?'

'No, I did not.'

'Do I understand you to say now that what took place was that you said, "It is terrible to have all these people killed and wounded", and he said, "That is the bomb we made"?'

'No. He said, "That is the bomb I made".'

With the waters well and truly muddied, Mr Lyons sat down, grateful at least that with her final words it appeared that the plural had been omitted from the bomb-making, thereby giving his client a partial escape route. Mr Lyons could only hope that when Mrs O'Hara was cross-examined by Mr Ward for the prosecution, no further oral cats would be let out of the bag.

In fact, Mr Lyons' fears were unjustified. Her only reference to her son-in-law was to the lining of the pit underneath the stairs, which Hewitt had already admitted. For the rest, she either blamed Richards or professed to having lapses of memory, and the prosecution did little to press home Mrs O'Hara's alleged culpability in the plot; with regard to who said what in respect of the purchase of the flour bags, Mrs O'Hara's memory was at fault once more.

As Mrs O'Hara was mercifully allowed to totter from the witness box, the last of the defendants, Mary Hewitt, took her place.

Examined by her counsel, Mr Winning, Mrs Hewitt described her marital circumstances and stated that the incriminating card from *Cumann-na-mban* came with a wedding present, a tablecloth, from a girlfriend. Her marriage to the hard-working Joseph Hewitt had been a happy one, and he had taken her out every night until the arrival of Richards – after which Richards was her husband's companion in the evenings.

So Richards was going to be made the villain of the piece; but in doing so, it was necessary for her to incriminate her husband. Having said that she had seen Richards opening a suitcase in the scullery, a suitcase containing white powder, she was asked, 'Did you say anything when you saw the white powder?'

'I never spoke to Richards about it. I spoke to my husband that night. I told him I saw white powder with Jim Richards in a case and I asked him what it was. He would not answer me. He would not tell me what the powder was . . . I asked him about a couple of days after whether that was explosive and he would not tell me; he told me that if I liked, I could go back to Ireland and that he would allow me £1 a week.'

Mrs Hewitt went on to say that she had asked her husband several times to get rid of Richards.

'What did he say?' asked Mr Winning.

'Well, he was a bit nasty with me. He just told me to get out.'

'Out of the house or out of England?'

'Out of his life.'

When she saw Richards digging the hole under the stairs Mrs Hewitt asked what he was doing, and he refused to tell her.

Mr Justice Singleton asked, 'Why did you let him dig a hole in your house?' to which she replied, 'Because if I had interfered with him, my husband would have been angry with me.'

Describing seeing Barnes for the first (and only) time on Monday, 21 August, she described him and Richards as being 'quite friendly, as if they knew one another'.

Regarding the acquisition of the flour bags, Mrs Hewitt told the court that it was Richards who asked her to purchase them, and that when she returned with the unsatisfactory items, both Barnes and Richards were present.

On the Thursday evening, when she returned from work at about 8.00pm, she asked her mother the whereabouts of her husband and was told he was upstairs. When she ascended the stairs, there was her husband in Richards' room with 'a strange man'; this was in complete contradiction to the evidence her husband had given.

The following day, when Mrs Hewitt came home for lunch at about 12.25pm she went upstairs to her bedroom; Richards and the strange man were there, she saw white powder and some tools on a box and asked what they were doing, and Richards told her they would not be long. Richards came downstairs in a hurry, saying he was going to get a bicycle. The strange man later asked Mrs Hewitt the time and upon being told it was five to one, 'He said Richards was a long time and he seemed agitated.'

But after Richards returned and both men went up again into Mrs Hewitt's bedroom, she followed them up the stairs and saw 'a brown paper parcel, a bit bigger than a boot box tied up in the middle of the floor'.

After she had returned to work she heard about the explosion from a colleague.

'When you heard there had been an explosion, did your mind go back to what you had seen in the house, or not?' asked Mr Winning, to which Mrs Hewitt replied, 'It did.'

'Perhaps you can tell my lord and the members of the jury why you should connect your house with that explosion?'

'Because when the girl showed me the paper it said about the bomb being placed in a bicycle.'

Asking about the statement she made to the police, Mr Winning said, 'Is there anything in that statement you wish to alter or withdraw?'

Mrs Hewitt replied, 'Yes. I said in that statement I knew what this man was doing, they were going to cause an explosion – well, I did not know.'

'Is this the passage you are referring to: "I did not go near the parcel. I was upset as I knew what they had done and were going to make an explosion, but I did not know where"?'

'Yes, that is right.'

'Later on, you say, "If I had known for sure what Richards and the other man were doing that morning and where the bomb was going to be placed, I would have surely told the police"?'

'Yes.'

In cross-examination by Mr Lyons it was made clear that at some stage her husband had expressed disapproval of Richards, telling her not to 'go messages for Richards' or any of the men who called, and that the only person she saw using the tools was the strange man.

'I am putting this to you, that you have never seen your husband handle any of this white powder at all?' asked Mr Lyons, and Mrs Hewitt dutifully replied, 'My husband never had any of that white powder on his person.'

'Or ever handled it?'

'No.'

'Or ever boxed it or unboxed it?'

'I never saw my husband with it.'

There was some fairly ineffectual cross-examination by Mr Ward for the prosecution which simply covered old ground, and with that, the case for the prisoners was closed.

But there was one point that, strangely, was not covered. All the other prisoners were asked if they were members of the IRA and all denied it (with the exception of Richards, who admitted it) – but not Mary Hewitt. And yet, by imputation, she had the strongest links with *Cumann-na-mban*, the incriminating card having been found in her bedroom. It begs the question, if she was not affiliated to that organization, why should they send her a card? It was odd – rather like an orthodox Jew sending a greetings card to a member of the National Front. Well, there you have it.

Chapter 28

The Summings-up and the Verdicts

The prosecution and the defence summed up the evidence, with Mr O'Sullivan saying little about the evidence against Richards, since the jury would have interpreted his evidence for themselves. Barnes, with his incriminating 'Dear Jim' letter, had gone up and down the country distributing the 'stuff', and Hewitt, Richards' bosom companion, had told his wife to 'get out of his life' and had known the where and when of the conspiracy to kill innocent people. He accepted the word of Mrs Hewitt and admitted that Mrs O'Hara was the first to tell the truth to the police, although she had left it to the last moment.

Mr Jenkins for Barnes and Richards made a particularly lacklustre speech, saying that Barnes had simply come to Coventry looking for work and that although Richards was the storekeeper for the explosives, his instructions were that human life was not to be endangered, and he was very sorry that it had been.

He also said that the bomb might have been poorly made, that it might not have been intended to explode when it did and that the jolting of the bicycle could have upset the mechanism.

Additionally, he stated there were two 2.30s – am and pm. This was what the actual bomber, Joby O'Sullivan, would say, many years later – that the bomb was supposed to detonate at 2.30 in the morning, thereby upholding the IRA's strict dictum regarding the sanctity of human life. Since he stated he intended to deposit the bomb at the police station, in those halcyon days when police stations were not only open 24 hours a day but were also fully staffed, this assertion can be effectively demolished.

But just to put into the waste-paper bin this oft-trotted-out piece of hokum, used extensively during this IRA bombing campaign – that bombs were timed to explode in the early hours of the morning – consider the following.

The alarm clocks used were analogue timepieces, that is, with rotating hands and a dial marked one to twelve.

Digital clocks display time on a 24-hour basis, in numerals or symbols.

The first digital alarm clock was not registered until 1956 in the United States of America.

Therefore, when the alarm was set on an analogue clock – as it was on the occasion of the Broadgate bombing – at, say, 1.00pm for 2.30, it was going to go off an hour and a half later; just like the three alarm-clock bombs which were set in London, the same day, to detonate at 2.30 at New Scotland Yard, the Bank of England and Westminster Abbey and which Detective Sergeant Len Crawford was fortunately on hand to de-activate. So no wonder that the heroic Joby O'Sullivan was jittery when Richards was slow in returning with his bicycle to transport the bomb.

Next, Mr Lyons for Joseph Hewitt – with no connection with the IRA – stated there was no evidence that he had taken part in the making of the bomb and added, 'I commend this man to you as no assassin but a tool and a fool if you like.'

Lastly, Mr Winning for the two women stated that they depended on Joseph Hewitt for 'life, lodging, board and happiness'. Was it likely that because they suspected that there were explosives in the house they would go to the police? It was impossible, he said, to conceive that the women, one with a small child, were taking any part in what was going on. It was a well-structured and a pretty convincing argument.

Mr Justice Singleton's summing-up lasted two hours and fifty minutes. It was remarkably fair and detailed. In explaining the law to the jury, he told them, quoting a stated case:

> If, when a prisoner did the act, he must, as a reasonable man have contemplated that death or grievous bodily harm was likely to result, he was guilty of murder but that if he could not, as a reasonable man, have contemplated either of those consequences, he was guilty only of manslaughter. If a bomb charged with some pounds of high explosive is placed in a street by day, or if it is placed in a building by night, must not everyone contemplate that it is at least likely to do serious injury to someone or to kill them? Can those who are proved to use such an appliance be heard to say: We did not think it was likely to cause any grievous bodily harm or death, therefore we ought not to be convicted of murder but only of manslaughter? The question again, is one for you. It is raised by the learned counsel, and far be it from me to trespass upon your province, but I do not disguise, or seek to disguise from you that I find it extraordinarily difficult to see how anyone using a bomb, inside or outside, particularly when it is placed in the street, how it can be said that those who used it for that purpose cannot have thought that grievous bodily harm or danger to life was likely. I do not withdraw the suggestion of counsel from you, but it may occur to you that in the evidence

> of each of these accused it is more likely to concern you as a question of murder or nothing, rather than to give rise to that in-between stage presented to you as you have heard it this morning. That is all I desire to say to you upon the law, apart from reminding you again that those matters which I have mentioned, have to be proved to your satisfaction before you can find a verdict against any one of them and the case against each one must be considered separately.

Dealing with the evidence against Barnes, he mentioned that Barnes had said he knew nothing about the purchase of the flour sacks but that the receipt for their purchase was in his possession and he gave it to his fiancée, Miss Keane, in London, to look after for him. There were the three packets, allegedly purchased in Oxford Street, found to contain potassium chlorate, the same chemical found in the suitcase he had allegedly lent to MacMahon as well as in particles on his hat, raincoat and dungarees. Mr Justice Singleton expressed incredulity regarding Barnes' copying of the letter from the notes which MacMahon had supposedly written out in the street, the deeply incriminating 'Dear Jim' letter of which Barnes had told Detective Sergeant Hughes, 'That is just a letter I wrote to a friend.'

'Was not MacMahon in Coventry?' asked the Judge rhetorically. 'The answer to Barnes' story must be no, must it not? Who was in Coventry? Barnes. Who got back from Coventry late that night? Barnes. Who then is writing that letter? Is there more than one answer, or is the answer the only answer you could put to it, really? Barnes.'

Richards' case was discussed at length, with the Judge reminding the jury, 'You notice how he put it – "I think it was a mistake the bomb went off in the middle of the day"; at that time, not that a bomb went off, but that it went off in the middle of the day . . . He knew the bomb was being made, saw the parts of it; he himself had a setter for the clock in his pocket when he was arrested. Did he know? Was he a party to that which was being done? Was it something which he must have known was dangerous to life?'

Next, Joseph Hewitt who, said the Judge, being the tenant of 25 Clara Street must surely have known what was going on. The potassium chlorate in his trench coat, the pit under the stairs and his explanations regarding the use of the tools found in his house which, said the Judge, 'were so foolish, you may think that either he is not being very accurate or else he is a fool – I almost said a half-wit – but these are matters for you, and you heard them . . . You may well think that Hewitt knew a good deal of what was going on. You saw him in the witness box. Did it occur to you at all that he had a more frightened look than some others?'

But in conclusion, Mr Justice Singleton said, 'I direct you that knowledge on his part of itself is not sufficient to justify a conviction for murder. There must be active participation in what was being done, coupled with the knowledge of what the likely result was.'

Finally, the Judge dealt with the cases of Mrs O'Hara and Mary Hewitt:

> They are mother and daughter. They may have known a great deal. They may have known a good deal more than they have said. You have heard them both give their evidence in the box, apart from one or two small occasions, clearly. You may or you may not have been impressed by it . . . I say again, that I think that you would hesitate a long time before you found those two women guilty of murder. It is for you and not for me.

The jury retired to consider their verdict at 4.10pm; they returned thirty-one minutes later to find Barnes and Richards both guilty of murder. Mrs O'Hara and Mary and Joseph Hewitt were acquitted.

The Clerk of the Assize said:

> Prisoners at the bar, Peter Barnes and James Richards, you stand convicted of murder; have you anything to say why judgement of death should not be pronounced upon you, according to law?

To this, Barnes replied:

> I would like to say as I am going before my God, as I am condemned to death, I am innocent and later, I am sure it will all come out that I had neither hand, act or part in it. That is all I intend to say.

Richards was silent, but as the Judge, with the black cap on his head was about to pass sentence, he interrupted with the words:

> My lord, before you pass sentence I have something to say. I wish to state, my lord, before you pass sentence of death on me, I wish to thank sincerely the gentlemen who have defended me during my trial and I wish to state that the part I took in these explosions since I came to England, I have done in a

> just cause. As a soldier of the Irish Republican Army, I am not afraid to die, as I am doing it for a just cause. I say in conclusion, God bless Ireland and God bless the men who have fought and died for her. Thank you, my lord.

It was Mr Justice Singleton's solemn duty to intone these dreadful words:

> Peter Barnes and James Richards, the jury have returned a true verdict according to the evidence. The sentence of the Court upon each of you is that you be taken from this place to a lawful prison and thence to a place of execution and that you be there hanged by the neck until you are dead; and that your body be afterwards buried within the precincts of the prison in which you shall have been last confined before your execution and may the Lord have mercy on your souls.

As the chaplain murmured, 'Amen' and the prisoners were led off to the cells, the Judge recalled Chief Inspector Parker and told him:

> I should like to express my admiration of the care and trouble which has been taken in this case and of the fairness too, of the other police officers concerned.

This acclamation was later echoed by the Metropolitan Police Commissioner, who awarded Parker yet another rare high commendation.

There were other indictments in respect of the three acquitted prisoners which, having been brought, had to be disposed of.

On 15 December they appeared, again before Mr Justice Singleton, charged with the murders of the four other people killed at Broadgate. Mr O'Sullivan offered no evidence on this indictment, and the Judge directed the jury to find them not guilty. They were also charged with five offences under the Explosive Substances Act, and on the Judge's direction, the jury found both women not guilty. However, it was not considered desirable that Joseph Hewitt should be tried at that assize, and therefore, on 6 February 1940 at the Old Bailey (and after careful consideration) no evidence was offered on a charge of maliciously causing an explosion and having explosive substances in his possession, and he was discharged.

When one looks at the evidence surrounding Joseph Hewitt, it is bewildering to see how he could have been acquitted of all charges. Since arriving in Coventry, his lodgers – at two addresses – had been at least two active IRA men, as well as Richards. At Clara Street, in addition to Barnes, there had been a steady stream of IRA visitors to his address, including 'Halfpenny' Jones. Despite evidence to the contrary, Hewitt had denied mixing cement in his garden but admitted making the concrete slab for the pit inside his house – the same pit of which he had initially denied any knowledge. He also denied any knowledge of how the tract, 'Break Connection with England' or the IRA song came to be in his bedroom, he disputed that the used soldering kit was his, after admitting it, and there was the evidence of the potassium chlorate being found in the pocket of his greatcoat. His wife had said that he had been in the company of Richards and 'the strange man' – that he denied – and when his mother-in-law had said that he and the same two men had examined the parcel containing the white powder, that, too, he denied. And although his wife had repeatedly asked him what the white powder was, he refused to tell her.

There may be a great many people reading these words who could come to the conclusion that Joseph Hewitt was an extremely fortunate fellow to be acquitted.

Be that as it may, he, his wife and mother-in-law were all deported to Ireland.

Chapter 29

The Appeals

There was outrage in Dublin amongst the ranks of the IRA; how could two of their innocent soldiers be convicted of murder when they weren't even there?

An exact parallel can be drawn between that case and the bomb explosion at the Ariana Grande concert in the Manchester Arena on 22 May 2017. The person who detonated that bomb (and blew himself to pieces) was Salman Abedi – no doubt about that. But his brother, Hasham Abedi, was just as guilty. He sourced the ingredients for the bomb, using email and online shopping accounts, and helped construct it. Hasham brought home an empty oil drum from his place of work to store the items; he ordered 55 litres of hydrogen peroxide and 16 litres of sulphuric acid for the bomb, plus 6 kilos of nails and 2,000 screws to use as shrapnel, as well as purchasing a car to transport it. When the bomb detonated, killing 22 people and injuring almost 1,000 others, Hasham Abedi was not even in the country – he was in Tripoli. But he was just as culpable as his brother, and on 17 March 2020 a jury at the Old Bailey took just five hours to find him guilty of all twenty-two murders and attempted murders.

So was consideration given by the IRA to offering up Joby O'Sullivan to the British authorities as being the person who oversaw the building and priming of the bomb, as well as planting it in Broadgate? Well, no.

What about Dominic Adams, who had played a decisive part in the plot? No, now he was chief of staff of the IRA he was too valuable to be spared.

Naturally, the two condemned men had to appeal, using the British legal system which they held in contempt, although on this occasion solicitors from Dublin were briefed and there is a possibility that IRA funds were used.

The appeal was heard at the London Court of Appeal (Criminal Division) on 22 January 1940 before the Lord Chief Justice, Lord Hewart, together with Mr Justice Hilbery and Mr Justice Hallett.

There could have not been a fairer, more open-minded Lord Chief Justice than Lord Hewart, who had held that post for eighteen years. Then aged seventy, he had been a Liberal Member of Parliament, and during his tenure as Lord Chief Justice he had quashed the conviction of one William Herbert Wallace for the murder of his wife. This was not on a point of law, or because of misdirection by the trial judge. The conviction was quashed because Lord Hewart felt that it was not supported by the weight of the evidence; in other words, that the jury was wrong.

It caused a storm of controversy, but Lord Hewart, whose axiom was 'Not only must justice be done, it must also be seen to be done', stuck to his guns. Therefore, the appellants must have felt that they were in with a fighting chance.

The grounds of appeal were that the Judge's refusal to grant the men a separate trial from the two women and his refusal to withdraw the women's case at the close of the prosecution had prejudiced their case, and that he had failed to point out the need for corroboration of the women's evidence.

In the case of Barnes, the Judge had failed to point out to the jury that Barnes' statement that he was not (and never had been) a member of the IRA had gone unchallenged. It was probably just as well, since Barnes had lied his head off during the trial, having joined *Fianna Éireann* at the aged of fourteen and three years later, in 1924, the IRA. Furthermore, he was the among the first to volunteer for active service in England at the commencement of the bombing campaign and was appointed Transport Officer, operating between Glasgow, Liverpool and London.

Moreover, it was said that Barnes' arrival in Coventry was not connected with any IRA activity, and he had no knowledge of any proposed explosions.

In Richards' case, his additional grounds of appeal were that the Judge had failed to point out the inconsistencies in Mrs O'Hara's evidence with regard to her police statement; this was a bit rich, considering that Richards admitted on oath that much of his statement to police was a pack of lies. Also, he had no knowledge that the bomb was going to be placed in a position where life could be endangered and, with barefaced effrontery, he claimed that had he known he would have taken steps to prevent such a calamity.

The appeal had as many holes in it as a colander.

The trial Judge had pointed out to the jury on three separate occasions the discrepancies in the women's evidence. A reason for not trying the defendants together was when one defendant sought to implicate another, said the appellants, but the evidence of the women was that they knew nothing about the plot. It was said that the Judge had failed to direct the jury that they should clear their minds of prejudice, especially since Richards had admitted being a member of the IRA; but, said the Court of Appeal, when had it been the law that a direction was defective because the Judge did not remind the jury that it should act without prejudice?

And concerning 'corroboration' and 'accomplice', all three defence counsel had given lengthy summings-up but those words were not uttered by any of them. Various points of law from stated cases were discussed (as they had been during the trial), but on 23 January 1940 the Lord Chief Justice delivered a judgement which finished with the words:

> In the opinion of this Court, on the facts in this case, the necessity for a warning with regards to the evidence of an accomplice did not arise. Even if it had arisen, it is manifest that there was ample and cogent evidence otherwise which made it clear what the verdict ought to be. There was ample evidence for that purpose apart from that which is said, wrongly as it appears to the Court, to have required corroboration. The summing-up of the learned Judge was careful, systematic and full and in our opinion there is no ground for the contention that it was defective in any of the respects referred to in the grounds of appeal.
>
> In our view there is no ground at all for the appeals which have been urged, and they are dismissed.

On Monday, 29 January, the Attorney General refused an appeal to the House of Lords, and President de Valera issued appeals, first to the Secretary of State for Dominion Affairs, Anthony Eden, saying, 'If these men are executed, the relations between our peoples will almost certainly deteriorate', and then, along with the Protestant Archbishop of Dublin, to Prime Minister Neville Chamberlain, asking each of them to intervene in the judicial process. The *New York Times*' view – with, no doubt, a healthy input of rhetoric from *Clan na Gael* – was:

> Opinion here is either that two innocent men will hang or that it is the partition of Ireland by the British who forced these young Irishmen to perpetrate such outrages. Anglo-Irish relations could markedly deteriorate through the hanging of these men.

Tom Barry, the Chief of Staff of the IRA, heroically offered to go to England and take Barnes' and Richards' place in prison until they could stand a 'fair trial'. Barry, who was said to have been opposed to the bombing campaign, had in the first six months of 1921 shot dead sixteen civilians accused of being informants, something he gloried in. In 1936 he was implicated in the murder of Vice-Admiral Henry Somerville, something he denied. But although his gallant gesture must have warmed the cockles of many a terrorist's heart, Barry knew full well that his empty offer would never be taken up by the British Government. This was in fact an exercise in hypocrisy, because he already knew that Joby O'Sullivan was the bomber. O'Sullivan had told him so – that is, if Barry wasn't already aware of it.

Former Dublin Brigade leader Simon Donnelly told a crowd, to their near-hysterical delight:

> We know very well what outcome we want to this war. We want the enemy, who has kept our people in bondage for 700 years and who continues to pour insults on us, to be pitilessly vanquished. Until such time as the Irish Republic is established, Ireland's youth will continue to sacrifice itself. If the Government does not bring foreign overlordship to an end, others must be entrusted with the task.

It made no difference whatsoever. The Prime Minister and the Home Secretary had made their minds up: Barnes and Richards would hang.

At 8.30am on 7 February 1940, the Roman Catholic priest who had administered the last rites left Winson Green prison, Birmingham, and at 9.00am the two men were hanged, simultaneously.

There was a strong police presence around the prison, but it was not needed. There were no demonstrations; the several hundred people who were present drifted away after notices were posted outside the prison at 9.07am that the sentences of death had been duly carried out.

That morning, the blinds were drawn at the Dublin Mansion House, and the committee who had worked for a reprieve met and issued a statement saying that England had demonstrated she cared nothing for the goodwill of Ireland. A march arrived at their offices carrying a black flag bearing a skull and crossbones, and a deputation met with de Valera's private secretary.

And following the last simultaneous hanging at Winson Green, the two men were buried in the confines of the prison.

Chapter 30

The Aftermath – Explosions and Arrests

It's now time to return to the activities of the IRA following the arrests in Coventry. On 11 September 1939, the Belfast express collided with a large coping stone laid on the LMS main line south of Hunton Bridge tunnel in Hertfordshire, and five weeks later, the Blackpool to London express struck iron rail chairs and a sleeper, which this time had been placed on the north side of the bridge.

There was a spate of telephone cable severings in London which coincided with incendiarism at a number of pillar boxes, also in London. These were at the junction of Hanover Street and Regent Street, at the corner of Jermyn Street and the Haymarket and also in Cockspur Street, all of which were extinguished by the Fire Brigade throwing sand on them; in the third fire, the remains of a balloon were found. A fourth fire at Upper St Martin's Lane was only discovered once it had burned itself out. The incendiarism spread to trains carrying mailbags, on the Euston to Wolverhampton and Euston to Liverpool express.

A party of terrorists took advantage of the wartime blackout on the night of 18 November by driving around in a taxi and depositing six acid bombs in London's West End. Two exploded at 8.30pm, in the Car Mart at the corner of Piccadilly and Park Lane and at Carreras, the tobacconists in Piccadilly, near Burlington House. As fire engines reached those two premises, two more bombs exploded, one at Scott's outfitters in Upper Regent Street and the other in an empty shop in Lower Regent Street half an hour later. An unexploded bomb was found on the pavement in Park Lane, next to the bank which had been wrecked by the explosion on 24 June, and a second one in a shattered shop window, also in Park Lane. Police Constable Bishop-Laggett from Vine Street police station, with great coolness and bravery, grabbed hold of it, ran across Park Lane and threw it into Hyde Park.

On the evening of Friday, 24 November, through till the early hours of the following morning, there was a succession of explosions – two police boxes and a telephone kiosk in Harrow Road, as well as a number of telephone kiosks near Marble Arch, were badly damaged. There was a fire in a pillar box and five telephone boxes were damaged in Birmingham; an explosive in a bin between two telephone boxes, detonated as a police officer approached – fortunately, he escaped injury.

The news of these explosions was immediately passed on to neighbouring police forces, and in Coventry a search was directly carried out which resulted in the discovery of a bomb behind a police telephone box outside the central fire station. The bomb, one of the balloon acid variety and contained in a coffee tin, was rendered harmless, and the Chief Constable of Coventry appealed to the local population to report any suspicious circumstances which came to their notice. Since the atrocity at Broadgate three months previously was still raw in their memories, it can be well imagined that that was a task which the public were only too happy to undertake.

Lord Dudley, the Midland Regional Defence Minister, was in consultation with the police chiefs within his remit on the Saturday morning, and at the same time a conference was held at Scotland Yard which resulted in Special Branch and Flying Squad officers raiding a number of suspect premises in North London and impolitely requesting the attendance of a number of persons at Cannon Row police station.

On 28 and 29 November there were more incidents: an explosion at Southampton's central railway station, another in the grounds of a building formerly used as a public library, and the severing of wiring in several more telephone kiosks. Parliament was informed that the costs of repairs came to £550.

* * *

Whatever possessed the IRA to send 16-year-old Brendan Behan to cause mischief in Liverpool, it can only be put down to the lack of available volunteers. Even at that tender age, Behan was susceptible to strong drink – he once famously said, 'I only drink on two occasions: when I'm thirsty and when I'm not' – and when under the influence in any number of public houses he had started spouting off about his proposed activities, this led Police Sergeant Earps to pay a visit on 1 December to his lodgings at Aubrey Street, Liverpool. There in a front bedroom he found Behan, holding a fountain-pen filler, standing by an open suitcase which contained a bottle of acid. Also in his possession were 20oz of potassium chlorate, sugar and sixteen balloons. Telling the sergeant that his name was Peter Russell and that he had only arrived from Dublin that morning, Behan claimed that 'the white powder' was for his ears and produced what purported to be a doctor's note to that effect. However, he later admitted to being a member of the IRA and that, given the chance, he intended to blow up buildings. Behan came from a family of republicans; as a boy he had joined the *Fianna Éireann* and was later recruited into the IRA. He had been trained in the use of explosives and earlier that year had been sent to London, where he was engaged in making up bombs.

He made a statement, in which he said:

> I have been sent over to take the places of Chris Kenneally, Nick Lynch and the others who have been arrested. I was to reorganize further operations in Liverpool. I intended to put bombs in big stores, Lewis' and Hughes', I think they call it. I was making some up to put in letterboxes tonight. I'm only sixteen and they can't do much with me.

When he appeared at Liverpool Assizes on 7 February 1940 he informed Mr Justice Hallett, 'I have no interest in the proceedings of the court', which was construed as a plea of not guilty. He did have sufficient interest to say that, with regard to his statement, 'I did not make such ridiculous assertions', but when he was found guilty, the Judge told him:

> Parliament, in recent years has taken an extremely lenient view of what ought to be done with young persons found guilty of offences. I cannot deal with you in a way I think you deserve, and I think you knew this before you started off on this expedition. You will go to Borstal detention for three years.

The account of Behan's arrest in his book *Borstal Boy* is markedly different to the facts as recounted at Liverpool Assizes.

* * *

There was more damage caused by incendiaries in Birmingham on 7 December; a woman was seen acting suspiciously in a clothing store, and after she left, a girl assistant searched a pile of goods where the woman had been standing and discovered two matchboxes, each containing a balloon incendiary bomb. Two hours later, half a dozen stalls in the Market Hall were found to be ablaze; over a period of thirty minutes it took the combined efforts of two air-raid wardens and the fire brigade to bring the fires under control.

On the day following the commencement of the trial of Barnes, Richards and others on 11 December, there were two cases of attempted incendiarism at an Oxford Street store, and three railway sleepers were dragged on to the Metropolitan railway lines at Rickmansworth; in neither instance was anyone injured, nor were injuries sustained two days later when incendiary devices exploded in a London cinema and at the Paramount and the Forum cinemas in Birmingham. In fact, they didn't even cause any panic.

With Christmas fast approaching, six postal incendiary units were found in the mail at Andover post office on 18 December, and two days later, another bomb, this one composed of gelignite, exploded at the entrance to Lewis' Stores, Corporation Street, Birmingham.

The following night, a parcel thought to be a Christmas present was found on a doorstep of a house in Cardiff; that, too, contained gelignite. On the same night, three incendiary bombs exploded in North London's Eversholt Street post office, where a worker was slightly burned. There were more explosions, this time at Paddington post office, where ten postal workers were injured, and a bomb was discovered at the Kingsway post office but caused no damage.

However, some 200 letters were damaged after five incendiary devices exploded at the sorting office of Birmingham's general post office. A temporary worker, a college student, received burns to his arms, but the fires were extinguished after workers smothered the flames with mailbags. More explosions occurred at a sorting room in a Wolverhampton post office and in a mailbag at the Great Western railway station.

At the end of the year, HM Inspectors of Explosives produced their sixty-fourth annual report, part of which dealt with the IRA campaign:

> During the year, 242 outrages or attempted outrages were reported to us from various parts of the country. Forty-one cases of illegal possession of explosives were also detected. These outrages caused the death of seven persons and 96 people were injured. The police made 128 arrests, 62 in London and 66 in the provinces. There were 96 convictions, 55 in London and 41 in the provinces. There is not the slightest doubt these outrages were part of a thoroughly well-organized conspiracy and the various persons taking part in it had received instructions of a very comprehensive nature.

And that, for 1939, was that. Even terrorists believe they have a right to celebrate Christmas.

Chapter 31

Terror in Oxford Street

The beginning of 1940 saw a lull in the IRA's bombing offensive, and there may have been several reasons for this. The previous month, a blackout speed restriction of 20 mph had been introduced which proved disadvantageous for terrorists wanting to make a quick getaway after a bombing expedition; and the rise in petrol prices could also have been injurious to the fragile IRA budget. Additionally, ration cards had been issued – sugar, bacon and butter were now on ration – which caused problems to those wanting to acquire a ration card or trying to obtain food without one. One more factor was that on 17 January 1940 the sub-zero weather caused the River Thames to freeze over for the first time in fifty-two years.

Extremely worrying for the terrorists was the fact that from 1 January Britain started conscripting two million men aged between nineteen and twenty-seven for military service; the thought of being questioned, with or without an identity card (they had been issued the previous September) was a chilling reminder to the IRA to stay out of the way.

So as well as speed restrictions to impede escape, a lack of food and freezing weather, the fear of being swept up to join the ranks of real soldiers was anathema to terrorists, and the IRA kept a low profile.

But with Christmas over, they felt that they really should renew their efforts, and on 2 February seven incendiary bombs were planted in the seats of buses belonging to the Birmingham Corporation. The first discovery was made by a cleaner at the Yardley Wood garage who noticed that a seat had been ripped open and found a small incendiary device hidden in the fabric; there was a sudden flash and the seat caught fire. Undeterred, the same cleaner found a second device in another bus, and the warning went out to other garages covered by the Corporation. One bomb was found at Harborne, one at Barford Street, another at Liverpool Street and two at the Midland Company's depot at Oldbury; fortunately, no one was injured.

Since it was felt – correctly – that nothing would save Barnes and Richards from the gallows, a series of explosions occurred as reprisals on 6 February, the day before their execution.

The first occurred at 11.40am, when a mail van from the Mount Pleasant sorting office arrived at Euston station. As the bags were being unloaded for dispatch to Liverpool and Manchester, one exploded, knocking to the ground the mail sorter carrying it and injuring him severely. Three other workers were also injured, and as they received first aid while waiting for an ambulance to take them to hospital, smoke was seen issuing from a second bag. There was panic among employees, passengers and passers-by, but all fortunately reached safety before the bag exploded.

At the GPO parcels sorting office at Hill Street, Birmingham, a postman emptying a bag of packages saw smoke rising from one of the bags before it exploded, injuring his face; a postal clerk's face was similarly burnt.

The explosion of a bomb contained in a brown paper parcel in the Newton Green sorting office, Manchester damaged a sorting trough, letters and parcels, and an unexploded incendiary bomb was found by an attendant in the main hall of the ground floor of the GPO at Liverpool; it was placed in a bucket of water.

A week passed without incident; then a bomb exploded at Rifle Crescent, Aston, Birmingham; windows were broken but no one was hurt. An hour later, however, another bomb which had been placed behind a glass showcase in the doorway of a shoe shop at the corner of Corporation Street and Bull Street exploded, injuring 24-year-old Charles Long, who was taken to hospital suffering from concussion.

In London, in the blackout on the evening of 22 February, there was an explosion in a cloakroom at Marble Arch at the corner of Bayswater Road and Hyde Park, where an Eric Tomlin was treated for shock. The blast was heard in Oxford Circus, and a sailor from HMS *Exeter* was stunned by the explosion. 'It sounded something like a depth charge going off and I was shaken for a moment', he said. A number of men from the cruiser *Ajax* as well as civilians rushed to the scene to help; and that was when the second bomb detonated.

It had been placed in a litter bin attached to a bus stop in Oxford Street. A middle-aged woman who was walking by caught the full force of the blast; she staggered on for a few paces and then collapsed. A young woman who was with her collapsed into the arms of two passing soldiers, having been blown to the ground; she repeatedly said, 'Don't take me away – I mustn't leave her!'

One of the soldiers had been accompanying 19-year-old Joyce Pearce, who said, 'We saw a vivid blue flash of flame. My friend grabbed me round the waist and pulled me several yards down the road to safety. When he found I was all right he ran back to help other men look after the injured woman.'

The explosion had shattered the windows of a whole block of shops, fragments of the bomb were discovered 50 yards away and passers-by were blown off their feet; women were screaming and several fainted. The scene was best described by Mr Alistair Mackintosh, a St John Ambulance man, who said:

> I was walking towards the shop when the bomb went off. A Red Cross man came staggering towards me and said, 'I am hit.' He fell to the pavement. I found that he had been seriously cut in the leg, head and hand and did my best to bandage him up. Then I found a woman leaning against the shop window and she said she had been struck in the leg. I examined her and found she had a large piece of metal about two inches long, embedded in her leg. It was certainly not glass and appeared to be a bomb fragment. With the metal still in her leg, she was assisted into an ambulance and taken to a hospital.

The man and the woman seen by Mr Mackintosh were the most seriously injured. The artery in the man's leg had been severed and he had lost a great deal of blood; the woman lost her leg.

In all, twelve people were injured by flying glass, including a war reserve policeman and Mr C. W. Rothwell, a taxi driver, who said, 'Bits of the litter bin hit me in the back.' Mr Rothwell's taxi was one of two that were hit by debris, which shattered their windows. Another man emerged from an amusement arcade as the bomb exploded; a piece of flying glass slashed him on the chin.

The injured were conveyed to St George's hospital, and a further three women and one man, all suffering from leg injuries, were detained at St Mary's hospital, Paddington.

Members of the public were heard to say, 'The people who did this deserve lynching.' They were sentiments that few would have disagreed with.

By coincidence, on the same day as the London bombings, a 15-year-old girl was released from Coventry and Warwickshire Hospital. She had been fourteen when, six months previously, she had been admitted to hospital, where she was treated for serious leg injuries. Her name was Muriel Timms and, as already mentioned, she had been grievously wounded in the bombing at Broadgate, Coventry. She was delighted that an ambulance was taking her home to Gregory Avenue, Green Lane, Coventry, although her joy was somewhat marred when traffic congestion forced the ambulance to stop in Broadgate, right at the scene of the explosion.

Chapter 32

Arrests – and the End of the Campaign

A week passed, and then there were incidents in Salford, where incendiaries exploded on buses within three days of each other, and two explosions in London, one at a store in Bayswater, another outside a Park Lane bank.

On 17 March, a bomb was thrown at a hut near Paddington Town Hall which was used as a dormitory for women telephone operators attached to the local ARP organization. Miraculously, none of the sleeping women was injured, although one had a lucky escape; she turned her head just as the explosion occurred and shards of broken glass embedded themselves in the pillow where her head had lain a split-second previously.

So who was responsible for the series of London bombings over the previous three weeks? Dan Keating was born in 1902 and joined the IRA in 1920. The following year, a Royal Irish Constabulary (RIC) officer was shot dead and Keating was thought to be involved, as he was five weeks later, when five more RIC officers were murdered. Five weeks after that, he was involved in a clash with the British Army – four soldiers were murdered. He was arrested and imprisoned (although not for those offences) during the next few years, and had later been instrumental in carrying out bomb outrages and establishing safe houses on the mainland but had then gone back to Dublin; in January 1940 he had been ordered to return to London. He established a unit comprised of himself, Terence Perry and Jack Daly, and their campaign commenced on 22 February at Marble Arch and Oxford Street. However, Perry was absent for the bomb attack on Paddington Town Hall. He had been instructed to travel 126 miles north.

But on the same day as that attack – coincidentally, St Patrick's Day – important arrests were made. These would be the last IRA arrests of this campaign, and they occurred at 39 Rupert Street, Nechells, Birmingham. James Hasty, also known as Arthur Fitzgerald, and Joseph O'Hanlon had lodged at that address since 27 January 1940; their landlady, Mrs Emily Wicks, charged each of them the princely sum of 6s 0d per week.

Hasty had left the house for a short absence but had returned on 15 March carrying a blue suitcase. It must have excited someone's interest, because in the absence of both Hasty and O'Hanlon, the premises was visited on 17 March by Detective Sergeant Hammond and Constable Riles, who searched the men's room and found the suitcase which had a raincoat belt around it and a label reading, 'Mr Perry, Belfast, Northern Ireland'.

Inside the unlocked suitcase was an attaché case which was found to contain twenty sticks of gelignite, a coil of fuse, eleven packets of powder weighing about 1lb each and 108 balloons. In addition, there was a five-chambered .32 revolver, a twelve-chambered .25 revolver and 105 rounds of assorted ammunition.

These items were removed, and later that evening, Sergeant Hammond returned together with Detective Inspector Mark Sellick and Detective Sergeant Bantock. Hidden from view, they waited until Hasty and O'Hanlon walked into the hallway, together with the 19-year-old absentee from London, Terence Perry. O'Hanlon told Mrs Wicks, 'We have a new lodger for you.'

'All right,' said the thrifty Mrs Wicks. 'Pay your rent!'

But there was little time for that, because the detectives swiftly nabbed the three men. A further search of the room was made which revealed fourteen detonators wrapped in a pair of socks in a washstand and three glass test tubes in an envelope addressed to Perry at a Belfast address. The men were led away to where accommodation would be provided for them at far cheaper rates than those demanded by Mrs Wicks.

They were a dangerous trio. Hasty had first come to the notice of the Royal Ulster Constabulary in connection with illegal drilling. Following the murder of a member of RUC, Constable Charles Anderson, on 9 October 1933, he and fifty other suspects had been arrested, and on 7 November 1933, for refusing to answer questions, he had been sentenced to one month's hard labour. Following his release, he was known to have associated with other members of the IRA, and in England he had been the subject of police enquiries since August 1939.

O'Hanlon had first come to England in 1936 and for fifteen months had been a member of the International Brigade fighting in the Spanish Civil War. Regarded as a 'fairly active' member of the IRA, his house in Belfast had been searched on several occasions and he had returned to Birmingham in July 1939.

It was thought that during February and March 1940, Perry – D Company, 1st Belfast Battalion, IRA – had taken a full and active part in terrorist activities and the procuring of explosives.

At the Police Court the three men had little to say, and Mr Dupré of the Home Office, who had examined the explosives – they were six times the amount needed at any one time for blasting in mining operations – told the Stipendiary Magistrate:

> They are highly dangerous. One powder, a mixture of potassium chlorate, sulphur and sugar, exploded while we were examining it. It would have exploded in any case, in a day or two.

Asked if they were still dangerous, Mr Dupré replied, 'Yes, if dropped.' The only missing bomb-making ingredient was sulphuric acid, which was easily obtained; the revolvers had been tested, and each would fire a bullet through two inches of wood.

Committed to Birmingham Assizes for trial and asked to plead to the indictment, Hasty replied, 'I didn't hear you. I don't know whether I am guilty or not. I don't care.'

O'Hanlon said, 'I am not interested.'

Perry remarked, 'The same applies to me – I am not interested.'

After pleas of not guilty were registered the three men adopted poses of sneering indifference, and after the prosecution evidence was heard they were asked if they wished to go into the witness box to cross-examine the witnesses. Only Hasty replied, saying, 'It would be a waste of time. We don't wish for leniency from this court at all.' He then said, 'I wish to address the jury' and still smirking, with his arms folded across his chest, he turned to the jury and said, 'All I want to say, is that, if it is for Ireland, the sacrifice will not be too great.'

After retiring for ten minutes on 16 July 1940, the jury returned a verdict of guilty. Regarding Hasty, Mr Justice Asquith was told by Inspector Sellick:

> The police are satisfied that he was actively engaged in the IRA campaign in Birmingham, and probably elsewhere. He is a cunning and dangerous man and nothing we have learned can be said in his favour.

Sentencing Hasty to ten years' penal servitude, O'Hanlon to eight years and Perry to six, the Judge told them:

> People who proceed against society with the help of dangerous explosives, even if their motive be some perverse misconception of patriotism, can hope for no leniency from any English court.

Tuberculosis claimed the lives of several IRA prisoners languishing in British gaols; Perry served just two years of his sentence before that disease ended his life at Parkhurst prison on the Isle of Wight on 7 July 1942. His remains were later interred at Milltown Cemetery, West Belfast.

So, given Hasty and O'Hanlon's stay in Rupert Street, were they responsible for planting the incendiary devices in the buses parked at the Birmingham depots, the explosion at the Birmingham sorting office and the explosions at the two shop fronts? It seems more than a possibility.

It was the swansong of the IRA bombing campaign; the day following their arrest, on 18 March, there was an explosion at the Westminster City Council Refuse Depot, where street litter was being dealt with, and seven sticks of gelignite were found in a litter bin in Grosvenor Place by a patrolling police constable. They were rendered harmless, and that was that.

Quite apart from anything else, the February thaw had brought flooding, and when meat rationing commenced in on 11 March, Britain was no place for a terrorist to tarry; besides, the police were on to Keating. He had sent Daly back to Dublin and then started destroying anything that incriminated himself; but before he could be arrested he was tipped off, escaped and was smuggled aboard a ferry leaving for Dun Laoghaire. During an interview on BBC Radio Ulster in 2007 – the year before his death – Keating boasted of his terrorist accomplishments, informing the listeners, 'No one got killed.' That must have been a great comfort to Maud Williams, Rosina Potter, Rose Cohen, Albert Roberts and the other eight people who sustained life-threatening and life-changing injuries as a result of Keating's intrepid 1940 bombing in Oxford Street.

The terrorists' final tally was 265 explosions or attempted explosions, 99 convictions, 117 people injured and seven innocent people killed; the deaths of the three terrorists in 1938 were regarded as 'own goals'.

Britain could now concentrate on defending itself against Nazi Germany; but where did Ireland stand in the conflict?

CHAPTER 33

The Nazi Connection

In 1937, the German Government had informed de Valera that in the event of war with England they would respect Eire's neutrality. However, the IRA had already made overtures to the Nazi party, and in particular to the Abwehr, the German intelligence agency, and this presented grave problems to both them and the Irish Government.

Irish politics were tremendously complicated, and the Abwehr simply could not comprehend them; furthermore, the IRA was not a sophisticated organization capable of liaising competently with the German intelligence network. The Abwehr was totally professional; they used complex codes – those used by the IRA were deciphered in double-quick time – and radio transmitters. Although the IRA demanded transmitters, the majority of its members had no conception of their use, or the discipline and ability to learn how to use them.

Additionally, the Abwehr were unable to understand why the IRA could not support de Valera; after all, he was a republican as well, wasn't he? But de Valera had turned his back on the armed struggle in favour of the ballot box. And the Prime Minister, Neville Chamberlain, hoping that in the event of war with Germany, Éire would come in on the British side, agreed in April 1938 to the unconditional return of three Irish ports which had been under British control. These were at Lough Swilly in Co. Donegal, and Berehaven and Cobh in Co. Cork.

Five months later, at Croydon Airport, Chamberlain triumphantly waved to a near-hysterical British public the 'piece of paper' which had been signed by him and Adolf Hitler, declaring that never again would their two countries go to war. But when the German Foreign Minister, Joachim von Rippentrop, later questioned Hitler as to the advisability of signing such a document, Hitler replied, 'Oh, don't take it so seriously; that piece of paper is of no further significance whatsoever.'

By the time realization had sunk in that there was going to be war with Germany, Chamberlain had to go cap in hand to de Valera to ask for the re-use of the ports. He was met with an unequivocal refusal. De Valera was not going to hand them back;

denying the use of them to the British would strengthen his agreement with Germany on neutrality. Poor, stupid Chamberlain; once more he had been royally shafted. With merchant ships in the Atlantic denied access to Lough Swilly, they were left at the mercy of the enemy. Berehaven and Cobh were strategically important sites from which Allied naval vessels could quickly reach Atlantic convoys; but denial of those ports meant that they would have to make far longer journeys from ports such as Plymouth.

Despite their misunderstandings, the IRA and the Nazi regime had initially become cosy bedfellows and were eager to do business with one another. In February 1939, a visitor called Eion Duffy had arrived in Dublin. He was, in fact, an Abwehr agent named Oskar Pfaus, and the sole reason for his trip was to make contact with the IRA. He met with Seán Russell and James O'Donovan, and the burning question was, could the IRA be used as fifth columnists in mainland Britain? In the event of war, would they attack the British war industries?

This appeared to be a heaven-sent opportunity for the IRA, and O'Donovan went to Germany in an attempt to set up a supply route for munitions and a cash flow, but without success. There was a second visit in April 1939, when O'Donovan suggested routes for weapons, money and transmitters; but that, too, proved abortive.

A third trip was made in August and also met with a lack of success. In fact, two days after his return from Germany, O'Donovan noted in his diary that the 'S' Plan was:

> hastily conceived, scheduled to a premature start, with ill-equipped and inadequately-trained personnel, too few men and too little money . . . unable to sustain the vital spark of what must be confessed to have fizzled out like a damp and inglorious squib.

O'Donovan was deeply disillusioned. What a pity that he didn't call a halt to proceedings there and then. It would have saved the carnage at Coventry two days later, plus the other injuries sustained in the remaining seven months of the campaign. But of course he didn't, and the reason is clear. In the same way that he knew full well that the British Government would not – in fact could not, even if they had felt so minded – remove British troops from Ireland as had been demanded, it didn't make the slightest difference. The murderous offensive had been planned for at least eighteen months, and come what may, O'Donovan, who loathed the British people, was determined to have his bloodbath.

But now, with war about to be declared between Britain and Germany, de Valera realized that Irish neutrality was threatened by the IRA, and the Irish police arrested leading members of the General Headquarters and seized a large amount of American dollars and correspondence documenting the IRA's proposed alliance with Nazi Germany.

Although some German agents were infiltrated into Eire from U-boats, they were arrested before they could make contact with the IRA. More arrests of IRA followed; and while the bombing campaign continued on the mainland, the terrorists needed more help. In October 1939, the IRA again made contact with the Abwehr, once more requesting guns, explosives and transmitting equipment, but again the request was ignored. Two months later, the IRA raided the magazine fort in Dublin's Phoenix Park and stole over one million rounds of ammunition. Within ten days the Irish Army and police had not only arrested IRA personnel but recovered most of the ammunition, the weaponry and, on 29 December 1939, the radio transmitter which had been acquired to contact the Abwehr. In fact, contact had not been possible; the transmitter lacked the range to reach Germany and had been used instead to broadcast local propaganda. However, O'Donovan had tried his best; a transmission log was later found in his house.

On 9 February 1940 the Emergency Powers Act was expanded to allow the internment of Irish citizens, and as the prisons at Mountjoy and Arbour Hill filled up, an internment facility was set up at the Curragh military camp. Barbed wire ringed the camp; living quarters consisted of Nissen huts with no heating and limited washing facilities.

Following an arson attempt by the prisoners, five IRA men were shot, and after two hunger strikers died there was a revenge attack on 25 April 1940, when a bomb exploded at Dublin Castle. The bomb had been placed in a lane off the lower castle yard at an angle between the house occupied by the housekeeper/guide, Mrs Smye, her husband and 12-year-old son, and the party wall at the back of the Garda barracks. The explosion occurred at 5 o'clock in the morning; Mrs Smye was cut on the forehead and the house was partially wrecked. The priceless blue and gold windows in the Chapel Royal were blown to pieces, as were the windows of the State Apartments, including St Patrick's Hall. The yard was littered with broken glass, plaster and masonry, and considerable damage was caused to the adjoining barrack offices and the sleeping quarters of sixteen detectives of the Special Branch; the five detectives who were injured received treatment at the depot hospital.

The scene was visited by, amongst others, de Valera and Mr MacEntee, the Minister for Industry and Commerce. The incident was the catalyst needed by de Valera; he stated in a radio broadcast that the IRA was jeopardizing Ireland's neutrality, stressed the danger of civil war and said that if the IRA persisted in trying to unseat the democratic Irish Government, there would be a risk of invasion. There was overwhelming support in the Dail and from the public, and with 640 Republicans interned, the IRA started to crumble – while support from the United States also began to fade. In June 1940, *Time Magazine* reported:

> Since 1938, the IRA's 7,500 youthful members (plus 15,000 fellow travellers) have followed the wild-eyed, bomb-Britain policy of 46-year-old, super-radical Chieftain Seán Russell. There is reason to believe that the intransigent IRA-sters are getting money from the Nazis, mostly by way of the U.S.

In June 1940, a suggestion was made to Dublin by the British Government that in exchange for the use of the Irish ports, plus Éire coming in on the British side during the war, there would be union with Ulster. De Valera would have none of it. He had already made it clear to the German ambassador in Dublin that if Germany invaded Ireland, he would fight them tooth and nail, with the British. However, if the British tried the same thing, he would join forces with the Germans to repulse them.

Irish neutrality was looking pretty shaky.

But what of Seán Russell, who had instigated the whole campaign? He had gone to Germany in May 1940 to meet the German top brass: the foreign minister, Joachim von Ribbentrop, and Admiral Wilhelm Canaris, head of the Abwehr, who would come to an untimely end following the failed putsch against Hitler on 20 July 1944.

Fluent in six languages and winner of the Iron Cross (First Class), Canaris was a brilliant intelligence agent and had run the Abwehr since 1935. Although Russell beseeched him to provide guns, explosives and transmitting equipment and stressed the IRA's willingness to attack British war industries, Canaris was distinctly unhappy with the situation, for the following reason.

Operation Sealion – Hitler's plan to invade England – had been formed in July 1940 but it never got off the ground. Therefore, if Britain was not going to be immediately subjugated by invasion, Germany's interest in Ireland waned. The Germans had never been particularly impressed with the targeting of civilian institutions and amenities under the 'S' Plan, and despite Russell's entreaties, could the IRA really be trusted to attack Britain's munitions factories and military aerodromes? They certainly hadn't so far. Should a portion of Germany's war budget be invested in supporting what would almost certainly be a lost cause? Because what Russell was certainly unaware of was Germany's already formulated plan to open a second front against its former ally, Russia, which was implemented five months later.

So – no. Canaris sent Russell home to Ireland in a U-boat, which left the port of Wilhelmshaven on 8 August. He was accompanied by fellow IRA man Frank Ryan, who had been extricated from Spain, where he had been awaiting sentence on death row for fighting with the International Brigades against Franco's forces.

But Russell never arrived. He died on 14 August, apparently suffering from stomach pains, and was buried at sea. A tragic illness, possibly a perforated ulcer – or something else?

To coincide with Russell's arrival in Germany, an Abwehr agent, Hermann Görtz, was parachuted into Eire and was arrested and interned a year later. Even though his radio transmitter was lost in the drop, did he manage to convey to Canaris his opinion of the IRA – that it was 'worthless'?

And if that were so, did the cunning little admiral, as he pondered the matter from his second floor office at SS Headquarters in Berlin's Alexanderplatz, decide to upset Eire's neutrality by permitting an out-of-control Russell to instigate a bloodbath?

Difficult to say.

But consider this. In the event of Germany winning the war, Ireland with its mild climate and lush green fields for crops and cattle-rearing would certainly have been subjugated by the Nazi jackboot, there's no doubt about that. A *Gauleiter*[1] would have been needed for Dublin, and it appeared that the post was a toss-up between Russell and Ryan. Additionally, there had been bad feeling between the two men. It has since been suggested by British intelligence that Ryan poisoned Russell; but in any event, the U-boat returned to Germany, taking Ryan with it. If Ryan did possess dreams of becoming Germany's puppet leader in Dublin, they died with him in Germany, in 1944.

By 1945 the IRA had lost momentum, and on 10 March a ceasefire was ordered. De Valera had taken a firm stance against the organization and used draconian powers to subdue it, but they paid off. The British police and security services had halted the IRA activities on the mainland five years previously.

---

[1] Head of a Nazi administrative district

Chapter 34

What Happened Next?

Thomas Hawkett, the courageous cloakroom attendant who dropped the bomb into a bucket of water, was awarded £5 from the Bow Street Reward Fund.

Dr H. E. Watts, the gallant disruptor of explosives, was later knighted, becoming Sir Hugh Watts, and died aged seventy in 1958.

Frederick Harold Dupré MBE, FCS, the Home Office explosives expert, was advanced to OBE in the 1948 New Year's Honours List. He died aged seventy-four in 1953.

Frederick Child, the recipient of the George Cross following the Hammersmith Bridge bombing, never married. He lived quietly with his sister in Shepherd's Bush until her death in 1964, after which he lived alone until his death, aged seventy-eight, in 1975. His George Cross, British War Medal, Victory Medal and Queen Elizabeth II Coronation Medal are privately held.

Leonard Burt, who had accompanied Mr Watts on his bomb-disrupting expedition in 1939, was appointed a Lieutenant Colonel in the Intelligence Corps for the duration of the war, catching spies and traitors. Afterwards he returned to the Metropolitan Police where, as a detective superintendent, he replaced Albert Canning MVO, MBE (now a chief constable) as head of Special Branch. Burt immediately strengthened the branch with the addition of a further nineteen personnel. He retired in 1958 with the rank of commander, having served for forty-six years. He had been commended by the commissioner on thirty-nine occasions and appointed a Member of the Victorian Order in 1947; seven years later, he was advanced to the rank of Commander of the Victorian Order. In addition, he was appointed Commander of the British Empire, and if that were not enough, the President of the French Republic conferred on him the *Légion d'Honneur*, the Queen of the Netherlands awarded him the Order of Orange Nassau and the King of Denmark made him a Chevalier of the Order of the Dannebrog. He died at the age of ninety-one, his retirement having lasted twenty-five years.

Robert Fabian's career flourished as well. Within a week of his award of the King's Police Medal for disarming the bomb near Piccadilly Circus he was promoted to Divisional Detective Inspector, and five years later he headed the Flying Squad. An intrepid investigator, one of his greatest successes involved the murder of Alec d'Antiquis; working flat out for twenty days, he caught the three men responsible. He retired as a detective superintendent in 1949, taking with him forty commendations from the commissioner, wrote three books about his experiences as a detective and found household fame as a result of thirty-nine television episodes of *Fabian of the Yard.* He died aged seventy-seven in 1978.

Fabian's contemporary in bomb-disarming, Len Crawford, was promoted following his £10 award from the Bow Street Reward Fund, and by 1945 he was back on the Flying Squad, this time as a detective inspector. There he would remain for the next four years, being much in demand as an undercover officer as well as using his courage and expertise in working with the highly secretive Ghost Squad. Having been commended on thirty-three occasions, he retired with the rank of detective superintendent in 1959 and died twenty-nine years later at the age of eighty-six.

Police Constable Ernest Hayward who, like Fabian, was awarded a King's Police Medal for neutralizing a terrorist bomb in Tottenham Court Road in May 1939, continued patrolling the war-torn streets of London's West End. His 26-year career had started at the end of the First World War; it finished at the conclusion of the Second. He received what was referred to as 'an ordinary pension' – for an extraordinary copper.

Margery Urquhart (she had graduated with a BSc in agriculture from Aberdeen University in 1935) continued working with Special Branch. Two months after having been promoted to woman detective sergeant she resigned on 23 July 1944, with the permission of the commissioner, to transfer to the Surrey Constabulary as a woman inspector. There followed other employments, including as a probation officer, before she became director of Grampian's social services. She retired in 1977, when she was appointed OBE; she never married and died in an Aberdeen nursing home at the age of ninety-four. She was the soul of discretion; following her resignation from the police, she never mentioned her activities with Special Branch.

Anne Winterbottom was promoted to woman detective sergeant in 1944 and eventually retired in 1964 having served twenty-seven years; she married, changing her name to Forbes-Wynton.

Of the Special Branch team, William Hughes was promoted to detective superintendent, awarded the BEM and retired in 1959. After five years in the Army, Sydney Barnes joined the police in 1919, aged twenty-five and in 1933 was posted to Special Branch, where in 1945 he was promoted to divisional detective inspector. Arthur Cain served for twenty-five years and retired with the rank of detective inspector; his retirement lasted twice as long as his police service. And William George Parker, the brilliant and much-commended murder investigator, served for twenty-seven years, retiring with the rank of detective superintendent.

So much for the good guys; now for the rest.

* * *

James O'Donovan was interned in Ireland between October 1941 and September 1943 and spent his time productively, training other inmates in bomb-making techniques and instructing them in the art of bellowing out Nazi marching songs, although the lyrics of *Wir fahren gegen England* (We're marching against England) must have left the vast majority of internees scratching their heads in bewilderment.

After his release he resumed his pre-war employment with the Electricity Supply Board, but with Germany's defeat looming he came to the irrevocable conclusion that there would never be a united Ireland – not with Germany's assistance, at any event. The man who was described by the Abwehr as their 'chief agent in Ireland' retired in 1962 and wrote various articles and his unpublished memoirs, before dying at the age of eighty-two of kidney failure in 1979.

Brendan Francis Aiden Behan was released from Borstal in 1941 and, aged eighteen, was deported to Ireland. During a gun battle with police the following year he snatched a pistol from an associate's hand, saying, 'Give it to me and I'll shoot the bastards!' and fired off shots at two officers. Arrested and sentenced to fourteen years' penal servitude, he was released when there was a general amnesty for IRA prisoners in 1946. In 1947 he was sentenced to four months' hard labour for attempting to free an IRA colleague from prison and, upon his release, another month's imprisonment for assaulting a police officer.

In between times he became a successful author and playwright, but his bibulous encounters with the law continued; at Bow Street Magistrates' Court in 1959 he was fined 5s 0d for being drunk ('No trouble, your Worship!' said PC John Dicks) and then, two years later, celebrated what he untruthfully stated was his fortieth birthday at Dublin District Court, charged with assault, threatening behaviour, malicious damage and assaulting a station sergeant and two constables with intent to resist apprehension, plus violent behaviour at College Street police station.

Two weeks later, in April 1961, he appeared in court in Toronto, Canada charged with assaulting the police, common assault and creating a disturbance.

But he was quite sober at a performance of his play, *The Quare Fellow*, when he met a playwright contemporary, Noël Coward, who thought he was 'really very beguiling' and noted in his diary, 'I think he was surprised that I could say fuck and cunt as easily and naturally as he could.'

Unsurprisingly, Behan died aged forty-one in 1964; he was accorded a full IRA guard of honour at his funeral.

Next, Dominic Adams, the purchaser of the carrier bicycle used to convey the bomb to Broadgate, who afterwards smartly vanished back to Ireland. He was later interned and following his release in 1945 was arrested for robbery with violence. Since this offence had happened in 1936, witnesses' memories were no longer as reliable as they had been nine years previously, and Adams was acquitted. In 1950 he was dropped from the General Headquarters staff of the IRA and returned to Ulster. Although he had been named in the newspapers at the time of the Broadgate bombing as someone the police wanted to interview – and this was even before Mrs O'Hara had made her dramatic revelation that Adams was involved – this was never followed up; one wonders why. One explanation is that Dominic Adams had become an informant for the British security services in exchange for his freedom; it may sound unlikely, but believe me, the ranks of both the Republican and Loyalist terror groups in Northern Ireland were (and still are) riddled with informers. If that was the case, it appeared to be a family trait; Adams' brother, Gerry Adams Sr., admitted that he had been an informant for the British for almost thirty years before his death in 2003 – and he had sexually abused members of his own family. He was nevertheless afforded an IRA funeral, but his brother Dominic, who died aged eighty-five in 2001, was not.

* * *

Although a committee was set up in 1949 to have the bodies of Richards and Barnes disinterred from their graves at Winson Green prison, it was not until twenty years later that this was accomplished. The bodies were flown to Dublin, where the coffins were met by relatives and an IRA guard of honour, and on 6 July 1969 mass was said at Mullingar cathedral, before a reputed crowd of 15,000 attended the funeral at Ballyglass cemetery.

And then, this happened …

On the same day as the funeral, the *Sunday Times* dropped a bombshell. They had accessed the Scotland Yard case papers and had discovered the identity of the man who deposited the bomb in Broadgate. Furthermore, they had tracked down Joby O'Sullivan; he was not referred to by name – neither was Dominic Adams – but under the guise of 'a nervous soldier of the IRA', he had decided to speak to the reporters. He told them that he had been trained in the use of explosives for only two weeks and was sent to Coventry alone, and this is what appeared about the Broadgate bombing in the newspaper article:

> 'As a soldier of the Irish Republican Army, there was nothing I could do but carry out my orders to the letter', he insists. Two days later, he kept a rendezvous outside Coventry Post Office with his director of training. 'We strolled down the street smoking cigarettes as if we had not a care in the world. Outside Montague Burton's tailoring shop in Broadgate, the other fellow stopped. "This is where you will plant the bomb", he said. "It will be in the carrier of a messenger boy's bicycle and you'll put the bike against the kerb at 2.30".' . . . The significance of the operation now sank in. 'Leaving a bomb in a crowded street is nothing but cold-blooded murder', he said. Coldly again, he was told, 'You'll do it because if you don't, you'll be court martialled and shot the minute you set foot in Ireland again.'

It was a typical criminal's way of playing down his culpability: a horrified reaction, followed by 'a big boy made me do it and ran away'.

He was persuaded – after a few drinks – to make a broadcast on RTÉ Radio, the Irish broadcasting station, again anonymously, in which he claimed responsibility for the Broadgate bombing, but this time saying that the bicycle had got trapped in the tram tracks and, fearing an imminent explosion, he had had to abandon it – once again endeavouring to minimize his guilt.

O'Sullivan's mental health had deteriorated over the years, due, his supporters would have pointed out, to beastly treatment during internment; but after spending several years as a guest of the Dundrum Criminal Lunatic Asylum, he died, a dribbling lunatic, aged seventy-two in October 1982.

So over the years various explanations have been offered: that the bomber 'panicked', that the intended target was the police station, the telephone exchange, the electricity station – in fact, just about anywhere except Broadgate.

The IRA repudiated the notion that it was a planned operation, conveniently forgetting the intended attack in London, on the same day, at the same time, using the same alarm clocks, the same tradesmen's bicycles and the same type of explosives which were planned to detonate at Scotland Yard, 10 Downing Street and Westminster Abbey. It is fair to assume that in that eventuality, there would not have been the five deaths that had occurred at Broadgate; there would have been hundreds.

Epilogue

So what brought about the end of the IRA's mainland bombing campaign? There are several explanations – one is that the operation simply ran out of steam, with a lack of funds and equipment, plus diminishing interest from Nazi Germany and over ninety of their most hardened members behind bars.

Next, the hanging of Barnes and Richards must have been a contributory factor. It was all very well to kill and maim innocent civilians and then roar 'God bless Ireland!' from the dock, but to get one's neck stretched was an entirely different matter.

Although the Luftwaffe's air-raids on Britain would not really commence until after the 1940 Battle of Britain (to be followed by 'the Blitz', concentrated attacks starting in September 1940), it was clear to everybody in the United Kingdom – and that included the IRA personnel on the mainland – that such attacks were imminent. It was one thing for the terrorists to be rudely awakened early in the morning by unfriendly detectives politely asking questions which they had no intention of answering about their possession of explosive materials. It was quite another to be subjected to sustained bombing by their former allies. So they sloped off back home to safe, neutral Éire, doubtless to be enormously delighted that by the end of the Second World War they would not be numbered among the 67,200 civilian fatalities sustained on the mainland.

* * *

Unlike Barnes' and Richards' re-interment, attended by 15,000 mourners who insisted that they were 'martyrs', the ceremony at Unity Lawn, Coventry Cathedral on 14 October 2015 was a low-key but an immensely dignified affair.

A memorial stone was unveiled by the Lord Mayor of Coventry, Councillor Michael Hammon, and the Very Reverend John Witcombe, the Dean of Coventry. It listed the names and ages of the five people killed at Broadgate, with the unpretentious inscription:

In memory of those who
were killed when a
terrorist bomb exploded
in Broadgate, Coventry
on 25 August 1939

It was a simple service, devoid of rhetoric, and members of the families of the victims laid single white roses at the memorial's base.

* * *

There is also a second memorial to the carnage. It is contained in the West Midland Police Museum and it consists of the remains of the carrier bicycle used in the bombing at Broadgate. The handlebars, the front wheel and the carrier basket are missing, and the remaining spokes on the rear wheel are distorted. It is contained in a glass cabinet, and when this is opened, it is still possible, over eighty years later, to detect the smell of burnt rubber and explosives.

Bibliography

Adams, T. Ian	*The IRA Bombing Campaign in England*	Spiker Publications, 2010 *1939–1940*
Adams, Ian and Wilson, Ray	*Special Branch: A History 1883–2006*	Biteback Publishing, 2015
Beveridge, Peter	*Inside the CID*	Evans Brothers, 1957
Booth, Nicholas	*ZigZag*	Little, Brown, 2007
Browne, Douglas G.	*The Rise of Scotland Yard*	George G. Harrap, 1956
Burgess, P. H. E.	*No Easy Way*	Privately published, 2009
Burt, Leonard	*Commander Burt of Scotland Yard*	Heinemann, 1959
Dillon, Martin	*The Enemy Within: The IRA's War against the British*	Doubleday, 1994
Dodson, Sir Gerald	*Consider Your Verdict*	Hutchinson & Co. Ltd, 1967
Enno, Stephen	*Spies in Ireland*	Macdonald & Co., 1963
Fabian, Robert	*Fabian of the Yard*	Naldrett Press, 1950
Fairfield, Letitia	*The Trial of Peter Barnes and Others*	William Hodge & Co. Ltd, 1953
Fido, Martin and Skinner, Keith	*The Official Encyclopaedia of Scotland Yard*	Virgin, 1999
Firmin, Stanley	*Scotland Yard: The Inside Story*	Hutchinson, 1951

Gosling, John	*The Ghost Squad*	W. H. Allen, 1959
Howe, Sir Ronald	*The Pursuit of Crime*	Arthur Barker, 1961
Hull, Mark M.	*Irish Secrets*	Irish Academic Press, 2003
Jackett, Sam	*Heroes of Scotland Yard*	Robert Hale, 1966
Kirby, Dick	*The Guv'nors: Ten of Scotland Yard's Greatest Detectives*	Pen & Sword, 2010
Kirby, Dick	*The Sweeney: The First Sixty Years of Scotland Yard's Crimebusting Flying Squad, 1919–1978*	Pen & Sword, 2011
Kirby, Dick	*Scotland Yard's Ghost Squad: The Secret Weapon Against Post-War Crime*	Pen & Sword, 2011
Kirby, Dick	*Scotland Yard's Flying Squad: 100 Years of Crime Fighting*	Pen & Sword, 2019
Lawrence, Jane R.	*From the Beat to the Palace*	Brewin, 2005
McKenna, Joseph	*The IRA Bombing Campaign against Britain 1939–1940*	McFarland & Co. Inc., 2016
O'Donoghue, David	*The Devil's Deal*	New Island, 2010
Payn, Graham and Morley, Sheridan (eds.)	*The Noël Coward Diaries*	Weidenfeld & Nicholson, 1982
Ryder, Chris	*The RUC: A Force under Fire*	Methuen, 1989
Shaw, Simon	*'Not Forgotten': the 1939 Bomb Attack*	Historic Coventry Articles, 2020
Sillitoe, Sir Percy	*Cloak without Dagger*	Pan, 1956
Thomas, Donald	*An Underworld at War*	John Murray, 2003

Index